HEDDLE NASH

Singing against the Tide

HEDDLE NASH

Singing against the Tide

Eleanor Allen

JUBILEE HOUSE PRESS

First published in Great Britain in 2010 by
Jubilee House Press
70 Cadogan Place
London SW1X 9AH
www.hauspublishing.com

Copyright © Eleanor Allen, 2010

The moral right of the author has been asserted

A CIP catalogue record for this book is available from the British Library

ISBN 978-0-956599-60-5

Typeset in Garamond by MacGuru Ltd
info@macguru.org.uk

Printed and bound in Great Britain by
CPI Antony Rowe, Chippenham and Eastbourne

For David, who so loved his father.

Contents

Introduction

He was dubbed 'Britain's finest tenor'; 'King of English tenors'; 'best-loved lyric tenor' – apologies for using such over-the-top-sounding clichés but try to explain Heddle Nash without them and it proves impossible. They happened to be true, and remained true, throughout a career lasting almost thirty years, from the late 1920s right down to the 1950s. He worked with most of the legendary names in the British classical music world of the twentieth century, sang in the inaugural opera season at Glyndebourne, made some of the earliest opera broadcasts on the wireless, and put in the very first flickering opera appearance on pioneering television. In fact, whenever there was a 'happening' on the British classical music scene (or most other music scenes for that matter), there – or so it seems – you would find Heddle Nash, not only enhancing but thoroughly relishing it.

Nash was born towards the end of Queen Victoria's reign, brought up in Edwardian times, fought in one world war, survived a second and lived into the era of Elvis Presley and rock 'n' roll, yet he died at the comparatively early age of sixty-seven.

As an opera singer he won so much acclaim at the Old Vic, the British National Opera, the Carl Rosa Company, Glyndebourne, Sadler's Wells and above all, Covent Garden, that his operatic career alone would have ensured him a write-up in the archives.

But he didn't stop at opera. Apart from the unforgettable quality of his voice, the remarkable thing about Heddle Nash was his sheer versatility.

Tack on the accolade 'one of England's finest oratorio singers' and already he's looking special, oratorio calling for a deep solemnity and repose in complete contrast with the flamboyant acting skills demanded by grand opera. According to the accompanist Gerald Moore, he was a self-declared 'best bloody Messiah in the country!'[1] Few would have disagreed. Many would have been keen to point out that, moreover, he was the finest exponent of Elgar's *Gerontius*. Yet he didn't scorn to tackle the light, melodious world of operetta and braved the harsh spotlight of the West End stage to win heart-throb status as a leading man. There were also appearances on the concert platform. Nash was a favourite with Proms audiences between 1927 and 1952, and he performed on so many concert platforms and gave so many recitals at so many music festivals and societies the whole length and breadth of the British Isles, there's a strong temptation to wonder if he had a double! Yet somehow he slotted in recordings for Columbia and HMV, plus those broadcasts on the wireless, becoming one of the best-loved singing voices in the home, pre-television.

If he had excelled in only a couple of musical genres, Heddle Nash would have to be classed as exceptional. To have excelled in so many was an achievement not matched by any other British tenor. Probably never likely to be either, in these days of increasing specialisation.

With so many achievements to his name, it comes as a bit of a jolt to learn that Nash himself viewed his singing career as 'a triumph over adversity'. And that he considered the German conductor Bruno Walter to have hit the spot when he observed, 'It is your misfortune, Heddle, to have been born in the wrong place, at the wrong time.'[2]

Starved of support and encouragement in his early days, devastated by his experiences in the First World War, he then found himself having to compete for the bread-and-butter singing contracts with the finest crop of tenors Britain has ever produced (Walter Widdop, Parry Jones, Frank Titterton, Webster Booth, Walter Midgely – those are just a few). And he always felt as though he was singing against the tide, which in the 1920s and 1930s especially, happened to be flowing strongly in favour of more full-bodied foreign tenors of the Gigli, Tauber, Martinelli and Borgioli variety. Heddle Nash's voice was pure perfection for Mozart, Handel and Donizetti, but – just his bad luck – the more baritonal Wagner roles were then in vogue. So instead of being able to glory in his gift, he was always struggling to lower his timbre.

And although, as a British tenor between the wars, it was possible to be loved at home – in Heddle's case 'cherished' even – you were also marked down *per se* as a bit 'lightweight' and inferior for the world stage. Especially in opera. Between the wars opera in Britain was in a precarious state, relying for

Heddle c 1930.

much of the time on the financial support of private individuals, and limiting a singer either to championing the cause of opera in English in the provinces, or at the Old Vic, or facing fierce competition from foreign soloists at Covent Garden and, later, at Glyndebourne. Bursting with colour and throbbing with passion, opera was considered to be an art form 'the foreigner' was not only steeped in, but genetically programmed to perform, while the white-corpuscled Anglo Saxon, fundamentally, was not. So no matter how much Heddle might make the most of any opportunity that came his way and 'fling himself on the fervours of the music'[3] or stride the stage being 'gallant, every inch of him'[4] as Des Grieux in *Manon*, or sing his heart out in near-perfect German and indulge in riotous by-play as David in *Die Meistersinger*, he could never quite live down the tag of being 'homegrown'. Yet despite such hostile times, he still achieved a remarkable career: to his patriotic pride, he would be flying the flag for England at Covent Garden or Glyndebourne in programmes otherwise dominated entirely by foreign soloists.

Because he sang very little outside Britain and his career coincided with a series of severe economic downturns – the Great Depression, the Second World War, and the Austerity years of the late 1940s and 1950s – he never made a personal fortune, nor managed to live a glamorous or flamboyant lifestyle. As for his private life, he largely kept it private. Few people ever realised that it was almost as full of comedy, drama and tragedy as the opera stage itself.

Unfortunately even the potted accounts of his life, on CD blurbs and the internet, don't always get the facts straight. To some extent the discrepancies might have been caused by the man himself; he was always in such a rush he could never spare much time to set down details. Like many top artists, he took no interest in collecting his own reviews. Only a handful of his letters seem to have survived, and those that do typically start with an apology for not replying sooner and are often signed, 'in haste'.

There is a telling business example addressed to the Columbia Gramophone Company Limited, dated 10 December 1935.[5] It was sent to Frederick Gaisburg, one of the pioneers of the recording industry, though it would seem that Gaisburg was still surprisingly hands-on, even in the most trivial financial dealings. Heddle is sending him a bill for the hire of a costume for some publicity photographs (to accompany the famous Glyndebourne *Così fan tutte* recording) which he has just unearthed from his stack of unanswered correspondence. After hoping that the *Bohème* recordings were OK, Heddle adds, 'Am just off for a week's concert work in the provinces,' before signing off 'Yours in haste':

Yet in spite of all the 'haste', being ever a perfectionist, he took scrupulous care to dot every 'i' and firmly accent *Bohème*, before finishing with a characteristically flourishing and self-establishing upswept stroke beneath 'Nash'.

His mind already seems to have been shooting away from the irksome task of writing formal business letters concerning the boring minutiae of professional life, and off to the place where his heart lay – those concert platforms, and the audiences eagerly awaiting him in the provinces.

Because, as his friend Stuart Hibberd, the well-loved BBC radio announcer of the same era once put it so succinctly:

'Singing was his life'

1

Out of Tragedy in South East London

A Londoner born and bred, he differed from other Londoners in that he had a good voice. [1]

'**U**llow – Heddle Nash speaking...' The telephone exaggerated his Cockney accent and highlighted his melodiously high-pitched tone. He used to joke that some callers, hearing him for the first time, had been known to mutter an apology and ring off sharpish – labouring under the embarrassed misapprehension that they had accidentally dialled up some warm-voiced East-End tart named 'Ethel Lash'.[2] The Cockney accent was lighter in his everyday speech, and when he sang there was no accent at all, just an echo of something down-to-earth and rooted; a faint suggestion in his otherwise exquisitely ethereal tenor voice of knowing-what-was-what, which came across as sexy and intriguing (and still does).

But he used to say that being born and bred almost anywhere else in the British Isles would have been preferable to South East London. From an opera singer's point of view, Heddle Nash might indeed have been born in the wrong country at the wrong time; as an oratorio and concert artist, he considered that he had been dealt the double whammy of being born in one of its least congenial spots.

He would have preferred Northern England, Wales, Scotland or parts of Ireland, areas where, in the first half of the twentieth century, they were proud of upholding their reputation as thriving, buzzing hotbeds of classical music, and not just for the elite: the tradition was deeply ingrained in the popular culture with choirs, brass bands, music clubs, concerts, festivals – all sorts of outlets for singing and music making. Heddle coveted the strong cultural base and loyal support those areas gave to their singers (the soprano Isobel Baillie claimed that in her early days as many as 90% of her bread-and-butter bookings came by word of mouth from her North Country connections). But his own home patch, composed of New Cross, Lewisham and Brockley, had only recently been developed and consequently had no established classical music tradition. Not having studied at any of the prestigious central music academies, he wasn't part of the main London music scene either. All his life Heddle would never lose the feeling of being out on a limb, having to struggle for work and recognition entirely on his own.

Yet ironically, in tracing the origins of Heddle Nash, it's not to South East London that we need to turn, but instead to one of the very areas he would have preferred himself, namely Scotland.

It was in the bustling and unlikely surroundings of mid-Victorian Edinburgh, in the year 1868, that by some extraordinary trick of fate Heddle's grandfather, Joseph Nash, a tin-plate worker originally from Somerset, happened to clap eyes on Maria Heddle, a servant girl from the Orkney Islands.

What had taken Heddle's grandfather to Edinburgh at that particular time remains uncertain, but it seems likely he had been lured up there by a brother-in-law in the zinc trade, boasting about big opportunities and rich pickings to be had in its flourishing economy.

The son of a poor agricultural labourer, Joseph had not been born with the elegant surname 'Nash' at all.[3] He had entered the world labelled with the far more rural-sounding 'Naish', in Tickenham, a village near Congresbury in North Somerset; an area noted in the nineteenth century for copper mines as well as for cider.

If he had followed the pattern of most young working men of the mid-Victorian era, Joseph Naish would never have strayed far from his Congresbury roots, let alone streamlined his surname and found himself a bride in Scotland. Members of the 'Naish' family bear witness to that fact; to this very day they still inhabit that same corner of North Somerset. But Joseph happened to have been born with a particularly ambitious and adventurous streak which led him, at around the age of seventeen, to shake the country soil off his boots and set out to better himself by following an elder sister, Amelia, and her entrepreneurial, zinc-manufacturing husband, up to London. It was in the great metropolis that his surname became 'urbanised' – the dropped 'i' presumably a result of Londoners assuming that when he said 'Naish' it was just the young man's drawling West Country way of pronouncing 'Nash'. For a few years he plied a trade as a tin-plate worker, hammering out cheap kitchen utensils – spoons, kettles, jugs and plates, while lodging with an Irish smith in the notoriously poverty-stricken courts and alleyways that made up Victorian Somers Town, just north of the Marylebone Road: the streets of London, as he would have pretty soon discovered, were not paved with gold for tin-plate workers. Low pay, fierce competition and miserable lodgings were a fact of life in the 1860s, and that particular part of Somers Town lay under the threat of demolition for the building of St Pancras Station. When his brother-in-law's zinc-manufacturing machinations took him and Amelia to Edinburgh in the mid-1860s, it's possible that Joseph welcomed the opportunity to follow and attempt another fresh start – he still had nothing to lose but his poverty.

Heddle's grandmother Maria, by contrast, came from the wild and windswept Orkney Islands, where 'Heddle' remains a common surname* as well as a place name. She had been born in a beautiful parish named Orphir, which lies mid-way between the Islands' capital Kirkwall and Stromness. Orphir was a lonely place back then, but destined to become a tourist spot, being blessed not only with breathtaking vistas over the historic natural harbour of Scapa Flow, but also richly scattered with ancient monuments. The parish is dominated by the old laird's Hall of Clestrain, and in the fields lie ancient Norse ruins dating back to the eleventh and twelfth centuries. There are the substantial remains of a round kirk, linked with the Crusades, and the foundations of the Earl's Bu (a drinking hall), excavated at the time Maria Heddle was in her early teens. The spot is steeped in both Celtic and Scandinavian folklore, legend and blood. Maria and her siblings would have grown up hearing yarns and songs passed down, about ancient battles, selkie folk from the sea,[3] phantoms flitting through the sea-misty twilight in the old kirk yard, and savage drinking bouts in the Bu, leading to scenes of violence, bravado, horrific deaths and brutal murders, all set down and embellished to the point of legend in the twelfth-century manuscript, the *Orkneyinga Saga* – and probably being re-hashed and going the rounds with added gusto at the time of the excavations.

Maria's childhood surroundings were rich in beauty, history, legend and

---

*Of Norse origin, like many old Orkney surnames.

bracing North Atlantic air – but little else: materially her family were as poor as Joseph's.[4] Her father managed to chip a living out of the local stone, as a mason, but one by one Maria's elder siblings had found themselves obliged to seek employment opportunities elsewhere. At some point in her mid-teens, Maria followed suit, quitting the Orkneys, most likely never to return.

Orphir c. 1900. Photographed by Tom Kent.

After crossing over to the mainland, Heddle's grandmother carried on south to Edinburgh, apparently following in the footsteps of a favourite elder sister named Jessie,[5] much as Joseph must have followed Amelia.

Maria had been earning her living surrounded by the thrust and commerce of mid-nineteenth century Edinburgh for at least seven long years or more before she somehow caught the eye of the young Englishman. At that point she looked doomed to a life of drudgery in domestic service. The age of eighteen had found her at the beck and call of a large, male-dominated household of flourishing house painters in Stafford Street, off the fashionable shopping thoroughfare Princes Street, in Edinburgh's New Town. By the time she met Joseph she had reached the advanced age (for those days) of twenty-four and must have been sick to death of 'doing' for others; desperate to acquire a hearth and home of her own while some trace of bloom still clung to her: getting married being virtually the only way a girl could escape from a life in domestic service in the 1860s. When she stepped up to the altar in Edinburgh in 1868, to knot her name and life to that of Joseph Nash, Maria Heddle probably suspected she was running a high risk of ending up over the border in England, even further from her Orkney roots. But the marriage must have seemed like a gamble worth the taking.

Joseph may not immediately have been aware of the fact, but the family he was marrying into harboured a special talent – for singing. Singing was in the Heddles' blood. It must have seeped in during those long, dark Orkney winter evenings when their ancestors gathered around the hearthside for companionship and entertainment, which took the form of drinking, story-telling and singing songs. When, in the words of the Orkney poet George Mackay Brown: 'a voice here and there was touched to enchantment by starlight and peat flames.'

Maria's elder sister Jessie, in particular – the one she had followed to Edinburgh, and who had subsequently married a bookseller there, named Mr Mackenzie – was certainly sometimes 'touched to enchantment'. She is reputed to have had such an exceptionally beautiful singing voice that echoes of it still linger on in Nash family memory. Untrained, it apparently possessed some of the same spontaneous qualities as Heddle's own. Later in life, when Jessie tragically became afflicted with mental illness, she ended up in an asylum. But there they encouraged her to sing, because when she sang, Jessie Mackenzie's hauntingly lovely voice is said to have had a strangely therapeutic effect – not only did it calm her down, there was an added bonus for the asylum staff – it soothed the other inmates too.[6]

> Now I have always thought there was a strong Celtic strain in Heddle's artistic nature. The imagination, the relishing of words, the streak of fantasy and a strange combination of downright earthiness with other-worldliness...[7]

Heddle certainly had his grandmother Maria to thank for his distinctive christian name. And on the Jessie evidence, it seems that his saga-and-folklore-steeped Orkney ancestors might also have handed down to him that plangent, centuries-old-familiar, minstrel's quality of tone, so often remarked on by critics down the years, ranging from Richard Capell to Alan Blyth (though all agreed he added a dash of some magically elusive ingredient that was all his own). Listening to his spell-binding recording of 'In Memory I lie beneath the palms' from Bizet's opera *The Pearl Fishers*, it's not difficult to imagine what Heddle's voice might have had in common with his Great Aunt Jessie's. Or why it was that his fan George Bernard Shaw (wearing his music critic's hat) once referred to him as an 'Orpheus'.*

Unfortunately Grandfather Joseph Nash's money-making schemes in Edinburgh must have floundered not long after he had married Maria, otherwise Heddle might have had his wish for more congenial surroundings and been born and bred in Scotland.

By 1871, accompanied by his Orkney wife, Joseph had made his way back to the English capital,[8] and the only changed element in his life, apart from his marital status, was his job description. From 'tin-plate worker' he had moved on to 'zinc-worker' (the bottom had fallen out of the tin kitchen utensils market by then). Eventually, as people started installing more bathrooms and indoor loos, Joseph attempted to keep abreast of the times, describing himself as a 'plumber and zinc-worker'. He would give the Nash family their first connection with the building trade, which would eventually feature strongly in the life of Heddle's father, and very nearly, Heddle's own. But all that hard work, with still nothing much to show for it, can't fail to have dampened the flame of ambition in a once-vigorous and enterprising man. It still seems to have smouldered on beneath his rough workman's clothing, and itched from time to time inside his hob-nailed boots, but disillusionment was gradually taking hold. Maria would watch her husband slowly falling victim to the soul-destroying Victorian working class curse of daily hard grind just to put food on to the table. Though Joseph would make modest attempts to freelance as a plumber – and one might have thought the opportunities were there – for some unknown reason, the business never seemed to prosper for him.

The area of South East London where Joseph and Maria had finally settled down was the newly developing working class area then known as Hatcham, on the borders of Deptford and New Cross, a spot that, surprisingly, had been given over to market gardening only twenty years or so earlier.[9]

They rented three rooms in a typical Victorian worker's house in Alexandra Street,[10] where the small terraced houses tended to be divided, as in this case, between two families, or rented by a family who took in lodgers to make ends meet. Like many other parts of Victorian Deptford and New Cross which managed to survive the Blitz, the area fell victim in the 1960s

---

*'As to the robust tenors who came between Mario and Jean de Reszke, the educated and carefully taught ones sang so horribly that they were classed as "goatbleaters": Heddle Nash is an Orpheus compared to Gayarre.' Article entitled 'We sing better than our grandfathers' published in *Everybody's*, 1950.

to slum clearance and the passion for building blocks of flats. In the parallel Vansittart Street, Joseph's brother-in-law and sister Amelia also settled down, his brother-in-law's grand schemes having apparently come unstuck. Later Joseph's mother would come up from Somerset and, for a year or two, somehow squeeze in with Amelia and her five children before returning to her roots.

It's still an edgy area, but it was even more so in the latter part of Victoria's reign. Venturing north or east, deeper into parts of Deptford, was best avoided. The Foreign Cattle Market – full of noise, stench and rough, loud-mouthed 'gut-girls' – had opened up on the site of the old Royal Dockyard and millions of sheep and cattle were being brought in by ship from abroad to be slaughtered in the former dockyard buildings. All around the area, heavy and unpleasant industries were growing up – engineering and chemical works; a tar distillery; a candle factory emitting vile smells; a glue works; timber yards and so forth, all attracting unskilled labour to the area. And not much more than a stone's throw from Alexandra Street ran the sooty railway.

Alexandra Street and Vansittart Street, however, determinedly clung on to their 'respectability', maintaining a general sense of orderliness – clean windows, scrubbed doorsteps, reasonably sober neighbours – all important when just one rogue neighbour could send the status of a whole street plummeting. Maria, with her just-off-Princes-Street background in domestic service, hopefully did her best to keep up standards, as far as was possible in a cramped space and with a shortage of cash. And she and Joseph were helped, at a time when many working class families were large, by having only two children to feed and clothe – a son, William (Heddle's father, b. 1870) and a daughter, Amy (b. 1872). Nevertheless, daily life would always be a struggle.

Although Charles Booth,[11] in his survey of the London poor in the 1890s, would place Alexandra Street in the 'Pink' category – 'Fairly comfortable. Good ordinary earnings', the family would have been uncomfortably aware that close by were older, 'Dark Blue' streets – 'Very poor, casual. Chronic want'. And even bottom of the scale 'Black' – 'Lowest class. Vicious, semi-criminal' – no-go streets of dilapidated houses where 'frowsy women gaped on the doorstep', shoeless, ragged children played in the street and where it might take up to twenty policemen to make an arrest. It was a constant reminder of what could lie in store for anybody who failed to work hard and seize their opportunities, or were unfortunate enough to be forced on to hard times by unemployment or ill health. Throughout all their precarious years of hanging on to respectability in Alexandra Street, anxiety must have been stalking Heddle's grandparents, swirling in with the Dickensian pea-souper fogs, hanging around in the noxious industrial vapours and breathing sooty breath onto Maria's window panes...

But in the year 1887, when Heddle's grandfather had hard-grafted his way up to the age of forty-five, poverty and despair at last succeeded in infiltrating even the respectable facade of 23 Alexandra Street. Their 'host' was the exhausted body and mind of Joseph himself. Like many other working men of that era, constant hard labour combined with a poor standard of living and unremitting anxiety appear to have completely worn him out; his business affairs had got into a mess; his health and mental state were on the slide; thwarted ambition was mocking and tormenting him into frequent nocturnal perambulations around the badly-lit industrial streets. His son William was only seventeen, his daughter Amy fifteen and his wife Maria forty-three when tragedy struck:[12]

FOUND DROWNED IN THE SURREY CANAL
On Wednesday evening Mr Cattar resumed an inquiry at the Railway Tavern, Hamilton-street, Deptford, on the body of Joseph Nash, aged 45, plumber, of 23 Alexandra-street, New Cross. Police-constable Bennett,

313M, was on duty on the towing-path of the Surrey Canal, near the Deptford Lower-road, on Wednesday, the 15 June and saw the body of deceased floating in the water, and he brought it to the bank, and conveyed it to the mortuary. Deceased was quite dead, but the body was warm. Police-constable Woodings, the coroner's officer, said when he saw the body in the mortuary the deceased had not been in the water more than an hour. Knew deceased had been despondent for some time owing to business troubles, and he had not been home all night on Tuesday, which was an unusual occurrence. He was perfectly rational when he left home on Tuesday evening. William Nash, son of deceased, who identified the body, said his father had never threatened to do himself an injury, and he could not account for his being found in the canal. Police-constable Bennett said he found the deceased at three o'clock in the morning. There was no watch or money on the deceased. Maria Nash, widow of deceased, said he had been mentally ailing for some time on account of business, and had been under the care of Dr. Illingston. He had left home a little past ten on the evening of Tuesday fortnight, but did not say where he was going. Expected him to return about one o'clock, as he would sometimes go for a walk and return about that hour. The next morning she heard he was drowned. Could not account for his being in the water. He had said on several occasions he would do for himself, as he could not stand it any longer. He had sickness and fainting fits. He had no business where he was found, but she had known him to walk in that neighbourhood. The Coroner said they were as far off as ever as to how deceased came into the water, and the jury returned an open verdict of "Found drowned, but how deceased came into the water there was no evidence to show."[13]

In those grim times, the canal was a favoured spot for unsavoury goings-on – muggings, accidental drownings and suicides. So much so that the Royal Humane Society had a string of places (mostly public houses) at intervals all along the Grand Surrey, where they stored drags and other useful body-recovery apparatus.[14]

Joseph's son William was an apprentice in the building trade by then and must have found himself thrust – as is obvious from his being the one to identify his father's body – into the role of man of the house. One questions whether, living in such cramped circumstances, Joseph really could have concealed from his son how deeply troubled he was. Perhaps the young man was in a state of denial about his father's desperation? Or maybe he was making an embarrassed attempt to protect the family honour when he gave evidence contradictory to his mother's? William would have been all too well aware that the tragic circumstances surrounding his father's death would leave behind the dreaded stench of scandal: an account of the inquest had appeared in a newspaper – the sad despair of their private lives had been laid bare for the whole world and his wife to pick over. In those days people were proud and guarded their privacy tightly: sometimes it was all they had worth guarding. So even if neighbours and relations had rallied round with help and sympathy, it would have seemed as though they had no shred of respectability left. Yet the family would have had little option but to bundle up their troubles and quiety 'carry on'.

Maria Nash now found herself widowed, as well as poverty-stricken, in the back-streets of industrial South London – a place that had already broken her husband's spirit. If she had found herself fervently wishing that she had never left the rural poverty of the Orkneys few would have blamed her – at least up there the air was fresh and clean, the views were spirit-uplifting, and washing could be hung out to flap unsmutted in the breeze.

But Maria had already been toughened by a life of hard work, so what she did was rally her resources and go down the route taken by many widows in those days (and immigrant wives in the East End right down to the present day): she started to take in dressmaking.[15] It was a simple matter in the 1880s to acquire a treadle-operated sewing machine, often a Singer, on hire purchase from slick salesmen who were only too ready to persuade a needy widow of its potential earning power (then sometimes unscrupulously double the h.p. rate and re-appropriate the machine if she got behind on the payments). Dressmaking, however, was not an easy option. As an outworker Maria would have been on piece-rate, hunched over her machine and treadling away for hours and hours on end, assembling a manufacturer's fabric cut-outs, expected to buy her own thread and buttons, and all for nothing more than a few shillings a week left to live on, after the deduction of overheads. Nevertheless, she would have found it preferable to working at the nearby glue works, or the other traditional means of support for a poor widow – the laundry. Fifteen-year-old Amy did what her mother had done before her and became a servant, leaving home to join a household over in nearby well-heeled Blackheath. In her dreams Maria must have been harbouring hopes of something better for her daughter.

Times could be said to have reached rock bottom for the Nash family in that summer of 1887. Yet before the century was out, they would each have picked themselves up and, on the surface at least, be well on the road to recovering the family's pride, in one way or another.

None more rapidly than the son, William. His father's tragic and igno-
minious end in the murky, industrial waters of the Grand Surrey Canal, as
well as his own inheritance of the ambition gene at maximum strength, must
have been what spurred him on. Not for him a life worn out by hard grind
and poverty; William resolutely set his sights on achieving what his father
had so abjectly failed at: being a success. In material terms he would never
look back.

And when William Nash had children of his own, he would take care
never to let slip to them any of the grim facts about their grandfather. Whether
he was driven by shame and embarrassment, or trying to shield them from
a harrowing tale, remains unclear. Whatever his motive, he appears to have
made a thorough job of blanking it out: there is no evidence to suggest that
any of his children ever got to learn about the dark family secret. As a result,
they never had the opportunity to realise how the fall-out from the tragedy
of Joseph Nash, their paternal grandfather, was still continuing to resonate
throughout their own lives.

In none would that be more strongly the case, than in the life of William's
eldest boy – the future tenor, Heddle Nash.

2

Growing Pains

By 1890, a mere three years after the family tragedy, Joseph's son William had already begun to feel confident enough about his own earning ability in the building trade to take on the added responsibility of a wife. And not just any old wife. He had picked out a Board School teacher named Harriette Carr, the daughter of a watch-maker and respected local businessman, John Carr, who had a shop in Deptford Church Street. Harriette was twenty-four to William's twenty and her family and educational background were both superior to his own.[1] But despite the knocks and deprivations of his early life, William had turned out to be not only dashingly handsome, he had somehow or other along the way acquired a cocky self-confidence, to add to a canny business brain. The pair set up house several streets further south from Alexandra Street, edging a little bit deeper into the more civilised New Cross area, where they rented three rooms in a house in Amersham Vale.* And, noticeably in a street where most residents were recorded as being 'employees', William was already showing his ambition by confidently ticking the 'employer' box and describing himself as a 'builder and decorator'.

William and Harriette were still living in Amersham Vale when their two eldest children were born; first a daughter, Winifred, in 1892, followed by

---

*Due to bombing in WWII and the clearance and regeneration schemes of the 1960s, the area is now unrecognisable. In the 1890s it would have consisted of two-storey terraced houses similar to those in Alexandra Street and Vansittart Street, generally occupied by two families, or one family with lodgers.

their eldest son – William Heddle Nash himself* – on 14 June 1894, coincidentally just seven years, give or take an hour or two, after the death of his grandfather.

There is sometimes confusion about precisely when and where the tenor Heddle Nash was born. Even the blue plaque on the wall of his home in Petts Wood gets the date wrong, giving it as 1895, whilst the first edition of the *New Grove Dictionary of Music and Musicians* stated 1896. But it's possible that Heddle himself helped to create the confusion by attempting to claw back a year or two of the four or five eaten up by the First World War. As for the place of his birth, it's listed variously as Hatcham, Lewisham, New Cross, Brockley or Deptford. Though he was actually born in New Cross, the old name for that area – still in use at the time – was Hatcham, while the ecclesiastical parish he was born in was Deptford St Paul; the family later moved to Lewisham, then to Brockley – hence the confusion.

By the time Heddle was six years old, in 1901, William Snr had moved his rapidly expanding family up a notch to Lewisham High Road, home to other self-employed tradespeople – greengrocers and small time 'manufacturers'. He had started describing himself by the grander term 'building contractor' and he was obviously taking full advantage of the turn-of-the-century building boom. Significantly, he even felt able to employ a live-in fifteen-year-old servant girl – a sure sign to the world of his respectability and upward mobility: his mother had been a servant, his sister had been a servant, now he himself could afford to employ one. The only fly in William Snr's ointment seems to have been the drain on his resources from eventually having six children to support (as well as, possibly, by that time, his mother). They were Winifred, Heddle, Leonard, Allan and Frank, and after a small gap, Douglas: a number somewhat above average at a time when, as more children were likely to survive into adulthood, upper working class and middle class families were tending to become smaller.

William Nash Snr's upwardly mobile ambitions were undoubtedly helped by his handsome and debonair looks. They were maturing well by then and showing no traces of the humble origins from which he'd so recently sprung. Those who can still remember him remark on his ability to turn heads and command 'Who's that?' attention when he entered a room, an attribute that would have served him well in the business world, as did his insistence on

---

*Though he would be known as 'William' throughout his early life (nicknamed 'Billie' by the family) it is less complicated to refer to him throughout as 'Heddle' – he would happily answer to any of those names).

The debonair
William Snr

always being immaculately and fashionably turned out – every inch the pros-
perous Edwardian businessman with his spats, walking cane, knife-creased
trousers, kid gloves and starched collars – enough to have made work-stained
Joseph immensely proud.

But Heddle himself, with his heavy-lidded brown eyes and heart-shaped
face, inherited his looks more from his attractive mother than his handsome
father. And it was Harriette who passed on to him, via the Carrs, a deep love
of learning and maybe, via her watchmaker father, a fascination for using his
hands to create objects that were miniature and perfect and which, in later
years, would result in some exquisite hand-written music scores. In overall
character, however, Heddle was more spontaneous, humorous and warmer
natured than his mother, who had a tendency to seem remote and constantly
up-tight.

But the fact that Harriette came across as up-tight is hardly surprising, given that her marriage to William Nash had turned out to be no easy ride. Coping with six children under the age of thirteen, five of them boys, keeping tabs on an expansive, ambitious and high-maintenance husband whom she suspected (rightly) of developing a roving eye, while at the same time running a dignified Edwardian household, would have given any woman a continual expression and stance of 'reining-in'. Also, she had been a Board School teacher, trained to educate the children in her care to be punctual, good mannered, clean, neat and obedient and to show respect for others – all of which she attempted to impress on her own children. Her teaching seems to have rubbed off so well on Heddle, he was still demonstrating a disciplined and cooperative approach in the 1930s, showing none of the self-obsessed waywardness of a hot-shot famous tenor, much to the approval of one of his fans:

> At this rehearsal with 200–300 people milling around, the producer – at one stage – stopped the performance with a cry from the heart! 'If only you would pay attention,' he said. 'Like Mr Nash! I only have to tell him once.'[2]

Not that Heddle was a goody-goody. From an early age he played out, roughing it around the streets of Lewisham with his brothers; always getting up to pranks, including one that he described as 'secreting half a brick inside gentlemen's up-turned top hats'![3] And he used to chuckle over the time he sang a solo of 'Land of Hope and Glory' with a bandage on his head, having narrowly escaped having his left eye put out by an air gun pellet. 'How sweetly that poor blind boy sings', he wryly quoted a member of the audience remarking. His niece Mary[4] describes how he was the quintessentially naughty choir boy. When the local vicar caught him and some fellow choristers larking around out of bounds, up the church tower, he gave them a sharp telling-off and sent them packing. But Heddle and his friends thought of a good jape to get their own back: when they reached the bottom of the the ladder, they removed it, leaving the vicar stranded. He was not amused. Nor were William and Harriette when they received a stern visit and Heddle was mortifyingly sacked from the choir. (Once the vicar had calmed down a bit, however, he realised he couldn't afford to lose his star singer and Heddle was quickly reinstated.)

How satisfying it would be to picture young Heddle, on his best behaviour, going round to call on his grandmother Maria in Alexandra Street, where she would feed his imagination with tales and legends from her own childhood in the far away Northern Isles. Unfortunately, that was not destined to be. The widowed Maria was no longer in residence. She'd suddenly upped sticks from industrial South London altogether, making it disappointingly doubtful that her eldest grandson ever got to know the Orkney grandma who had given him his memorable middle name and also, most likely, his precious gift for singing. Maria had not gone back to Orphir (a return had probably never been on the cards: her mother had died and her father re-married, introducing into the cramped household a new wife over twenty years his junior, along with her own aged father, thereby laying hands on a dowry of a few acres of farm land). Not back to Edinburgh either. The place where Maria had unexpectedly gone to live out her days was down amongst Joseph's family roots in Somerset! And her name had even reverted to the drawlingly rural 'Naish'.[5] She had given up dressmaking by 1901 and was describing herself as living on her 'own means', which might have involved a helping hand from William. Such was her indomitability she survived right down to 1924, outliving Joseph by a full thirty-seven years, until she was finally laid to rest in his home town of Congresbury. Heddle's aunt Amy had also moved west by 1901, exchanging domestic service in Blackheath for a job working in a bakery in Clifton, Bristol,[6] quite near to her mother, which at least gave her independence and must therefore be considered a slight step up.

Heddle's father William, however, resisted the temptation to join the family drift back to the West Country. His single-minded commitment to following his father Joseph's youthful dream of establishing a flourishing line of metropolitan Nashes seems to be what continued to spur him ever onwards and upwards. Something was certainly driving him. Throughout Heddle's childhood, his father's building firm, William Nash Builders, based in Deptford, at Creekside and Childers Street, would continue to prosper and expand at an incredibly successful rate.

William Nash Snr had apparently inherited quite a useful 'Heddle' singing voice himself. And although all his and Harriette's children were born talented, Winifred, Douglas and Heddle were the ones who also inherited a bent for music. Winifred would eventually become a concert party pianist, known by her married name of Winifred Vernon. But Douglas, although he was also born with a lovely singing voice, showed no interest at all in using it, eventually going to work quite happily in the Foreign Department of Barclay's Bank. Heddle, by contrast, used to declare that, even when he was quite small, he was always singing and making it apparent to both his parents that their eldest son had been blessed with a rare natural talent. Apart from finding an invaluable outlet in the church choir, he claimed to have been in

big demand at the local children's parties which flourished among well-to-do tradesmen's families around Edwardian New Cross, because he could be relied on to deliver such a good 'party piece' (at a time when homemade entertainment was the norm and children were expected to stand up and give a recitation, sing or play an instrument). His rendition of 'Cherry Ripe' in particular wowed his future wife, Violet Pearce, then aged only three (or so she later claimed) when he sang at one of her big brother's parties.[7] But, whenever the subject cropped up, Heddle would always rubbish any 'twee' image of himself by pointing out how his boy's eye had always been firmly fixed on the rewards of jellies and blancmanges. (Food would always figure largely in Heddle's life, even more so after he'd endured near-starvation in World War I).

With six children to cater for, and probably nursing the attitude that he had managed darned well himself without the benefit of more than a rudimentary education, William Nash Snr naturally sent all his children to the local state Board School. When the time came, Heddle was enrolled at the nearby Blackheath Road London County Council School.

Blackheath Road would provide young Heddle Nash with his education up to the age of eleven. It was a typical-looking red brick and high-windowed Victorian Board School,[8] set up to provide an education in the '3 Rs' for the working classes. But, like certain other LCC schools, it was proud to be progressive: in addition it offered manual training; the older girls received lessons in useful 'plain cookery' while the older boys, for two and a half hours a week, had training in woodwork, including drawing, handling different types of wood, and sharpening and caring for the tools; all designed to train their eyes and hands to 'habits of accuracy and neatness'. When Heddle saw what special significance was given to woodworking at Blackheath Road, the tempting array of tools the older boys could get their hands on, combined with opportunities to learn advanced skills, along with the outlet it offered for individual creativity, the appeal of woodwork became firmly lodged in his mind. Wood became a passion. Carpentry and joinery would give him an intense satisfaction throughout his life, and a feeling of total relaxation. It was a skill, moreover, that he would have in common with many others in the music profession, most notably the aptly-named conductor Sir Henry Wood, known to have been proud of some excellent restoration carpentry work on his own house.

Another benefit for Heddle in his LCC Board School education – never fully appreciated by him – was that it immersed him even further in the rough and tumble of South East London. The extra-curricular education he picked up in the asphalt playground probably offers another likely key to the 'downright earthiness' in his voice, along with his casual use of 'bloody' and – said to have been much appreciated by his fellow artists – flashes of clever and cheerful Cockney wit.

But by the age of eleven he was starting to get big ideas. He fancied moving on to a school that could offer him more than just a basic education in reading, writing, arithmetic and woodwork. He had proved his native intelligence by passing his Junior County Scholarship, in May 1905,[9] and that seems to have heralded a period of thwarted and frustrated ambition, which brought him into conflict with his father. Heddle never went on to sing as a chorister at Westminster Abbey, as is sometimes stated. Maybe the mistake arose because, according to his family, he was clever enough to be in the running for a scholarship to Westminster School.[10] He is said to have been thrilled, and curious, to sample what such a famous educational estab-lishment for the upper classes might have to offer – maybe he already had an inkling, even at the age of eleven, that a Board School education was never going to get him very far in the cultural circles of class-ridden Edwardian England. (Even Edward Elgar had to struggle all his life to throw off his provincial tradesman's son image and live down the fact that he'd left school at fifteen with little or no classical education.) But William Snr, either by design or accident (he claimed 'accident'; Heddle – frustrated, disappointed, and knowing by then exactly what his dad was capable of – always suspected 'design') lost him the chance by failing to turn up in time to get him to the interview. It would be understandable if William, given his own shaky start in life, had considered the posh portals of Westminster School a step way too far, too fast, for his eldest son, but unfortunately he appears to have failed to communicate that fact to Heddle. All that the eleven-year-old perceived was that he had been clever enough to win a big opportunity, but instead of being proud and supportive, his dad had badly let him down. The incident rankled, in the way such incidents do in the mind of a clever eleven-year-old who had been hoping to win his father's approval and respect.

Eventually Heddle was found a place at Mercers' School, which at that time occupied buildings at Barnard's Inn in Holborn.[11] Mercers' was more in line with William's expectations, not only because there was less expense involved, but because it was geared to turning out boys for the 'useful' and money-making world of trade and commerce, an area in which he felt at home. In 1905, the same year that Heddle passed his Junior County Scholarship, the London County Council had approached Mercers' to enquire if they would be willing to accept some of the holders of their Junior Scholarships. After some discussion, they decided to admit a few LCC Scholarship boys experimentally that year. Those would have included Heddle.

Scholarship boys in general can expect to be looked down on in fee-paying establishments, which is enough to rattle any boy's pride, but Heddle's especially, since by that time he probably came from a more well-to-do background than many of the fee-payers themselves (the building firm was still going from strength to strength). And a more Arts-based education (he showed a remarkable flair as a linguist) was what he knew himself to be cut out for. But again that lay way too far outside his father's comfort zone. He did allow Heddle to stay on at Mercers' until fifteen, whereas William might himself have been out earning a wage by the age of ten, or even younger,* so he probably considered he had done pretty well by his eldest son (they had no sixth form then at Mercers').

Heddle would always have a hang-up about his education. Perhaps in later years, when he began to mix with the elite of the music world, he was made uncomfortably aware of cultural gaps or of committing embarrassing gaffes. It must have galled him to think that at a time when he could have been storing knowledge useful to him in the world of the arts, he had been learning how to survive in commerce. In later years the comment was sometimes made, perhaps with peevish intent, that in manner he was, 'more like a businessman than an artiste'. In fact his school days seem to have been such a sore spot with Heddle (perhaps there was even more to the matter than we know)

---

*Education to the age of ten did not become compulsory until 1881, by which time William would already have been eleven.

that he felt driven to do better by his own two boys. Providing them with the best education he could afford, to give them an opportunity to be whatever they wanted to be in the world, without having to struggle, became one of his main motivations in life and his top, and heavy, financial priority. And because he seems never to have got over the lonely, chilly feeling of having grown up lacking affection from a remote and busy father, Heddle made sure that, in addition (though he was constantly busy himself), his own sons knew that they basked in his affection and approval.[12] John (who went on to become the well-known baritone John Heddle Nash) would be immensely proud to perform with his dad in the 1950s, while David's judgement of him today is: 'A most wonderful father', so he obviously succeeded.

It seems a pity that William Nash Snr glossed over his own difficult past. Where they might have sympathised, all his sons, like Heddle, grew up seeing him only as a self-centred, ruthless and overbearing man, hung up on success, and none of them apparently liked him very much. But it was Edwardian England and, especially after having joined the middle classes, William would not have felt it necessary as a father to take pains to 'relate' to his sons. The fact that he himself had been brought up as an only son might also have contributed to his innate self-centredness, as well as exacerbating his inability to come to terms with having no less than five boisterous sons of his own to deal with. It's possible that, for William, the strongest relationship in life would always remain the one where he played the son himself, and that achieving success for the sake of wiping out the circumstances surrounding his own father's life and death loomed vastly more important to him than achieving success for the sake of his own sons. Interestingly, the only child with whom William Nash Snr seems to have struck up any real rapport was the girl, his daughter Winifred.

By this point in the life of most artists, a figure has emerged who has spotted their potential and stepped in to lend encouragement and generally give them a push in the right direction; a teacher, a friend of the family, a relative, or, as in the case of Caruso and of the English soprano Maggie Teyte, a rich benefactor who, by sheer luck, has happened to hear them singing. But for Heddle Nash there came no such early supportive figure and no such luck. Nowadays, of course, financial support from the state would be available for such a promising talent as his, but not back then.

After Mercers' he apparently made a bungled attempt to win a scholarship to the Royal College of Music, which shows how strongly his inclinations already lay in a musical direction. But that ended in yet more frustration and disappointment, due to an 'administrative mix up' that has never been

65 Wickham Road.

properly explained.[13] Ironic, considering the fact that years later he would teach there. Had his attempt been successful, he would have been a contemporary of the composer E J Moeran (later a friend) and have made all sorts of contacts who might have made his future path a bit smoother. But instead, the place where he was destined to pursue his further education was the Department of Technology at the local Goldsmiths' College in Lewisham.[14] There he bowed to what seemed like inevitability: he started to prepare himself for a life in William Nash Builders, and he achieved First Class in Building Construction and Drawing in the examinations of 1911.[15]

Heddle's father had plenty of cash at his disposal by then and could have helped to further his son's musical ambitions but, perhaps understandably, he preferred to splash out on bricks and mortar and generally up-grading the material quality of his life. First he moved the family to a more spacious and up-market abode in Tyrwhitt Road, and then a step up again, into Wickham Road.

Wickham Road, Brockley, represented an Edwardian arriviste's dream. A number of owners and managers from the nearby industrial areas of Deptford and Bermondsey lived there. It was still not too far from their sources of wealth, so they could remind themselves on a daily basis and with considerable satisfaction, just how far, in material terms, they'd come. Yet it was lined with seriously large houses, many of them detached, with curved driveways and surprisingly spacious gardens, all breathing an air of back-slapping opulence. Lillie Langtry, the famous beauty and mistress of Edward VII, lived for a time at 42 Wickham Road. When William moved his family into number 65, on the corner with Glensdale Road, it impressed all his children, especially because of its extensive gardens, boasting no less than three greenhouses growing grapes and exotic vegetables and needing the services of a full-time gardener.[16] Though some excellent single-family-occupied houses still exist in Wickham Road today, its character has been changed somewhat by years of multiple occupation, and bombing in World War II. Number 65 itself, like the houses in Alexandra Street, Amersham Vale and Lewisham High Road, has gone, replaced by a large block of flats. But with a little imagination it is still possible to picture the area in its polished and starched, well-heeled Edwardian hey-day.

Heddle remained at home in his late teens, being employed by his father in the building firm – an occupation he seems to have enjoyed well enough because he continued studying for further qualifications. But under the surface all was far from well. The surroundings were opulent, but the cold remoteness appears to have been on the increase between his parents, as well as between father and sons. Heddle, being by nature warm, affectionate and full of mischievous humour, seems to have turned to his brothers for a feeling of closeness and identity. He had great affection for all his brothers, but the one to whom he was closest at that time was the one only twenty months his junior – Leonard, a sensitive-looking boy who was also a keen woodworker.

The inherited family urge to sing and perform was also increasingly agitating in Heddle's blood. At the age of twelve, under pressure of homework, like so many boys, he had chucked the church choir. After that, in his own words, he had been, 'discouraged from singing'. And yet 'out of evil came good,' he decided. 'I consider this saved my voice, such as it was. It was left alone, to grow as it would.'[17] Now, in an amateur way, he began to sing again, in local choirs and at local events, if ever he got the opportunity. But for Heddle, the opportunities in South East London were few and far between, and in any case, that increasingly wasn't enough – a bit like sitting a water-colour artist down in front of a magnificent landscape with a pencil, but denying him a paint palette. He sensed that he had been blessed with a unique gift – something that made him special – and the urge to have his voice trained, enabling him to use it to the full, was something that constantly itched away at him. Yet despite his father's ever-increasing wealth, no money ever seems to have been forthcoming for singing lessons. William Snr, blessed with a not-half-bad 'Heddle' voice himself, is known to have viewed singing as nothing more than a 'hobby', never likely to lead to a serious, money-making occupation suitable for a man, like building. And of course, there were so few outlets for opera singers in England, he had a strong point. Added to which, he was notoriously tight-fisted when it came to personal cash handouts to any of his family (perhaps he had the feeling that only he could be trusted). Even his wife, in later life, had to resort to blackmail to squeeze some out of him, threatening to make his meanness on the home front a matter for the public domain.[18] Whatever his father was paying Heddle at that point, it seems reasonable to assume it wouldn't have been enough to give him the feeling that he had much independent lee-way. And there's a tale about how, around that time, when William Snr was playing a recording by Caruso, he flung at his son the taunt: 'Why can't you sing like that?' To which Heddle quietly retorted: 'I can!'[19]

But it wasn't until the summer of 1914, just before his twentieth birthday,* that Heddle finally found an opportunity to have his voice trained. He happened to hear that the local conservatoire at Blackheath had some singing scholarships on offer and took the plunge, going along to audition at the nearby Eltham branch. It's said that he hit on the idea of treating it as a bit of a joke, not wanting his family to suspect how important it was to him, just in case he came unstuck! A famous mezzo-soprano named Marie Brema was adjudicating that day. Brema had had a most impressive international singing career herself, having had the honour of being one of the first English singers invited to perform at Bayreuth, and having sung to great acclaim at the Metropolitan Opera House and at Covent Garden. She had also had the distinction of singing the part of the Angel in Edward Elgar's first airing of *The Dream of Gerontius* at Birmingham in 1900, when she had been the only component in the whole disastrous performance to win any critical approval. Heddle must have been mightily impressed when he turned up to find himself auditioning for Brema. Yet, when her fine-tuned ears heard Heddle audition with 'Waft Her, Angels' from Handel's *Jeptha*, she was also impressed by him. She not only awarded him one of the scholarships, he claimed that she remarked prophetically – 'A real tenor at last'.[20]

Blackheath was just one of the suburban conservatoires set up towards the end of the nineteenth century to provide a grounding in music and the arts for the local community. And all Heddle had was a half-scholarship for a handful of singing lessons. Nevertheless he was elated by this first real bit of recognition. It seemed as though the opportunity he had been secretly craving – of training to sing to a more professional standard – actually lay within his grasp.

But even that wasn't to be. Heddle often said that if anything could

---

*Heddle later tended to deduct a couple of years and state that he was 18.

happen to stop him having a career in singing, it happened: this time it was a world war.

He celebrated his twentieth birthday in June 1914. He received the confirmation of his scholarship early in July 1914. On 4 August 1914, Britain went to war with Germany.

What price singing lessons in the country's hour of need? Heddle enlisted in the army.

3

The Dark Valley: 1914–1918

Instead of taking a tram over to Blackheath to sign on at the Conservatoire, the young, silver-voiced Heddle Nash found himself heading for Blackheath to volunteer as a soldier at Holly Hedge House, the headquarters of the 2/20th Battalion London Regiment (Blackheath and Woolwich). Alongside him were his younger brother, Leonard, aged eighteen (the only one of his brothers old enough to enlist at that point) and their mate Bob Jones (who would later become his brother-in-law).[1]

He was probably reassuring himself that he wouldn't be missing out on much; the whole country was optimistically expecting a quick victory and the phrase on everybody's lips was 'over by Christmas'. He could even have been anticipating returning to civilian life without having committed a single hostile act, able to take up his singing scholarship with a clear conscience, secure in the knowledge that merely by enlisting he had 'done his bit' – a demand being made on all youthful consciences by Lord Kitchener's infamous recruiting campaign. Deep down Heddle might already have been harbouring doubts about soldiering but physically he was perfect recruitment fodder: just twenty years old, about five feet nine inches tall[2] and fully fit. And newspapers like the *Daily Sketch* were firing off all those bullying headlines: 'We think that every able-bodied man between the ages of twenty and thirty should enlist!' And everywhere he looked hoardings would have been screaming at young men of 'honour', like him, to defend their 'hearth and home' by fighting 'the Hun'. Under all that pressure, and with mates, relations and neighbours descending on the recruiting offices *en masse* to join

up, it's understandable that any doubts he might have had got the elbow. It was all very black and white and *Boys' Own* stuff in those early days. If England badly needed him, Heddle, ever patriotic and gallant, would not be slow to respond.

During the first days of the war, all musical activity in England had abruptly wound down anyway. All the major musical events planned for the autumn had been cancelled on patriotic grounds, sending jobbing musicians and students rushing off in their droves to enlist, for the sake of the cash, realising there would be no prospect of work or study in the near future. Even renowned composers like Ralph Vaughan Williams and Gustav von Holst were stepping up to do their bit.

Vaughan Williams (with whose music Heddle would later become closely identified) was over forty and a pacifist, but that didn't stop him enlisting straight off in a non-combatant role in the field ambulance corps. Holst, aged thirty-eight, had to drop the suspicious 'von' and convince the authorities that he wasn't a spy before he was eventually accepted for war work. Young George Butterworth, perhaps best known for setting the poetry of AE Housman to music in 'A Shropshire Lad' and 'Bredon Hill', enlisted early and was tragically killed in 1916 in the Battle of the Somme, aged just thirty-one, his death being generally regarded as one of the greatest losses to British music in the First World War. The composer EJ Moeran (who would later dedicate to Heddle the song 'Diaphenia') collected a piece

Heddle centre back, Bob to his left, Leonard to his right. Like many of his fellow recruits, HN is armed with a cigarette.

of shrapnel in his head, close to the brain, and it would plague him for the rest of his life.

But when the War unexpectedly rumbled on way beyond Christmas, the nation inevitably started to feel in need of a spot of music to boost morale. Ivor Novello quickly obliged with his enduringly popular 'Keep The Home Fires Burning', which made him a fortune. The great Irish lyric tenor John McCormack recorded what proved to be two of the biggest hits of the War – 'Tipperary' and Haydn Wood's haunting 'Roses Of Picardy', while Caruso's rendition of 'Over There' garnered the same sort of enthusiasm as Luciano Pavarotti's recording of '*Nessun dorma*' for BBC TV's coverage of the 1990 FIFA World Cup. The operatic singer Maggie Teyte (dubbed the Pocket Prima Donna, and later to play Butterfly to Heddle's Pinkerton) joined music-hall stars in the recruitment drive by recording, 'Your Country Needs You'.

But it was the great contralto Clara Butt (great in all ways – she was 6' 2" tall with an enormous chest and a voice to match) who was the most zealous, booming forth her patriotic rendition of Elgar's 'Land of Hope and Glory' at concerts which raised thousands of pounds for The Red Cross. Elgar himself, although the war saw the revival of his 'Pomp and Circumstance March' was, at fifty-seven, ill and in a low state for much of the war, though he still conducted at numerous performances. He also composed a few patriotic pieces, among them 'Carillon', in support of the Belgians, which, by coincidence, happened to be based on a poem written by Émile Cammaerts, none other than the son-in-law of Marie Brema, the mezzo-soprano who had selected Heddle for the singing scholarship.

Heddle, of course, was still nothing more than a young Cockney apprentice in the building trade. But family legend has it that while they were serving in France, Bob Jones had access to a portable gramophone and that on one occasion Heddle started casually singing along with Caruso. The next thing he knew (according to an account smacking rather of the movies) a group of his fellow servicemen had gathered round and were egging him on with encouraging comments: 'Hey – you could earn a living doing that!' and so forth – words which he took very much to heart. Years later he recalled also taking part in an informal camp concert party: 'sang once in the desert with a military band outside Beersheba...' he wrote, 'to see if my voice still functioned'. He specifically mentioned performing 'Take a Pair of Sparkling Eyes' and 'My Dreams'.[3] 'This,' he added, 'to everybody's astonishment'. So he obviously hadn't lost the urge to perform, even at what must have been a particularly low point in his life.

Both Heddle and Leonard trained as army signallers. It's not certain whether they had displayed some particular aptitude and been prevailed on, or whether they felt that learning the rigmarole of the signaller's art would be more congenial than getting stuck into the purely physical aspects of soldiering – bayonet and rifle training – aimed directly at killing. But it was a risky assignment they were embarking on, given the fact that in the early days the signaller's role hadn't moved with the times and was hopelessly unsuited to trench warfare. Crazy as it sounds, in 1914 the signaller was still being trained to stand in full view of the battlefield waving his arms around to spell out his message with blue and white flags – an open invitation to enemy snipers, if ever there was one.

Fortunately, by the time the Nash brothers were dispatched to the front line in 1916, the problem of exposure had been solved. Battery-operated signalling lamps were being issued, for use from trench to trench, which could be operated from cover and read using a periscope. But transmitting up-front on the battlefield was still a highly dangerous activity; one of the enemy's top priories being – obviously – to put a stop to it. During quiet times the signallers would have been positioned back in the reserve trenches with other specialist troops, but even there they would have found themselves a target for shelling and snipers. Later, when telephone communication came in, they would have been involved in the hazardous business of laying and maintaining the cables, often crawling around in No Man's Land, as well as keeping the equipment in good, functioning repair[4] – frustratingly not as easy to accomplish in the mud and chaos of the trenches as in the misleadingly clean, orderly training conditions. In an offensive, their position would have been right up front – in the thick of things. Needless to say, many signallers lost their lives.

Both brothers entered as privates, but Leonard, although twenty months younger and more docile-looking than Heddle, seems to have been more enthusiastic about soldiering, getting promoted to lance corporal, over his brother. Bob Jones showed the most potential – he thoroughly took to army life – and was eventually made a sergeant. Heddle himself, though in looks and intelligence appearing to be excellent officer material (even to the Black-adder-style mustache, and being noted afterwards for his gallant mien on stage) entered as a private and after four years of service, resolutely left as one. He had very soon come to detest the war; as for authority – he developed a hatred so strong it would lodge in his gut for the rest of his life. The brutal punishments he would witness being handed out, especially in the Near East, aroused both his deep anger and revulsion. Later he would emphasise to his

At Sutton Veny: Heddle flanked by Leonard and Bob Jones.

sons that no way could he ever have issued orders that entailed sending men to certain death for little gain. And he mentioned how difficult it had been for him, taking orders from officers whom he despised for their appalling ignorance and total incompetence. Being at the bottom of the social heap in the class-ridden army of those days, patronised, and having to watch officers helping themselves to the best of everything in the officers' mess, while the men were suffering hardship, was difficult for his kind nature and strong sense of fair play to swallow.[5] Although he was spoken of throughout his life, even in the highly competitive music world, as an exceptionally kind and tolerant man, always full of encouragement, fun and high spirits, his wartime experiences left him with a short fuse for any petty official – or high-up for that matter – showing blatant discourteousness, or trying to throw his weight about.*

Not only did Heddle and Len train together as signallers, they were still allowed to operate together as a pair when the battalion was sent to the front, the shocking belief in WWI being that a volunteer would be prepared to commit more of himself if he was fighting alongside somebody for whom he felt a strong attachment. But Heddle would have fully endorsed the comment: 'I decided that to go into action with one's own brother was an unnecessary cruelty, an anxiety to be realised only by those who have had that particular experience.'[6]

On 26 June 1916, after training at Betchworth, followed by intensive training for the whole battalion at Sutton Veny on Salisbury Plain, they were taken down to Southampton where they embarked for Le Havre – the Nash boys' first time abroad. They must have found it a strange introduction to foreign parts: a train journey packed into horse-boxes followed by long, weary route marches through pouring rain, from one spartan billet to another, until they finally reached the front line on 4 July, at the notorious Vimy Ridge.

Few personal details have survived about Heddle and Leonard Nash's time serving with the 2/20th Londoners, but it's possible to piece together a clear picture from general accounts, in particular from the history of the 2/20th Battalion London Regiment written by Capt. W R Elliot in 1920,[7] in which he made use of the detailed log books. Elliot makes several specific references to the Nash brothers, pinpointing exactly where they were and what was happening to them. But for the early part of his army life Heddle is mostly seen not as an individual, but as part of the regiment. Elliot describes what they endured on Vimy Ridge, referring to the 'inevitable stagnation of mind and morale' during long periods in the trenches, with no opportunity to attack or advance; the necessity to achieve psychological domination of No Man's Land by constantly making dangerous patrols and tunnelling; the hard physical work on building and maintaining trenches,

---

*Even Churchill and Roosevelt, in Southampton, allegedly. They were carrying on a loud conversation and causing a distraction at an official dinner in the 1940s: 'Gentlemen, have the goodness to listen when I'm singing to you...' (DN).

dug-outs and barbed wire entanglements in 'conditions indescribably horrible', in 'mud, slush and danger, with the ever-present possibility of the bomb or "Minnie" or shell which might come at any moment and blot out a dozen men' and – worst of all – the strain of knowing that 'companies would have to muster at short notice and give a hand in repelling the enemy from the front line'.

Where he mentions 'the two brothers Nash' specifically, Elliot reminds us that if the Hun artillery 'strafed' and the telephone cable was cut, it was the signallers' job to crawl out into No Man's Land and repair the wire while 'runners' maintained communication. The work in France was light for the communications section, compared to that demanded of them later, yet 'never a day passed without some call upon the courage and endurance of the Battalion telephone operators and linesmen. The 2/20th owed much – very much – to its signallers'.

During September and October the Battalion carried out several offensives and lost 51 men and suffered 192 wounded at Vimy Ridge. Then, towards the end of October, when all general leave was suddenly cancelled, rumours started to fly that they were being re-deployed to the Somme. But, to general surprise, it wasn't the Somme they were heading for: they were about to be shipped off to join the British Salonika Force in Macedonia.

It was in that far-flung theatre of war that Heddle Nash would experience one of the most defining moment of his life:

> ...when the people of Verona met Dante in the streets of their town they pointed at him saying, 'there goes the man who has been to hell'. After listening to *Gerontius* we are apt to think that Elgar too has passed through the dark valley before his time – and beyond as far as human thought or imagination can reach.[8]

Little did F Bonavia, who wrote those words, realise it, but they applied equally well to the man chosen by Elgar himself, in 1931, to sing the part of the dying knight in his *Dream of Gerontius*. In Macedonia, at the tender age of twenty-two, Heddle Nash would pass through his own 'dark valley' – both literally and metaphorically.[9]

Macedonia was an unknown land. The boys learned that it lay somewhere to the north of Greece and would take a jaw-dropping six days by sea from Marseilles. But they knew nothing about the climate or conditions of warfare – or even why they were being redeployed there. 'Wait and see' was the policy – not one likely to have inspired confidence in young volunteers who had envisaged that fighting in 'foreign parts' meant crossing the Channel to Belgium or France.

One wintry evening in late November, the Nash brothers found themselves embarking for the port of Salonika, with around two and a half thousand other anxious territorials, mostly from London, all crammed on board the *Ivernia*, a former Cunard luxury liner stripped of her 'luxe' to transport as many as possible. By the time they had slipped out into the dark waters of the Mediterranean, the atmosphere on board had sharpened into one of belt-tightening apprehension – all wondering not only when but if they would ever get to see 'Blighty' again: the Mediterranean was infested with German U-boats and they were being stalked. Their first long, zig-zagging sea voyage turned into a test of the young men's nerves as well as their stomachs. Although they eventually made it safely, if wretchedly, to Salonika, they had had a narrow squeak: a fact borne out by the torpedoing of the *Ivernia* on her very next voyage, when she sank, after frightening and chaotic rescue scenes, off the Greek coast, leaving a 'horribly empty sea'.[10] This incident of a luxury liner-turned-troop-carrier being sunk shortly after he had been on board would have a strange echo for Heddle in 1940, in the Second World War.

When the 2/20th arrived at Salonika, the Macedonian climate straightaway let rip in the form of a ferocious night-time gale, flattening tents and flooding the camp. They soon learned that they could also anticipate septic sores, influenza and malaria-carrying mosquitoes. Creature comforts would at times be non-existent. Links with home would be extremely tenuous, though absolutely vital. All the supplies – every single thing to keep them going, from tins of milk and bully beef to letters and ammunition – had to run the gauntlet of those German and Austrian U-boats and then, due to a lack of suitable roads or rivers for transport, be carried on the backs of pack mules. As for going on leave to Blighty – forget it. Even a spell of hospitalisation would get them no further than Malta. Captain Elliot couldn't have made it clearer: 'The way home was barred to all.'

They still had no clue why were they there. On the Western Front the situation had seemed pretty clear-cut: Heddle, Len and the rest of the Battalion were at least doing what they had volunteered to do – fighting the Hun. But in Macedonia they found themselves stuck in a side-show, fighting Bulgarians – nicknamed 'Johnny Bulgar'. No idea why, and no means of escape.

Once they got up to the front line and saw the tactical situation, the boys were in for an even ruder shock: the British position looked completely hopeless. 'Johnny Bulgar' had already grabbed every single important geographical feature. And he'd had time to get thoroughly entrenched and wired in. Captain Elliot of the 2/20th summed it up yet again, 'Wherever one looked, he (the enemy) was on the mantelpiece and we were on the carpet... He held the healthy heights; we had to be content with the plain and the still more malarial Struma Valley.' From their vantage points the enemy could spy on every movement the British troops made along the plain, almost back as far as Salonika.

Only two clear alternatives presented themselves: withdraw, or launch an offensive. And the latter looked nothing short of suicidal.

Such was the position Heddle and Len found themselves stuck in at the start of the new year, 1917.

In the meantime the 2/20th were ordered to dig in, sit tight and be on twenty-four hour alert. Dire enough, but then they came in for the most miserable and helpless night and day the Battalion had ever known. While camping in an unhealthy, mosquito-ridden spot adjoining a canyon, inauspiciously named 'Dead Man's Ravine', a blizzard got up and laid about them for a whole twenty-four hours, while all they could do was huddle in their collapsing bivouacs and feel grateful that at least the enemy hadn't seized the opportunity to attack and annihilate them.

In April, the High Command finally took a controversial decision. Presumably they'd failed to come up with any more ingenious or inspired ideas, because they decided to go ahead and launch a British offensive. To the 2/20th they allotted an equally controversial role: carrying out what was euphemistically referred to as a night-time 'demonstration raid' on a position that completely dominated the British lines – nicknamed, for obvious reasons, 'The Nose'. The fact that The Nose had already been 'poked at' twice before by the British, and both times proved to be impregnable, didn't matter. Actually capturing it was not what the plan was about. As Captain Elliot pointed out,

> The objects of the 2/20th operation were stated to be: the capture of prisoners and identifications, the destruction of the enemy's trenches, and the infliction of casualties; but the main objective was to make the enemy believe that the principal British attack was coming at that point, so as to distract his attention from the real centre of operations, which was some miles further east.

In other words, the 2/20th had been selected as decoys. They were even instructed to set about erecting a dummy camp to exaggerate their numbers and attract enemy attention.

The Nash boys drew a short straw, being selected to take part in the raid, fixed for the night of the 24 to 25 April. There would be three assault parties, each made up of around fifty men. Heddle and Leonard were allocated to the centre party. Already they would have been out in No Man's Land endangering themselves by laying and maintaining the telephone wires, and during the raid they knew exactly where they would be positioned – right up-front with their equipment, alongside the officer in overall command, Captain Watson. It's not difficult to imagine what thoughts the boys would have been attempting to blank out as they waited for off on the edgy evening of 24 April.

In Macedonia, No Man's Land was an undulating valley roughly a mile wide. The parties couldn't 'jump off' from the trenches and go straight into a Western-Front-style attack. First they had to cross that mile under cover of darkness and position themselves in front of the barbed wire. During the previous twenty-four hours the artillery had arranged to cut six gaps in the wire, and once all three parties were in position in front of their gaps, Captain Watson would send the signal 'Vimy'. Then the British artillery would open up to give them a covering barrage as they charged (with apparently suicidal intent) through the wire and threw themselves into the enemy trenches. That was the plan.

The night in question turned out even darker than anticipated – absolutely pitch black, and all three raiding parties apparently encountered difficulty right from the start in trying to stumble their way over the rough terrain of the valley. Then when they finally made it to the enemy's complicated barbed wire entanglement, at 10.40 p.m., the scouts couldn't locate the gaps! No wonder – the Bulgars had slipped out and, despite machine-gun fire, managed to repair them. As the parties fumbled around in the dark, in increasing consternation and frustration – searching for gaps that weren't there – the Bulgars, having been set up to expect trouble, started sending up coloured Very lights. By 10.55 p.m. the enemy were on to them. They announced the fact with a murderous barrage of heavy trench mortars and simultaneously switched on three powerful searchlights. No Man's Land suddenly lit up as bright as day. All three raiding parties at the wire were caught in the searchlights and Heddle and Leonard were in the nightmare situation of finding themselves sitting ducks.

Not that the boys would have been able to give the situation much thought. Captain Watson urgently needed his 'Vimy' signal sent back to Battalion Headquarters and there was that to attend to. Their signal apparently got through because the British barrage opened up in seconds. But the two parties on the flanks were being so heavily pinned down by enemy fire, they couldn't even attempt to tackle the barbed wire. It was left to the centre group alone, apparently with the aid of wire-cutters, mats and a wooden ladder, to make inroads into what proved to be five thick belts. At one point the wire was too thick for the cutters and they had to blow a gap in it with a Bangalore torpedo before finally – those of the party still left standing – actually reached an enemy trench – only to find the Bulgars had planned a 'welcome' package: they had packed it in places with yet more wire and withdrawn to a higher position from where they started hailing down trench mortar bombs, machine-gun bullets, rifle-grenades and rifle fire... Yet incredibly the remains of the raiding party managed not only to get into the trench, but to set about trashing it, and they remained in there for a full thirty minutes, before Captain Watson ordered a withdrawal.

It was logged as 2.25 a.m. when the battle-stained survivors finally reported back to camp:

17 men had been killed outright
2 officers and 68 other ranks were reported wounded.
2 later died of their wounds.
3 men had been taken prisoner of war.

Only one in three had returned intact.

Lance Corporal L G Nash was tragically not destined to be among them. The 'Signalling Corporal and most gallant and reliable NCO', was last seen alive, reported Captain Elliot, 'in the middle of the enemy's barrage, attending to the signalling wire from Captain Watson to Battalion Headquarters'.

Leonard had just celebrated his twenty-first birthday.

Heddle spoke – though never in any detail, as men didn't in those days – of operating with his brother at the moment when he was killed by a bomb from one of the trench mortars. Those bombs were said to travel relatively slowly, sometimes giving the men a chance to see them coming and dodge. It's possible Len was too preoccupied with the telephone wire to notice it.

Heddle also spoke about how close to death he had been himself that night. For three days afterwards, he said, the trauma of the experience sent him completely out of his mind. There was no safe refuge for his thoughts: he couldn't draw comfort from his own survival, nor reap any consolation from his own bravery. How could he when Len was his younger brother and he had come back without him? A lonely, hollow sense of guilt took hold, as it did with many men facing a similar situation – why him, not me? And a deep reservoir of grief, bitterness and anger built up inside him which would never completely drain away.[11]

It was this experience that would give Heddle Nash, perhaps uniquely among those who have ever attempted to sing the part of the dying Gerontius, his own first-hand glimpse of hell:

> Nash's '*Novissima hora est*' is the most moving and most beautiful of all, and the ensuing phrases, up to when Gerontius expires, make me really believe that he is 'wearied' and at the end of all he can bear.[12]

Captain Elliot later went on to tell the tale of how the Divisional Commander, watching the raid from Brigade Reserve at 'The Crag', and seeing the spotlights playing over the men as they 'went over', remarked that he had never expected to hear any of them had managed to reach the enemy trenches. Elliot adds,

> Viewed in the light of the considerable difficulties attending it and the fact that the enemy had already made elaborate preparations to meet the raiders (as indeed he was meant to do) [*sic*] the operation was generally believed to have proved the fighting qualities of the Battalion.'

He believed it to be one of their finest 'achievements'. But one must remember that he was writing only shortly afterwards, in 1920.

In a letter, the Brigadier informs the C.O. that he has 'much pleasure in drawing the special attention of the High Command to the gallantry displayed by this party, whereby the instructions controlling the enterprise were carried out, and the enemy led to believe he was being seriously attacked.'

Those words would have left a nasty taste in Heddle's mouth, if he ever read them. Especially when added to the fact that the major offensive on the right flank – the one for which the 2/20th Battalion's raid had been a decoy – failed to attain any of its objectives. The enemy strongholds were left just as firmly as ever in the hands of the enemy. And when the 2/20th was withdrawn from Macedonia two months later, their presence had made no obvious difference at all to the overall situation.

> Coming to terms with the war meant honouring the lost loved one as a hero whose cause was worthy. Death had to have justification, for futility combined with loss was too much to bear.[13]

Yet the best thing that Captain Elliot could find to say about the Black-heath and Woolwich Battalion's stint in Macedonia was: 'the absence of malaria among the men had been noteworthy'.

It must have seemed to Heddle that Leonard wasn't just a brother dead: he was a brother wasted.

Although he was still in a state of shock and grieving over his brother, and with none of the rest or counselling he might have received today, Heddle had no choice but to 'stick it'. He accompanied his battalion from Macedonia into Egypt and Palestine; and fought in the bloody Battle of Sheria, 'a contest between the British bayonet and the Turkish bullet' which 'the British bayonet won'; then on a nightmare march through Palestine to fight for the recapture of Jerusalem. It was an horrendous time for all concerned, but especially for a young man who by then had turned so anti-war and all it stood for.

All the troops were discouraged by the fact that the British press, and therefore the public back home, were showing little interest in or apprecia-tion for their heroics. Nobody in Britain seemed to understand what they were going through. In fact, the accusation was even being levelled at them that they were having a 'cushy' time, basking in the sunshine, while soldiers on the Western Front – up to their necks in mud – were getting on with the 'real' job of winning the war.

Transportation was an issue again. Pack-mules had been exchanged for camels, which had to carry not only the army's food and ammunition, but also, crucially, all the water, for both men and horses. There were dire shortages again – never enough of anything – water, food, equipment, cigarettes, sleep or rest. On the trek to Jerusalem, when they had to plod ten miles or more at a stretch under a scorching sun with heavy packs on their backs, their boots started falling apart and sore and badly blistered feet became a serious problem. Heddle's feet would never recover. Later, if he was performing a role that called for him to dance elegantly – for instance Eisenstein in *Die Fledermaus* – he would have to bind them up beforehand with elasticated bandages.[14]

Food was a totally inadequate supply of bully beef, biscuits and jam. And without enough water to drink in the scorching heat, men's tongues started to swell up and their lips turned purple. Heddle told his sons that if you had gone without food or drink for three days at a stretch, as he had in Palestine,

Heddle showing the strain in Palestine.

what your body craved most wasn't a banquet of rich, elaborate food and drink: it was just prison fare of bread and water.

Needless to say, there was no water to spare for washing bodies and clothes, sometimes for weeks on end, leading to infestations of lice, which cunningly laid their eggs in the seams of clothing, where it was almost impossible to get rid of them. Heddle, like all the men, broke out in boils and sores, not just due to the lice, but also to infected water, lack of fresh vegetables, and mosquito bites. Sand got into the sores and wounds, and flies settled on them and turned them septic.

The fighting was ferocious and bloody hand-to-hand stuff with rifles and bayonets, dodging snipers and 'killing or capturing every Turk in the vicinity'. It's impossible to understand how Heddle, mentally off-programme, managed to cope. There were constant calls on the Battalion's worn-out supply of courage and bravery, under conditions where they knew that being killed outright would be preferable to being wounded and running the risk of a slow, agonising death under the blazing sun. The sort of atrocities they witnessed caused even the hard men in the regiment to cry out in their sleep.[15]

And then there was the discipline: the bitter feeling Heddle constantly harboured that many of the officers were totally incompetent, and yet must still be obeyed – at all costs. One form of punishment he witnessed that rankled in his mind for years, was called Field Punishment Number One. For such offenses as getting drunk or giving lip to an NCO, a soldier could find himself bound crucifixion-style to a wooden stake or a cart wheel and left there for two or three hours a day, over a period of several days.[16] Heddle could never come to terms with officers treating their own men like that, especially young volunteers.[17]

When the Battalion finally fought its way to the outskirts of Jerusalem, Heddle took part in the historic assault on the Holy City. But the men apparently felt like anything but heroic crusaders about to create history. On the eve of the battle they were more concerned about the weather. The temperature dropped dramatically. Driving rain set in and a heavy ground mist created an eerie atmosphere in the hills where they were camped. They shivered the night away in their light-weight uniforms, some still in drill shorts, with no greatcoats or blankets and only 'iron' rations – and an extra supply of rum. Yet they knew, come dawn, that they would have to face ferocious hand-to-hand fighting with fearless Turks, who were determined to hang on to the city. When the assault came next morning the 2/20th were on the right flank and were the ones most exposed to heavy machine-gun fire, rifle fire and shrapnel. Miraculously, Heddle somehow managed to scrape through alive and physically intact – yet again – and the 2/20th's 'gallant assault' was later said to have delivered 'the decisive blow which forced the capitulation of the city'.[18]

Oddly enough, one of the Blackheath and Woolwich's chief claims to fame afterwards lay not in their 'gallant assault', but in the actions of two of their mess cooks. Straying off with their dixies in search of water after the battle (to make the officers some celebratory cocoa!) they found themselves approached by a group of civilians from Jerusalem, holding a white flag. To their amazement, the cooks found they were being invited to accept the surrender of Jerusalem! Overawed, they scarpered! It was left to others to squabble over who would be photographed accepting the historic surrender. Much to Heddle's lasting disgust and that of his comrades, after all the

Londoners' ferocious fighting, they were deprived of the honour, which fell hypocritically to the Australians.

Heddle went on to engage in yet more heavy fighting in Palestine before the 2/20th Battalion was eventually redeployed to Europe – to fight some more on the Western Front...

But Heddle's health succumbed at last. He had been exposed to battle conditions for far too long. No man has an endless store of courage and endurance, and he had been given no opportunity to replenish his. Given also how disillusioned he'd become, when almost every action must have gone against the grain, it is difficult to conceive how he'd forced himself to keep going for so long.

He was laid low by pleurisy in the end, the result of damp, miserable conditions in the French trenches. His family were shocked when he arrived back home a 'broken man'. He was gaunt; hollow-eyed, covered in boils and sores – and stuttering badly. At Lewisham Military Hospital they issued him with a shapeless uniform of 'hospital blues' – a public sign that a man had 'done his bit'. Then they set about nursing his body back to health – so that they could send him back to the front again! But by that time he felt so fervently unable to cope with going back, he actually attempted to thwart their efforts by surreptitiously rubbing dirt into his sores – to no avail. Back he was eventually sent, to France. But the gods must have been watching over Heddle, because somehow he managed to survive until the end of the war.

Heddle's body, however, had taken so much punishment by then that he would never be really fit again. And, along with thousands of other young men, he had taken up smoking as one of the few relaxations available when things got too boring or too awful. If cigarettes were in short supply – frequently the case in the Near and Middle East – then he would roll 'smokes' out of bits of old newspaper filled with tea leaves and sealed up with the ubiquitous plum jam. He never lost the smoking habit, being unaware in those days of any potential danger. Indeed, having a high voice which was easily affected by colds, he claimed that smoking helped to keep cold and flu germs at bay and was therefore good for him! He'd smoke anything that came to hand – cigarettes, pipe, cigars – but tragically it gave him – eventually – lung cancer.[19]

As for his mental sores, no healing hand could deal with those. The description of his general condition sounds as though he was suffering from combat stress – given the misnomer 'shell-shock' back then. But there wasn't much understanding or sympathy for the condition and, if recognised, it was

In 'hospital blues' at Lewisham – in need of TLC.

rarely treated. In fact, when treatment was given – sometimes even involving electric shocks – it was often worse than the malady itself.

Inevitably Heddle's mental sores took far longer to heal than his physical ones. And even when they did heal over, they left indelible scars.

For the ex-soldier, the war experience was a fully laden pack which he could not easily discard.[20]

Exhaustion, deprivation, stressed-out senses on high alert in situations where someone is constantly trying to kill you, can trigger off unusual responses, especially in the mind of a sensitive and intuitive young man. While he was out in the Middle East, Heddle had started to be plagued by a strange phenomenon: he seemed to be suffering from premonition, or second sight. He started to foretell, with uncanny accuracy, the death of certain friends and comrades, and he found that as unnerving as it was isolating.

But on returning to England, Heddle was soon to discover that he wasn't alone; his mind wasn't the only one that had been fine-tuned by war into picking up wave-lengths out of range to normal men under normal circumstances.

The poet Siegfried Sassoon was another who had experienced much the same phenomenon. He too had lost a brother and, on the night before his best friend was killed in action, Sassoon had had a premonition. He poured out his feelings in one of his shortest, but most powerful poems, 'The Dug Out'.

So many people, from all walks of life, were struggling to come to terms with the tragic death of loved ones or, worse still, loved ones 'missing in action, believed dead', it's perhaps little wonder that the war period and its aftermath saw a surging interest in Spiritualism. Some of the most prominent people and most brilliant minds of the day were involved, including Sir Arthur Conan Doyle (already a convert before the War), the eminent physicist Sir Oliver Lodge, Rudyard Kipling – even Siegfried Sassoon's mother. They had all lost sons, Kipling most famously, due to a poem he wrote about his loss, entitled 'Have You News of my Boy Jack?' which was also set to music and sung by Clara Butt.

Hoping to find answers to the questions that were preying on their minds, and maybe even find some comfort from beyond the grave, people started seeking the help of mediums. Tales started circulating – about dead soldiers reappearing in their old homes, or making shadowy, mysterious appearances in family photographs. Others were reported to be appearing on the battlefield to warn their ex-comrades of imminent and unexpected dangers. And there was the famous tale of the Angels of Mons, when English bowmen from the battlefield of Agincourt were said to have intervened during the terrible British retreat. That proved to be purely a tale of fiction, but a surprising number of people wanted to believe it was true. And there were many other accounts of spiritual interventions on the battlefield which were claimed to have been witnessed by whole groups of men together.

It's not surprising that Heddle Nash should have been in sympathy with the Spiritualist Movement, given the mood of the times and his own 'curse' as he always called it, of second sight. He showed his support in an active way by singing at the Marylebone Spiritualist Association's concerts when they took place at the Queen's Hall.

Intriguingly, an incident occurred, not in a spiritualist, but in a public concert at the Albert Hall – years after the Great War – which left a strong impression on him. He was being bedevilled by the notoriously bad acoustics while he was singing under the baton of Sir Adrian Boult, and he felt himself getting into a state of rising panic, uncertain which note to pitch after a ten beat silence following an overture. But suddenly, he felt as though a calming hand was resting gently on his shoulder. He instantly relaxed, found the right note and continued singing with an enormous sense of relief and well-being.

After the performance, a woman who had been sitting in the audience came round to his dressing room. She was eager to tell him that she had witnessed something very strange. Was Mr Nash aware, she asked, a little tentatively, that while he was singing, a young man wearing army uniform had put in a fleeting appearance on the platform at his side?[21]

From the significance Heddle attached to the incident, it's obvious that the tragic loss of his brother Leonard was a hefty part of his 'war experiences pack' that never got any lighter as the years wore on.

Not, one suspects, that he would ever have wanted it to.

4

Not So Merrie England: 1918–1922

It had been an eventful war for the entire Nash family. Heddle's brothers Allan and Frank, too young to enlist at the opening of the war, had both gone off to fight eventually. The only child left at home was Douglas because Winifred had married a year before the war, in 1913 (Douglas was still aged only fourteen in 1918). After the tragedy that had robbed them of Leonard, they must have been constantly dreading the arrival of another fatal telegram at Wickham Road.

Allan had had a narrow squeak. He had joined the navy and been involved in a dramatic escape at sea up at Scapa Flow, within sight of his grandmother's old Orkney home – though Grandma was probably the last thought on his mind as his ship battled with the icy waters of the North Atlantic. Frank had been involved in a dangerous escapade in France. Like many boys, he had lied about his age to join the army, then been captured and sent to a prisoner of war camp – escaped – and, in true dramatic style, been hidden and aided by a French farmer. It must have felt strange for the brothers to find themselves reunited and back at home after more than four momentous years apart, each now carrying his own separate memory pack and all struggling to come to terms with Leonard's eerily empty place. Yet the boys remained close and they would stay that way for the rest of their lives.[1]

Despite being full of relief at having these three combatant sons back home intact (more or less intact in Heddle's case) Harriette couldn't have been in the best of spirits because she was nursing a few private problems, caused by her self-centred, unpredictable and now frequently absent husband.

In 1918 William Nash Snr was forty-eight and a wealthy man. In business terms, he'd had a most excellent war. The building firm had flourished, picking up all sorts of lucrative jobs, including, some said, repairing damage caused by Zeppelin bombing. But right out of the blue, or so it seemed, he had made a momentous decision: he would sell the business, retire early and start enjoying his wealth. In his mind there must always have lurked the spectre of Joseph, fished waterlogged from the canal aged forty-five after a life of hard labour and little fun.

Because William himself would have started work at an early age, he must already have put in way in excess of thirty years. Now he was determined to seize some well-earned enjoyment while he was still in his prime, and with the hearty appetite to savour it to the maximum.

What he intended to do was pursue certain interests that had been gradually developing in his life – namely, horse racing, snooker and – astonishingly – living the life of a fashionable man-about-town up West. Believe it or not, this man of many surprises had become a member of the sumptuous RAC Club in Pall Mall, famed for its green-shaded snooker tables, smoking rooms and marbled Turkish baths – all providing a feeling of well-being and offering excellent away-from-home facilities and freedom from domestic hassle. Contacts in the sporting world must have been his entrée to this gentlemen's club world in which he now found himself to be very much at his ease. Mentally – if not geographically – he had now travelled about a million miles from the despair and poverty of his youth.[2]

His absences from Wickham Road were fairly frequent at that time because he was either at his club or travelling from racecourse to racecourse, betting, some claim, with huge success, though not according to his grandson David, who maintains that Grandpa Nash warned all his sons against the pursuit: 'Never bet on horses!' He claimed that even with his expert insider knowledge of the turf, he only just broke even.

And then there was the lure of those excellent snooker tables at the club. The amazing William seems to have done little by half – even when it came to potting balls. In snooker there was such excellent prize money to be pocketed that it seems possible he amassed some of his wealth from snooker as well as from building. Eventually his name would even go down in the annals of snooker history. In 1926 William Nash achieved the distinction of becoming Amateur Snooker Champion of England – and that at a time when a professional championship did not exist! To win the coveted title he defeated an opponent named Fred Morley 383–356 3–4 in the final.*

---

*For snooker fans: William won the title on aggregate, as was the rule at the time. There

Money-making prowess, sporting prowess (he was a talented amateur golfer and cricketer too) – as though all that didn't distinguish him enough, William also became a prominent Freemason and eventually founded a lodge, the Sir Francis Drake Lodge at Deptford. Into a life packed out with business and leisure pursuits, he also somehow managed to slot in the time to function as a local Lewisham councillor and it is said that he turned down the position of mayor on no less than three occasions.

Poor old Joseph would, one suspects, have been proud and thrilled – doing whatever was the 1920s equivalent of punching the air, had he lived to see the day. But it was a crushing list of achievements for a man's own sons to live up to!

A true Edwardian entrepreneur, combining enormous vitality and intelligence with a Midas touch, William Nash Snr was evidently a thoroughly charming man, yet at the same time he could be mean, selfish and unscrupulous – hardly surprising that none of his sons could ever force much liking for him. And only Winifred turned out to share her father's keen interest in playing the Stock Market. When he died, it was to her that William left his shares, and – much to the disgruntlement of her brothers – she's reputed to have done very well out of them.[4]

The sale of the family firm would, of course, have had a devastating effect on Heddle. As the eldest son he had been brought up to expect to play a leading part. And all through the war he had believed that he had the security of a job to come back to. While in Belgium, waiting to be demobbed, he had actually hired a room overlooking a parade ground to study for some building exams he intended to take when he returned to England. Sometimes he used to tell an anecdote about an incident he had witnessed at that time. He would incorporate it into his concerts when about to sing the words, 'I will arise and go unto my father'. Apparently one wet and windy day he was idly watching some troops out on the parade ground, when a farrier sergeant lurched out in a drunken state to take charge. In a stentorian voice Heddle overheard the sergeant roaring at the men, 'I will go unto my father and I will say – "Father – Stand at.... Ease!" Upon which, he fell down in a drunken stupor.

had apparently been rumblings about this rule for several years and it was as a result of this victory in 1926, when William Nash won the title even though his opponent had taken four frames to his three, that the rule was finally changed. (3)

Stage-struck Violet c. 1921.

But on finally being demobbed in 1919, it came as a powerful shock to Heddle's system to learn that suddenly there was no family firm to join – because his dad had disposed of it. Heddle could not have been deprived of his safety net at a worse time – just when his health was wrecked, he was stuttering badly, and to top it all, even if he had been able to summon up the strength to go job hunting, the whole country was in the grip of mass unemployment.

Only one bright spot illuminated those depressing post-war days as

Heddle reeled around, struggling to get fit and to pick up the threads of civilian life: he had found romance. An attachment had flared up between him and Violet Pearce, his little fan from the children's parties. On one of his leaves home from France he had called to visit her brother. But it was an all-grown-up-and-blooming eighteen-year-old Violet who had bounded to the door. Propping himself up weakly on the family's doorstep was this wan-faced, stuttering, heroic combatant – obviously a case in dire need of 'comforts' and a good slice of a girl's 'War Effort'. For her, she claimed, in those heady, emotionally-charged wartime days, it was 'love at first sight'. She lost no time in scooping him up and lavishing on him some hearty TLC.

The Pearce family and the Nash family lived within half a mile of each other (the Pearces at Jerningham Road) and Violet's brother had been Heddle's best friend in the church choir. Her family were also well-to-do local business people, the owners of Pearce Signs of New Cross, which would later become Britain's leading sign maker (noted particularly by the public for having produced the moving neon sign of a workman climbing a ladder, which was quite revolutionary at the time, and attracted people into the area specifically to stand and watch it). The Nash boys were impressed by the Pearces having private tennis courts, which they let out and which Violet had the job of organising. William Nash Snr himself thoroughly approved of his son's forging a close connection with Pearce Signs, Mr Pearce Snr being, in all respects, a man after his own heart.[5]

The young Violet was pert, vivacious, loved to sing, and was into amateur theatricals. Possibly she was also stage-struck, because in 1921 she went on tour as a soubrette. She claimed to have done so purely to find out what it would be like to be 'the wife of a performer', but actually sampling squalid, crowded dressing rooms and depressing digs – the provincial norm – seems a bit extreme and unlikely for a well-brought-up girl at that time, so one suspects strong theatrical ambitions of her own. She certainly always enjoyed having a hands-on role in Heddle's theatrical world.

Back in 1920, however, Heddle, whose stutter had improved but was not yet cured, was encouraged by Violet to audition for the Wimbledon Amateur Operatic Group's production of Edward German's patriotic operetta, *Merrie England*. He landed the prestigious role of Sir Walter Raleigh, a role he would reprise on the professional stage, to huge acclaim, many years later and in the aftermath of another war, in 1946. And by lucky chance the composer in person happened to drop by for a performance. After hearing Heddle sing 'The English Rose', German made a point of publicly singling him out for lavish praise, an act said to have rather disgruntled his fellow performers. But

it was exactly the sort of encouragement Heddle needed at such a low point in his life: it made him feel that a professional singing career might just be a possibility.

As his health started to improve (singing in *Merrie England* is said to have cured his stutter)[6] Heddle, encouraged by Violet, became increasingly certain that his way ahead lay in taking up the singing lessons he had won before the war. They were still his for the taking; scholarships having been respectfully kept open for all holders who had been snatched away to fight and were fortunate enough to return to claim them (which must have meant that a good few were going spare).

Heddle was probably also thinking along the same lines as many other

The great Marie Brema.

young men of his generation: that, having so miraculously survived the carnage of war, he owed it to himself and to those who had died, to use his gifts to do something special with his life, if he could.

And so it was that Heddle Nash finally presented himself at Blackheath Conservatoire to study singing – six years late!

Some sources claim that he actually studied there with Marie Brema, but Blackheath have no evidence that she ever taught there, though she is known to have taught in Manchester. She signed Heddle's scholarship certificate, but only in the capacity of a visiting adjudicator. The mezzo-soprano would have been into her seventies by then, though strong on experience. Heddle would have found Brema (née Minnie Fehrmann and born in Liverpool) still a forceful personality. In her day she had been especially noted for her performance as Brunnhilde – a part to which she had brought not only a splendid vocal interpretation, but also her striking physical stature – she had been one of Queen Victoria's favourite singers, and it was said, in awe, that her booming voice packed the capacity to 'blow the queen out of her chair'. She had also been a highly active Vice President of the Actresses Franchise League before the War, playing a militant part in campaigning for votes for women. And there's a tale of how she dealt with a heckler in Paris who expressed a dislike for her repertoire: fastening her eyes on him, she fairly bit out the words. The audience cheered her.[7]

Heddle, always noted for his boyish high spirits and sense of fun, would certainly have had a few 'Brema' tales to tell. But the only comment anybody remembers him making about his Blackheath lessons was bland and diplomatic – 'a grounding that would stand me in good stead when I went on to do further study later' – nothing could be a more definite indication that some worthy, but colourless, singing coach and not the great Brema herself had taught him. (One should not, of course, rule out the possibility that Heddle subtly bandied Brema's name about himself at some point in the early stages of his career, to give his initial training a bit more clout.)

While he was still studying at Blackheath, Heddle started to pick up one or two paid singing jobs at various venues around South East London: 'trying to find someone to pay me for singing a few songs' was how he put it. But he was only pocketing the odd guinea for each performance (payments seem to have always been in guineas in those days). And the bookings were still way too few and far between to have given him any feeling of security about actually being able to make a living as a singer. He was already starting to have regrets: 'I should have had the full, proper musical course.'[8]

He was still living at home in Wickham Road, trying to build up his strength, so if any bit of spare cash came his way, he would spend it on tickets for the gallery at Covent Garden. Perched up there was where he first heard Maggie Teyte (probably in 1922) singing in *Madame Butterfly*, as part of the British National Opera Season. When he returned home he is said to have raved about the performance, and especially Maggie Teyte's voice which he thought 'just magnificent'. He was probably indulging in fantasies – Pinkerton! The glittering world of Covent Garden! Maggie Teyte! If only...[9]

In the meantime, in common with many other future stars,[10] Heddle managed to get himself a summer booking with a pier-end concert party, and in the summer of 1921 off he went to hone his skills at Shanklin, Isle of Wight. Although he might not have realised it at the time, this first experience of performing to a holiday audience would prove invaluable in future years; the particularly close and warm rapport he had with his audiences became one of the qualities for which he is best remembered. The following year he picked up more work, touring with what he described as 'Gaieties around England',[11] about which one would love to know more, but unfortunately he left no details. He had to wait for a further year before his singing career finally took a significant turn and he was able to experience the joy, elation, and sheer rocket boost to his ego system, of managing to land – at long last! – his first substantial, professional contract.

Optimistically, Heddle told himself that he could now call himself a real singer. This contract finally gave him the confidence to put the war behind him and start moving his life forward. On the strength of it, the first thing he did was rush off and marry Violet Pearce, at St James' Church Hatcham on 7 April 1923. A whole five years had elapsed since their romantic wartime reunion; though that was not so unusual in those days, when a man was expected to take on full financial responsibility for his wife, and there were many men who found themselves in Heddle's position in the post-war years – too skint to afford one.

Heddle and Violet on their wedding day, at St James Hatcham.

In that burgeoning spring of 1923, Heddle – or William Nash, as he was still known – then proudly sallied forth to make his first big professional stage debut: singing in Italian opera – at the Scala!

5

Opera with Strings Attached

Few people realise that Heddle Nash's first substantial professional engagement was singing major roles in Italian opera at the Scala...

Too good to be true?

Well, for Heddle there were bound to be a few snags. For a start it wasn't La Scala Milan that was giving him his first real step on to the professional ladder – it was the Scala Theatre in Charlotte Street, off the Tottenham Court Road. A rather self-important Edwardian edifice that somehow never quite lived up to its grand pretensions by taking off as a flourishing theatrical venue, it stumbled along, turning into a cinema in 1911; then back into a theatre (hosting mostly amateur productions); then ending up as a cinema again, before finally meeting the unhappy fate of being demolished in 1969 following a fire to make way for an apartment block.[1] But in 1923, the Scala was alive with the sound of opera and young William Heddle Nash was being given the opportunity to cut his professional teeth with a top-notch Italian company, from Rome...

Snag number two: it wasn't traditional grand opera. It was comic opera; a genre with roots that could be traced right back to mid-eighteenth century Naples. It cocked a snook. It was grand opera adapted to entertain the common man. Using a potted and often highly sentimentalised version of the plot, it took all the stylistic grand operatic gestures – all the chest-beating, eye-rolling, hand-wringing and bosom-heaving – and parodied them.

Snag number three: Heddle did not actually get to appear on stage; the parodying was not being done by humans, it was being done by a troupe of puppets.

Most Famous Puppets

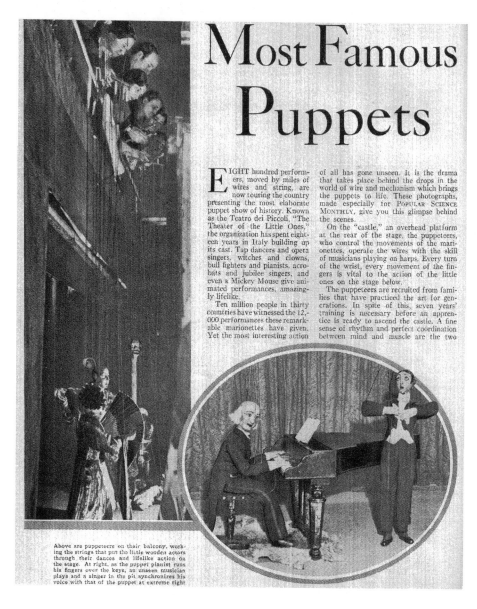

EIGHT hundred performers, moved by miles of wires and string, are now touring the country presenting the most elaborate puppet show of history. Known as the Teatro dei Piccoli, "The Theater of the Little Ones," the organization has spent eighteen years in Italy building up its cast. Tap dancers and opera singers, witches and clowns, bull fighters and pianists, acrobats and jubilee singers, and even a Mickey Mouse give animated performances, amazingly lifelike.

Ten million people in thirty countries have witnessed the 12,-000 performances these remarkable marionettes have given. Yet the most interesting action of all has gone unseen. It is the drama that takes place behind the drops in the world of wire and mechanism which brings the puppets to life. These photographs, made especially for POPULAR SCIENCE MONTHLY, give you this glimpse behind the scenes.

On the "castle," an overhead platform at the rear of the stage, the puppeteers, who control the movements of the marionettes, operate the wires with the skill of musicians playing on harps. Every turn of the wrist, every movement of the fingers is vital to the action of the little ones on the stage below.

The puppeteers are recruited from families that have practiced the art for generations. In spite of this, seven years' training is necessary before an apprentice is ready to ascend the castle. A fine sense of rhythm and perfect coordination between mind and muscle are the two

Above are puppeteers on their balcony, working the strings that put the little wooden actors through their dances and lifelike action on the stage. At right, as the puppet pianist runs his fingers over the keys, an unseen musician plays and a singer in the pit synchronizes his voice with that of the puppet at extreme right

Podrecca puppets June 1933

Heddle had been engaged for his voice alone. He had been hired to spend the entire performance throwing it from the shadowy obscurity of the orchestra pit, along with a soprano, baritone, contralto, bass, and an orchestra numbering the grand total of five. Meanwhile up on stage his embodiment, in the form of a wooden marionette, sang in synch., trembled with emotion, hogged all the limelight, milked the applause and took the bows. And since most of the marionette operas Heddle performed in[2] had more than one tenor part, he was having to adapt his voice, not an easy thing for a singer to do, for it's far harder to disguise a singing than a speaking voice.

But Heddle's experience was not quite as hopeless as it might sound. There were some compensations. For a start, it wasn't just any old marionette company he had fallen in with: it was Vittorio Podrecca's magnificent 'Marionette Players', or as they were better known, the 'Teatro dei Piccoli' – 'The Theatre of the Little Ones'. Heddle might have been lending his voice to puppets, but they were rather special ones. And even though England had its own strong tradition of puppetry, everybody seemed to be in agreement that London had never before seen such an amazingly complex and skilful display as Podrecca's. The show was destined to become the most celebrated puppet show in the entire world, even if, unfortunately, it would also turn out to be one of the last.[3]

We are so used to seeing sophisticated puppets nowadays, employing all sorts of special effects and technical wizardry, that it is hard to explain what all the fuss was about. To say that the Podrecca puppets were impressively large – about one metre tall – and dressed in perfectly scaled-down costumes and accessories, with expertly carved and painted heads and hinged jaws so that their mouths could open and close for the all-important synchronisation with the singing – that's not exactly capturing their magic. To grasp fully the superb wit of their movements and to appreciate the uncannily life-like fascination they still have for an audience, even today, it's really necessary to see them in action. (At the time of writing, that was possible on the internet.)

The show took place on a small stage roughly two metres high by six metres in length. Standing out of sight on an overhead platform, a team of puppeteers – of whom Podrecca boasted that they been recruited from Italian families who had practised the art for generations – operated the strings 'with the skill of musicians playing a harp'.[4] It might take as many as four puppeteers to handle the strings of just a single figure, with perfectly coordinated movements. The stylised gestures of grand opera so perfectly suited these marionettes that an American critic later pointed out: 'when they imitate human beings, they come to grief. But when they travesty them, they are delightful.'[5]

The ebullient Dr Vittorio Podrecca (a doctor of Law) had first launched his Teatro dei Piccoli in Rome in 1914, but the outbreak of war had forced him to put it on hold. Its re-launch could not have been more fortuitously timed; the show perfectly captured the zeitgeist of the early 1920s. Surprising as it might sound, war-torn Europe had seen a resurgence of affection for puppets. It's so easy to forget how life in the trenches was far from being all blood, guts and non-stop action, how there were long periods of doing absolutely nothing but wait around, in a state of either severe nervous tension, or plain boredom, when even puffing on a cigarette couldn't fill the gap. Instead of just twiddling his thumbs, a soldier with a spark of creativity could put them to better use. With a sharp knife in his pocket, a fragment of wood and whatever useful scraps he could lay his hands on, he could relieve the monotony by whittling himself a puppet. The craze caught on in prison camps where some prisoners managed to contrive little rudimentary theatres and put on shows. Creating objects they could breathe a semblance of life into, in the middle of so much carnage and destruction, must have felt quietly spirit-uplifting – like giving fate a sly kick up the backside.

But Podrecca's puppets not only appealed to the emotions of post-war Europe: they soon started attracting a strong intellectual following. The marionette show that Heddle had joined might have been steeped in the traditions of the past, but it turned out to be surprisingly avant-garde. Not that he would have realised that beforehand – he would have been just glad of a job – any job.

All sorts of famous people in the artistic world went along to see Podrecca's show and wrote him fan letters, including the great Italian actress Eleonora Duse, who wrote: 'I envy you. I'd like to be the leader of a marionette troupe, too. Your actors don't speak and they obey. Mine speak and don't obey.' George Bernard Shaw, after seeing the London performance, pointed out that you could pack the puppets away after a rehearsal, thereby 'saving all manner of complaints and gossip' (he was obviously ignoring the orchestra pit!)*

In 1923 the words 'modern' and 'mechanical' went hand in hand. In London and New York the Tiller Girls were thrilling audiences with their synchronised high-kicking dance routines, echoing the movements of machinery, while a whole string of classical composers – Stravinsky, Schoenberg, Strauss, Falla, Satie and Respighi – were all being inspired by the movements of marionettes. Another critic pointed out that while Dr Podrecca's puppets were more lifelike than any before him, in ballets such as *Petrushka* and in some silent films acting came closer to marionette movements.

Otto Respighi had written a new marionette opera especially for the Podrecca puppets, premiered in Rome in 1922,[6] and it was said to have been

---

*It would be interesting to know if Shaw, who became a great champion of HN, ever learned of his connection with Podrecca.

one of the highlights of the 1923 London show. A little fairy opera in three acts, named *La bella dormente nel bosco*, it was based on the seventeenth-century tale of the Sleeping Beauty by Charles Perrault. Respighi seems to have been having a bit of fun, filling it with all sorts of witty allusions to contemporary composers – Verdi, Debussy, Massenet, Wagner, and Stravinsky himself – apparently to the delight of intellectuals in the audience. He had even slipped in an up-to-the-minute fox-trot. All of which led another critic of the time to point out that in *La bella dormente nel bosco*, Respighi 'spoke to the musically literate and illiterate with the authentic voice of contemporaneity.' In other words, Heddle had found himself at the cutting-edge, even if being a voice double for puppets was not quite what he had originally had in mind to kick-start his career.

Following the chaotic and unspeakable conditions he had endured during the war, and all the uncertainties he had been struggling with in its aftermath, Heddle must have slotted into the behind-the-scenes camaraderie and orderliness that characterised the Podrecca troupe with a deep sigh of contentment. He would certainly have thoroughly approved of the way the puppets were so beautifully cared for, each with its own protective cloth bag, and how, if any repairs were needed, they would be carried out immediately, with meticulous care. Such was the sense of expertise and quiet dedication to the art in Podrecca – every man and woman doing their bit without any fuss, but with supreme skill and dedication, that one wonders whether Heddle's own belief – that excellence in performance should be merely the base line – was reinforced by this early encounter with the behind-the-scenes attitude and expectations of the 'Teatro dei Piccoli'.[7]

The show eventually moved on to the Coliseum, then briefly went on tour. It was while playing the Palace Theatre in Manchester that a crisis of some sort occurred among the singers – only vaguely explained by Heddle – but as a result, he claimed to have found himself having to sing in no less than four different voices 'to save the show'! In the hopes of duping the audience into believing that there was a full complement of singers in the orchestra pit, they improvised a 'thicket of greenery' and concealed him behind it. But according to Heddle, the show nearly ground to a halt anyway: the orchestral players and the conductor were so convulsed by silent hysterics at the strangled voices emerging out of the singing bush they could hardly manage to keep playing.[8]

Young, talented and ebullient, William Heddle Nash appears to have fitted into the troupe so well that, come the end of the summer when the group split into two halves, he was invited to stay on and accompany one half on their next engagement. The venue can't fail to have added an incentive when he agreed – they'd been signed by up by the legendary American producer Charles Dillingham and were heading for no less a place than New York – capital of The Jazz Age and, in the early 1920s, the most vibrant up-beat city in the world.

It is an intriguing thought that the only time this man, who was to become one of the finest lyric tenors of the twentieth century, made landfall in the USA to sing was as part of a travelling marionette troupe!

An excited Violet found herself travelling with Heddle on their big adventure with the 'Teatro dei Piccoli' on what appears from the family

album to have been a fun-packed voyage across the Atlantic on board the SS *Celtic*. Who knew what the American opportunity might lead to and how long they might spend in the USA? The Podrecca company's arrival in New York was noted in the *New York Times* on 6 September 1923 under a small heading, 'ITALIAN MARIONETTES HERE: Company Brings 500 Puppets to Perform in Classical Operas.' The article adds that the puppets were accompanied by sixteen members of the Theatre.

The 'Marionette Players' opened in New York after only four days for settling in and rehearsing, on Monday, 10 September at the miniature rooftop theatre (appropriately just renamed the Frolic Theatre) situated on the rooftop of the fabulous New Amsterdam Theatre on West 42nd Street. In the main theatre below and just a week later, Jerome Kern's show *Sally* was booked to open for a return season, while the following month the show *Runnin' Wild*, which introduced the Charleston, would open on Broadway. Heddle and Violet must have been thrilled to bits at suddenly finding themselves slap bang in the middle of the dazzling burst of creativity that was New York right then, anticipating maybe settling down to a long run, and planning...

Podrecca troupe on board SS Celtic, bound for America. A gaunt Heddle (with longer hair) bottom right, Violet centre back (in white hat).

But alas – they were in for a swift and bitter disappointment. New York in 1923, unlike London, wasn't in the mood for Podrecca. Heddle's own theory was simply this: 'The Americans had seen a similar marionette show only recently, and they always want something new'.[8] So the show bombed. It closed after only sixteen performances and the company was temporarily disbanded.*[9]

Heddle returned to England, his brief flirtation with America over almost before it had started. In the autumn of 1923, it was back to depressing, fog-bound old London again.

His life seemed to be rapidly ticking away – he was twenty-nine already! Yet there he was – jobless again, still penniless and still despondent: 'I had not improved in singing', he recalled, and now he had a wife to support.

It seemed he could forget about natural talent – no matter how prodigeous – it was becoming frustratingly obvious to him that he was never going to have any sort of career in singing without more training. The harsh truth of the matter was that a few singing lessons at the provincial Blackheath Conservatoire were never going to get him much further than the orchestra pit. And he coveted far more than that. It now dawned on him forcibly that he needed to train with one of the big, prestigious names in the operatic world; and at that time the mecca for fledgling singers was Italy. More and more his thoughts kept turning yearningly towards Milan. But at that point he couldn't even afford to pay the rent, so dreaming of coming by the sort of financial backing that training in Italy would entail must have seemed like utter madness.

---

*Podrecca's flirtation with New York wasn't over, though. It might take another ten years and many other tours around the world, but eventually 'The Theatre of the Little Ones' did finally manage a triumphant return in 1933. In the meantime plump, beaming impressario Podrecca had obviously come to realise that in America even 'small' benefits from being hyped up 'big'. Publicity boasted-up the facts that the organisation had spent eighteen years building up the cast; had entertained ten million people in twelve thousand performances in thirty countries, and had brought with them no less than eight hundred performers, moved by 'eighteen miles of wire and string'. No wonder they were now being referred to as the most elaborate puppet show in history. Ignore them who dared! Their repertoire had also widened and now included crowd-pleasers such as the Mad Pianist, in a tail coat, the Large Soprano, with a heaving bosom and extending neck, and an extraordinarily life-like, wiggling and shaking, laquer-haired Josephine Baker. They toured the country and 'succeeded hugely' before storming Manhattan in January 1934.[10]

Yet miraculously, as Heddle's spirits steadily declined into a state of total despondency, help did come his way – at last. It came in the form of a cash hand-out from a totally unexpected source. A fairy godfather suddenly appeared on the scene, waving a magic cheque book, and muttering, 'Thou shalt go to Italy, Billie!'* It was none other than his erstwhile tight-fisted father, William Nash Snr.

It's not possible to say for certain what had brought about this unexpected, career-saving gesture. Heddle held the opinion that a friend might have 'had a word'. But one would like to think that William had finally succumbed to twinges of guilt about his sons facing the horrors of the Great War while he was making money hand over fist, then selling off the family firm, and that he was now, belatedly, trying to make amends. On the other hand, he thoroughly approved of Heddle's choosing to marry into Pearce Signs and was obviously concerned that his son should have the financial means to support Violet, for whom he seems to have had a personal regard. Furthermore, William Jnr had now proved that he might, just might, with a bit of backing, actually be able to make some money – and maybe even some sort of career out of singing.

Whatever the motives, William's grand gesture took the form of the gift to Heddle of a four-figure sum – a huge amount in those days. It was a gift that he would, eventually, out of fairness, extend to each of his sons when they married.[11]

For once in his life Heddle must have been speechless. The gift meant, of course, that he would for ever after feel beholden to William, but that caveat was one that probably would not have troubled him too much at that particular moment.

He seems to have wasted no time at all in setting plans in motion to travel to Milan, nor in fixing up lessons with one of the finest Italian heldentenors[†] of his day, Giuseppe Borgatti, renowned for his performance of Siegfried under the baton of Toscanini at La Scala and for creating the title role in Umberto Giodano's *Andrea Chénier*. At that point Borgatti was acknowledged to be one of the finest and most prestigious singing teachers not only in Italy but the world.

Heddle and Violet, their optimism tanks thoroughly replenished, had their bags re-packed and were heading joyfully (Heddle's sudden onset of flu not withstanding) for Milan, even before the topsy-turvy year of 1923 was out.

---

*The spelling that Heddle's father and Violet used for Billy.
†A tenor voice suited to grand, heroic roles.

6

Milano to Columbia via the Old Vic and the Pier Pavilion: 1923–1925

The time spent in Italy sounds like a two-year-long rehearsal for some of Heddle's more romantic leading roles. Picture a charming old cobbled back street, the Via Castel Morroni.* There, at number 6, the young couple found rooms to rent with a window opening on to a little cast-iron balcony, above a chemist's shop. And their landlord, Signor Cecciare, was also a perfumier who bubbled up flowers and plants on a distillation still down in the basement, to concoct his own essential oils. When Heddle needed peace and quiet, away from the noise, heat and olfactory overkill of the city streets, he would climb up the cool stone steps to the roof of Milan's magnificent Gothic cathedral, the Duomo, find a quiet, shady spot amongst the spectacular forest of carved and fretted spires and pinnacles, and settle down to learn his parts, in Italian.[1] And naturally, whenever he could, he seized the opportunity to take in concerts at (the real) La Scala, to hear Toscanini conducting – 'simply marvellous with an orchestra,' he would later enthuse, 'we have no one like him' – and to pick up tips from hearing the cream of Italian tenor talent of the time, including Pertile and Fleta.[2]

But for a time, he recalled being 'in despair on hearing the singing. I was watching the best opera in the world, and thought all opera was like that – magnificent colours and production with full engineering resources backed by the Government'. He declared himself bowled over by Verdi's *Aida*, with 'four elephants'; Wagner's *The Valkyrie* with 'real horses', and as for the crowd scenes in *Rigoletto*, they left him gasping – 'just wonderful'.[3] But above all, he

---

*Flattened by bombing in WWII.

Borgatti, Violet and Heddle holding out a wine glass.

had – at last – got the opportunity for serious study, under the tutelage of the great Borgatti.

Born of humble origins, Giuseppe Borgatti was still an imposing man, and he had retained his impressive acting skills. At the peak of his singing career around the turn of the century, he had tackled all the major Wagner tenor roles to great acclaim, and had enjoyed the distinction of being the first ever Latin tenor to be invited to sing at the Bayreuth Festival, in 1904. But three years later he had started to go blind. Heddle always claimed that the blindness had been brought about by a safety-curtain tragically striking him on the head while taking a curtain call. Whatever the truth of the matter, when he was finally forced to retire from the operatic stage, Borgatti had set about cultivating a second very successful career as a singing teacher, while at the same time remaining active on the concert platform – he was still in very good voice. Heddle held the opinion that the gradual deterioration in his sight had led to the development of an intense feeling for the beauty of sound and nuance of expression. When Borgatti sang 'Spring Song' from Wagner's *Die Walküre* he used to say, 'you could feel the spring changing into summer'.

At first Heddle found himself, most frustratingly, not allowed to sing at all. Then he was given just five hours vocalisation each day.[4] He had to be patient – it would prove to be a very gradual process. Yet it was during this period that he was learning how to 'colour' his own voice, to such famously soul-stirring effect.

Teatro Carcano
publicity flyer
1924.

When Borgatti felt that his pupils had made sufficient progress, his next step was to introduce them to the public by giving them a slot in one of his concerts. Not only excellent training, because it involved learning to sing with a full orchestra (which Heddle had never done before) but also a sharp incentive. Heddle was apparently first awarded that honour in the latter part of 1924, when Borgatti included him in several concerts in Milan, Bologna and Turin, the first concert believed to have been in September 1924 in Milan, when he sang an aria from *Il barbiere di Siviglia* and took part in duets. In a second concert, in October, he was to be found singing a more adventurous repertoire, which included arias from *Mefistofele*, *L'elisir d'amore*, *Manon* and *La Bohème*. By December, at the Teatro Comunale of Bologna he was contributing to a highly varied programme of Reyer, Puccini, Donizetti, Massenet, Bizet, Verdi and Wagner.[5] All just the sort of excellent experience and confidence boost he needed, in addition to being a tremendous thrill for a young tenor.

As for the opera stage, Heddle eventually got a crack (literally!) at that too. Various versions are told of how, and precisely when, his major chance occurred, but it is generally acknowledged to have been some time in 1925, and at the Teatro Carcano in Milan. The following account is based on a mixture of both Heddle's and his family's recollections:

Heddle's opera debut in Milan came about in just the sort of clichéd way that every young singer dreams about. In his case, though, it turned out to be even more memorable than he could have imagined:

A tenor at the Carcano having been struck down by illness one day, right at the eleventh hour, the manager, in sheer desparation, despatched a hurried message, by 'sweating lad', round to Heddle's lodgings. Could he possibly get himself round to the theatre – on the double – to fill the breach?

The part so suddenly going begging was none other than the plum role of Count Almaviva in Rossini's *Il barbiere di Siviglia*! And hadn't Heddle already sat among the spires learning it in full, in Italian, in preparation for just such a golden opportunity? Yet even as he hot-footed it across town to the theatre, with Violet in tow, he was well aware that singing in Italian before an opera-steeped Milanese audience at such incredibly short notice was going be an almighty challenge.

He made it, panting, backstage, with barely half an hour before curtain up – only to be flummoxed by a purely practical problem: in those days Italian singers were expected to provide their own props – he had none. There was no alternative but to go dashing round the other singers' dressing rooms, begging and borrowing all the bits and pieces he needed – sword, boots, gloves, wig (not ideal, but would have to do...) – whip... He was congratulating himself on having managed pretty well and almost ready to go on, just struggling into his shirt, when he suddenly discovered that the one he had been handed had no essential jabot (ruffle down the front). Panic stations! Here Violet proved her worth. Inspired and resourceful, she whipped off her white silk underskirt, snatched up a pair of scissors and a needle and thread, and set about cobbling one together. She was still attaching it to Heddle's front at the moment they caught the strains of the orchestra striking up – the overture! .... It was so touch-and-go, Violet later claimed, as she jabbed in those final few frantic stitches, that for the rest of her life she would never be able to hear those opening strains of the overture to *The Barber* without breaking out in a cold sweat.

As for Heddle himself, he was either so impressed by the Italian singers' dedication to providing themselves with the correct props, or else he experienced such a colossal surge of humiliation at having to appear in front of an audience in – of all places, Milan – wearing not only a make-do wig, but with a strip of his wife's underskirt tacked to his front, that it had a profound psychological effect. Either way, throughout the rest of his career, he would become noted as a stickler for insisting on authenticity in both props and costumes.

And his actual performance? That would turn out to be nearly as full of drama as the opera itself. What occurred next was to become one of the most often repeated tales about Heddle Nash. The soprano Isobel Baillie recounted how 'everybody' was gossiping about it when she arrived in Milan to study shortly afterwards, in the summer of 1925:

> I first heard the unusual name of Heddle Nash in Milan when some of
> my fellow students asked if I knew of him. After admitting that I did not
> they gleefully told me how he had apparently used a whip on some other
> member of the cast. Whilst this was in accordance of the stage directions

Heddle had, it appeared, scared everyone to death by displaying far more abandon than even the most temperamental Italian.[6]

What on earth had caused Heddle, on such an important, career-building occasion, to behave so seemingly out-of-character as to lose his temper on stage with a whip, thereby earning himself the nickname with the Milanese audience, '*Il matto Inglese*' – 'The mad Englishman'?

His jabot? His wig? No. It appears that the looks of withering scorn being so openly flung at him by the bass singing the part of Bartolo were expressions of severe resentment about the plum role of Almaviva having been given to a parvenu Englishman. At the point when Bartolo has to fetch Almaviva a slap across the face, Heddle would later wryly describe the action as 'having something of realism in it'. And when he then fell into the common trap for a foreigner, of mispronouncing the word *biglietto*, the bass triumphantly seized the opportunity to belittle him even further by striding over to the footlights and loudly mimicking the mistake, thereby drawing loud guffaws from the audience. Such uncouth behaviour, quite justifiably, roused Heddle's professional outrage. Not only that – it combined with his *amour propre* (he really prided himself on his linguistic skills). Add a hearty dash of 1920s chauvinism, and you have a volcanic mix. Publicly make fun of him – for being an Englishman? And that from a member of a nation commonly berated at the time for having put up such a sorry show in the War – after all he had been through?*

At the point where the stage directions instruct Almaviva to 'torment Bartolo', Heddle, having found himself at the receiving end of yet another heartily authentic slap around the face, and by that point boiling over with rage and resentment, decided enough was enough. About time he injected his own dash of realism. So that's when he let rip with his whip. And legend has it that he dragged out 'the torment of Bartolo' right up to the end of the scene, and that he mercilessly pursued a ducking, weaving and, by then, hotly protesting Bartolo, around the stage, aiming extra flicks and lashes whenever the action allowed him even half a chance – not quite in the 'spirit' of the stage directions. But this provoked display of temperament thoroughly appealed to the amused and applauding Milanese audience who were a party

---

*Late entering the war and turning against their former allies the Austro-Hungarians and Germans to side with the Allies, the Italian army were said to have suffered a notorious disaster at the Battle of Caporetto when 300,000 of their troops were lost – 270,000 of them, it was said, not to death or injury, but to surrender as prisoners of war, or to desertion...

to it all. (The incident seems not to have done Heddle any harm with impressionable young English sopranos either: 'All this made me most anxious to meet him and hear him sing,' Isobel Baillie comments, rather roguishly. But when she finally did meet him, she was 'astonished to discover a handsome man with riveting brown eyes and a gentle manner.'[7])

Heddle himself used to smile with modest satisfaction when he referred to this incident, which he described as 'the battle in Act Two'. And he commented that he 'always got on fine with Italian male singers' after that.

He performed at two more Borgatti concerts in August and September of 1925. But time was flying by – he had been in Italy for almost two years. Everything had gone perfectly to plan; his voice had benefitted enormously from the Borgatti training ('solved voice production in one and a quarter years' he reported) and he would always carry great affection for Borgatti; he had picked up a few valuable tricks of the trade, and doubtless a few Latin on-stage wooing techniques. But money – a perennial problem for Heddle – was starting to run out. Added to which Violet had just announced that she was expecting their first child and that she wanted the baby to be born in England. Forced to take stock, Heddle reluctantly realised that he would have to draw his colourful and instructive interlude in Italy to a close and return home – echoes of John McCormack and his wife Lily who had been obliged to abandon singing lessons in Milan for precisely the same reasons, twenty years earlier.

The time had come for Heddle to make a bid for recognition in his own country. But not – and he was absolutely determined about that – as Guglielmo Nasck, *tenore* – nor Nasch, nor even Gnasch – all of which versions of his name are said to have appeared on programmes in Italy. Not even as Edele Nascio, a name later jokingly suggested by George Bernard Shaw, to emphasise the fact that to be successful as a tenor in England at that time, a foreign name – especially an Italian one – was considered essential.[8]

Following in the tradition of many singers, he decided to adopt his family-rooted second name to give himself a ring of added distinction and gravitas.* Otherwise, he'd fight for success while proudly proclaiming himself to be precisely what he was – Heddle Nash, English tenor.†

'I'll show them an Englishman can sing as well as these foreigners!' he is said to have resolved.

---

*Sims Reeves (John); Parry Jones (Gwyn); Webster Booth (Leslie); Stiles-Allen (Lilian) etc.
†An appealingly modern clash of images – Heddle: a weaving term invoking down to earth skills and ancient crafts; Nash: a name synonymous with Regency beaux and elegant urban architecture – it could not have suited him more if he'd invented it.

Relaxing outside an Italian café.

NASCK GUGLIELMO·TENORE

Composers and musicians have always starved and, as this is a sentimental country, we think the tradition should be continued.

(Sir Thomas Beecham)

Heddle and Violet returned to London full of optimism in the autumn of
1925. They found furnished rooms at Micheldever Road, Lee Green, just
south of Lewisham in South East London; a street of brick Edwardian
houses with autumn-dank, privet-hedged front gardens, all heavily staid and
suburban compared to the ancient walls of lively Milan, where just strolling
the crowded streets had felt like taking part in the chorus of a grand opera;
where Violet had constantly complained that her bottom was being 'pinched
black and blue' and Heddle had bought a sword stick out of bravado. Lee
Green was also a fair distance from the heart of the London music scene. But
the rooms belonged to the friend of a relative, and as such, they came encour-
agingly cheap and just about affordable for a young couple precariously down
to their last few pounds.[10] Plenty of trams plied in and out of central London
in those days, and it was at this point that Heddle settled down to a pattern
of travelling to his music, little suspecting that he would carry on doing so for
the next thirty-five years!

Heddle was aware that his next priority, after accommodation for himself
and his pregnant wife, was to get an agent. He would never be able to pull in
the prestige jobs without one. Naturally he set his sights on the most obvious
firm – he optimistically determined to try for the famous Ibbs & Tillett of
Wigmore Street.

Many of the country's biggest musical events of the 1920s – the Glasgow
Choral and Orchestral Union Concerts, the Handel Festivals, Leeds Triennial
Musical Festivals and so forth – drew soloists, sometimes all their soloists,
from Ibbs & Tillett. And the firm already had most of the leading singers of
the day on its books – Walter Widdop, Muriel Brunskill, Frank Titterton,
Isobel Baillie, Parry Jones, Roy Henderson… all singers with whom Heddle
would later go on to perform, and in many cases form personal friendships. As
Christopher Fifield points out: 'For most of the twentieth century, from 1906
until 1990, Britain's music profession had its equivalent of Marks & Spencer,
Bradford & Bingley or Fortnum & Mason, namely the artistes' management
agency Ibbs & Tillett, or, as it was affectionately (always?) known to many
musicians on its books in its last years, "Fibbs & Toilet".'[11]

Pumped up with enthusiasm and confidence after his Italian successes,
Heddle hurried along to be auditioned for Ibbs & Tillett, as part of a 'batch',
on 2 November 1925, at Steinway Hall in Central London. Only to discover

that they were not immediately blown away by his talent! Instead of recognising that one of the about-to-be greatest lyric tenors of the twentieth century had just walked through the door, and signing him up on the spot, his unique qualities went only partially recognised: 'a very good voice singing upper notes. Sings opera and oratorio equally well. Think highly of him. Audition Mills, Boosey, Wood, BBC', said the okay but not wildly enthusiastic audition notes.[12] 'Very good' – whereas the word 'excellent' was used to describe two sopranos who auditioned that same day, both of whom sank into oblivion. No mention was made of his youthfully handsome physical appearance either. And apparently Ibbs & Tillett were unswayed by his Italian successes. They sniffily declared themselves reluctant to offer immediate work to an 'unproven newcomer' advising him, as Heddle himself put it, 'to run away and make a name for myself in England,' and come back to them when he had done so.[13]

What a blow. Heddle left the Steinway Hall with all the jauntiness knocked right out of him. Things were not going according to plan.

It was the old Catch 22: get a few jobs under your belt and some good reviews, then you'll get an agent. But of course, all the best jobs go to artists who already have the backing of an agent... What Heddle desperately needed at that point was the magic ingredient every artist, no matter how talented and how expertly trained, needs to succeed – a stroke of good luck.

In the meantime, having no local support he could call on, he set about the morale-destroying task of hawking his talents round the musical venues of central London. He had spent two years training in Italy and used up his windfall – for this? Christmas was fast approaching, despair was setting in again; there was also the little matter of a baby on the way...

But one dreary Thursday, after a particularly demoralising morning, or so the story goes, he was heading back to Lee Green empty-handed and deep in thought – probably worrying about where to drum up some immediate cash – on a tram, whose route lay over Waterloo Bridge and along The Cut. At that moment Fate didn't so much strike Heddle, as give him a hefty nudge. The tram was rattling past the Old Vic Theatre, when he just happened to jerk up his head and glance out of the window. A large sign on the front of the theatre leapt out at him. What it said was, Shakespeare and the classic plays. Operas in English.

Inspired by what he described as 'the courage of desperation', he leaped off the tram at the next stop and ran back to the Old Vic's stage door, which just happened to be standing open. 'If you're here for the audition, you'd better hurry up, it's nearly over!' the stage door keeper is reputed to have shouted, waving him straight through. Next thing he knew, Heddle – probably, he realised, mistaken for somebody else, but who cared – found himself up on stage, being auditioned.

Miss Lilian Baylis, lessee and manager of The Old Vic addressed him, 'I won't hear you sing a whole aria,' she's reputed to have told him (as later recounted to Violet). 'Just let me hear your top notes.'

'So,' Heddle said, 'I just ripped off some B flats, Bs and high Cs.'

'That's fine,' Miss Baylis responded. Then she went on to explain that she was having a bit of trouble with one of her tenors who was, apparently, 'playing her up' by refusing to attend rehearsals. 'Could you sing the Duke in *Rigoletto*?' she demanded. Heddle was astounded, but of course he found the words to grab hold of such an amazing chance. 'Splendid!' she cried. 'You won't let me down, will you? I'm afraid I can only pay you five pounds'. And then she took the young tenor aside and on the spot she carefully counted out the precious pound notes into his needy hand, one by one.[14]

But there was something Heddle had not revealed to the formidable Miss Baylis: although he had learned the part in Italy and knew it thoroughly, he knew it only in Italian! Back at Lee Green, he had to sit up all night, learning it in English. But he was young and eager etc. In less than a fortnight, on 3 December, though declaring himself to be 'nearly unconscious with a terrible cold' (this from the survivor of ferocious warfare!) he went on stage and gave a sparkling performance as the womanising Duke of Mantua. It was a good thing that he had done his homework though, because – he was never quite sure how it came about – it turned out that Miss Baylis had got all the leading London critics to venture out, not only south of the river, but through a pea-souper fog to hear her new 'silver-voiced tenor'.[15]

To his great excitement, Heddle turned out to be an immediate hit with both audience and critics alike, not only because of his voice, but because of his handsome looks. In those days tenors had a tendency to come in rather stout, stuffy and self-regarding packages – heroic only if you kept your eyes shut – so at the sight of Heddle striding on to the stage, the audience immediately sat up and took note. In the words of the *Daily Mirror*: 'great was the sensation when this slim, handsome man strode on to the stage and began to sing'.

'Mr Heddle Nash, a tenor with a truly beautiful voice, sang at the Old Vic performance of *Rigoletto* last night,' reported the *Daily News*.[7] 'Mr Nash bids fair to be one of the finest lyric tenors of the day, if he will only look to his extreme low notes and get a little more ring in his upper ones.

No wonder the Old Vic audiences went crazy over the new tenor. Such a suave *legato*, such perfect ease of diction and assured bearing have rarely been heard here of late'.

Other newspapers carried similar enthusiastic notices. So great was Heddle's excitement at 'waking up next morning to find myself famous', that in a fit of youthful bravado, he is said to have dashed straight over with no less than eleven crits. to Ibbs & Tillett's offices and placed them with a flourish on Mr Tillett's desk. But the agent was still not bowled over. 'How much did you have to bribe them?' Heddle always claimed was Tillett's frustratingly dry response.

'They were rather grudging and not very helpful,' adds David Nash. 'Eventually they did take him on, though. I think the first booking they gave him was for three concerts at Llandudno Pier Pavilion Theatre.'

Back on the pier again? This time up in North Wales? Before snorting in disgust at what appears to have been a morale-shattering put-down for a burningly ambitious young tenor, it is as well to point out that in the year 1926 such a booking was not quite what it now seems. Between the wars all British seaside resorts were flourishing places. And the top ones – Llandudno, Scarborough, Eastbourne, Blackpool and Douglas Isle of Man – boasted large and well respected summer orchestras. The seaside promenade concert was, in fact, a popular British summertime entertainment with all classes of society. A family who had spent their day on the beach would shake the sand out of their hair and go off to a classical music concert in the evening. Not in some hall tucked away up a side-street either, but in a fine and imposing theatre – as in the case of Llandudno – flamboyantly placed right there, on the Prom or the Pier. Classical concerts wouldn't be replaced by the more familiar seaside variety shows until the second half of the 1930s, and until then the summer concerts attracted big names. Holiday-makers got the opportunity to see and hear such first class talent as Dr Malcolm Sargent, who was at Llandudno himself, conducting for the 1926 and 1927 seasons, and he was followed there on several occasions by Sir Adrian Boult. So in the summer of 1926 Heddle was glad to take up Ibbs & Tillett's booking at Llandudno and he made a big success of the concerts there too. In fact, the theatre manager was so delighted with him that he gave Heddle a friendly word of advice, 'He took to my father,' says David Nash, 'as most people did, but asked, "Why did you charge so little money?" My father explained it was the first concert he had done through Ibbs & Tillett, who had never even told him how much to charge. The theatre manager put him straight and they became great friends. At least two lots of summer season concerts became regular bookings and, as a family, we took our summer holidays there almost every year right up to the mid 1940s.'

But although Heddle Nash would go on to be be represented by Ibbs & Tillett for the next thirty years or so, the relationship never warmed into a close one. Being known for his boyish delight in word-play, it's certain he would have had a good chuckle over 'Fibbs & Toilet'. In *The Creation* he would often refer to Uriel as 'Urinal'. And once he quipped in his light Cockney tones to the rather self-regarding tenor Frank Titterton – bemoaning at the time the fact that because there were more letters in his name than in 'Heddle Nash', Heddle's always appeared bigger on the advertising literature – 'So why not shorten it then? To Frank Tits?'[16]

And he would have endorsed the words of his friend and colleague Isobel Baillie: 'I often wonder if the public realises what a crucial role the agent plays in shaping an artist's career and subsequent fortunes. In retrospect I'm sure my agents could have secured far more than my top fee of forty guineas.' On one occasion they discouragingly told her, 'Ah, Miss Baillie, at present you're an attraction, but not a draw'.[17]

In the meantime, after his success in *Rigoletto*, Heddle had been invited back to the Old Vic during the 1925–26 season. He jotted in his notes sometime afterwards, 'Mr Corri[18] said, "The man's mad! But he gave me *The Magic Flute* to sing in a fortnight's time."'

He went on to sing a number of other roles in English to great acclaim, including Faust, Pinkerton and Tonio in Donizetti's *The Daughter of the Regiment*. He was building up quite a fan base by then, which both flattered, and amused, him. He never took that aspect of his work so seriously that he lost the ability to poke fun at himself. So it seems he was quite happy to recount to a group of colleagues the tale of what occurred one evening in his early days of appearing as Faust.

He had caught the last bus home as usual, the expense of a taxi being 'unthinkable'. Also as usual, it was packed out, so he found himself having to strap-hang in the aisle. Lolling below him on the side bench were three pretty girls who, it gradually dawned on him, had been to the performance – and were discussing it. He pricked up his ears, naturally, and suddenly he was rewarded. 'But didn't you just love Heddle Nash?' 'Ooo – yes! He was wonderful!' breathed another, in the sort of starry-eyed way that gave Heddle the impression she might have more in mind than just his singing... He was mentally preening himself and indulging in a furtive, self-satisfied smirk when the third girl chimed in and took the wind right out of his sails. In a bored, knowing voice she exclaimed, 'But my dears – have you met him?' She allowed a pregnant pause before sighing, '*So* disappointing!'

After repeating this tale in her autobiography, Isobel Baillie, being such a great fan of Heddle's herself, couldn't resist the kind urge to make amends by adding her own comment, 'I for one can honestly say that Heddle did not once disappoint me in anything he did or sang throughout his glorious career' – which perhaps comes across to the modern ear as a little more suggestive than she obviously intended!

Heddle continued to perform at the Old Vic to great acclaim until 1929. He was in his element there. His unique talents and high spirits combined to make him a favourite both on stage and off. Operas at the Old Vic were always sung in English at the insistence of Lilian Baylis, who was famously keen to continue the tradition started by her aunt, Emma Cons, of offering afford-able but first class cultural entertainment for the benefit the working people of London – originally the shop workers, clerks and typists who lived locally in the Waterloo area. To keep the price of tickets down and thereby ensure that audiences really would be all-inclusive, she ran the theatre on a shoe-string. The scenery and seating were improvised – ginger-beer crates allegedly played a role – and the pay for her performers was notoriously poor. Her most often repeated prayer is quoted as being, 'Dear God, send me good tenors (or actors, depending on who was repeating it), but please send them cheap.' How she must have been rubbing her hands in glee at having got Heddle for a fiver!

Yet it was generally agreed that the atmosphere in the theatre sparked and crackled. One night she would put on Shakespeare, another night ballet, the next opera and so on. Heddle thoroughly appreciated being part of such a vibrant scene – apart from those occasions when he arrived to find that the ballet dancers from the previous evening's performance had left the dressing room in chaos – 'Messy lot, ballet dancers!'[19] he used to exclaim. Instead of a large, expensive orchestra, they worked sometimes with just two pianos and the brilliant resident conductor Charles Corri. Heddle claimed that music critics would snootily cross the River to Waterloo prepared to sneer at the arrangement but went away silenced, 'it was that good'. He rubbed shoulders with some of the soon-to-be-great young actors who were also lured there to perform in Shakespeare, including Edith Evans, Ralph Richardson and Laurence Olivier. And on one memorable occasion he ran into the great Australian soprano Dame Nellie Melba:

Madame Nellie Melba, on one of her many farewell tours, was booked to sing in *Bohème*. She wanted, as part of her rehearsal, to have the stage all to herself to check all the furniture and props. My father (Heddle) was deputed to keep the stage clear of anyone. When he saw a little old lady 'with a face like a sergeant major' (his words) and explained why she must leave the stage, she replied that SHE was Madame Melba and went on to bounce up and down on the stage bed, saying, 'I once put me bum through one in Texas'.[20]

There are many anecdotes told about Lilian Baylis and her inspirational, if thoroughly unconventional, approach – she seemed to encourage them – it was good publicity. Heddle used to recall how she added to the informal, family-like atmosphere prevailing at the Old Vic by providing fry-ups for her impoverished young artists, doing the cooking herself on a little portable spirit stove in the wings. After the deprivations of the War, Heddle thoroughly enjoyed his food and felt that being thoroughly stoked up was essential to give him the stamina to sing. He was especially partial to a fry-up, so he for one would have been grateful for a good tuck-in before catching that late-night bus or tram back home to Lee Green. (Violet was doubtless equally grateful.)

But there was one occasion when Miss Baylis felt driven to put her frying pan to a different use: 'My father's part of Tamino in *The Magic Flute* was, apparently, particularly successful. Nevertheless, when he missed a stage entrance (the worst crime you can commit in the theatre[11]) Lilian Baylis chased him all over the place brandishing a frying pan! He only escaped by taking the last refuge available to a man – he hid in the Gents!'[21]

Unfortunately one (alleged) high-spirited encounter with a certain Shakespearean actress was not taken quite so lightheartedly by Heddle when an account of it later appeared in print in 1944. In a book written by the actor Esmond Knight, Heddle was absolutely furious to discover that certain elements of an anecdote about himself, presumably added for the sake of upping the entertainment factor, were totally untrue. He thought it such a slur on his gentlemanly reputation that, urged on by his family one suspects, he brought a libel action against both the author and his publishers, despite the fact that Knight had recently been injured in the war.[22] The action was settled out of court, but certain sections of the press obviously had a field day.

Under the heading 'Star hadn't the Falstaff touch', the *Daily Mirror* reported thus:

'Mr Nash is not a man who addresses women domestic servants as, "Ullow, you old cow," and smacks them on the buttocks'
This statement was made in the High Court yesterday by counsel appearing for Mr Heddle Nash, operatic tenor, in the settlement of a libel action. Mr Douglas Lowe (for Mr Nash) said a story about Mr Nash in the book was entirely untrue. It ran:
'Heddle Nash was another who first began to attract public attention at the Old Vic. Heddle, apart from his great ability as a singer, possessed a charming gaiety.
'Climbing the stone stairs to the rehearsal room one day, he was

suddenly confronted by the vast posterior of one of the leading Shake-spearean actresses.

'She, having dropped her bag, was on her knees busily engaged in assembling the scattered contents.'

Now here comes the addition that Heddle found so offensive:

'Heddle, thinking she was one of the cleaners, fetched her a resounding thwack. "Ullow, you old cow," he hailed her. "Having a nice clean up?"

'The actress indignantly replied, "I will have you know I am a member of the Old Vic Shakespearean Company."'

Throughout his life Heddle was described by the women he worked with as 'always the gentleman'. Yet to attract unwanted publicity by bringing a court action over this matter seems somewhat unHeddle-like and demon-strates just how hopping mad he must have been, even though his anger may have been stoked by others. And imagine the ill-concealed smirks and sniggers when the details were read out, not to mention some light-hearted speculation among the public at large about the identity of the well-endowed actress. (Note that Mr Esmond Knight, who went on to become a renowned actor, was just starting out at the Old Vic in the 1925/26 season, billed as a 'dancer' in *The Daughter of the Regiment* in which Heddle was starring, and he went on to act bit parts such as 'extra' and 'messenger' in a number of Shakespeare plays that season.)

The eventful year of 1925 was rapidly drawing to a close. But still it held one more ace up its sleeve for Heddle. As a result of his impressive debut at the Old Vic, a letter plopped through the door one morning inviting him to make a test recording – for the prestigious Columbia Record Company. Columbia had most of the top conductors under contract – Sir Thomas Beecham, Dr Malcolm Sargent, Bruno Walter – so the invitation must have caused huge excitement in those rented furnished rooms in Lee Green. In the 1920s the gramophone was a main affordable source of home entertain-ment on a par with television today (available with no deposit and 2/- a week on the 'never-never'). The public's appetite for records was enormous and Heddle's desire to be taken on by Columbia must have given him pins and needles in his vocal chords.

He sang Cadman's beautiful love song 'At Dawning' for the test. The late music critic Alan Blyth quotes the critic and conductor Trevor Harvey as saying: 'there was no one like Nash to interpret a love song', and Blyth adds that in this recording the inflections Heddle gives to the words 'I love you' let us know just what Harvey meant. 'In this performance, one immediately hears that peculiarly plangent sound that Nash always produced and was so admired... The simplicity and spontaneity of the performance are obvious'.[23] Heddle would go on to sing 'At Dawning' in a film in 1945 – of which more later – and he was to record it again in 1952, so it both began and rounded off his career. In the final recording he would bring 'a lifetime's experience to interpreting it'.

Columbia Records were sufficiently impressed to sign Heddle up, and they broke the good news just one week into the new year of 1926. The contract was for the period of one year, with the option of extending for a second. He was to make twelve titles at a fee of five guineas each, in addition to a royalty of 5% of the retail price.[24] This was not only an honour for him, it was also a tremendous opportunity for those members of the public who were unable to attend one of his live performances to hear that unique voice. But the 'fortune' Heddle might have envisaged in the euphoria of the early days would need heavy sales if it was ever to accrue. His second recording for Columbia, in April 1926, was '*Una furtiva lagrima*' from Donizetti's *L'elisir d'amore*, which he sang in a fine Italianate style. Apparently it achieved good sales so rapidly – around 4000 copies in a month (earning him, at a rough estimate, £4.2s.0d) that Columbia were immediately encouraged to make more recordings with him. Other recordings that year included '*La donna è mobile*' from *Rigoletto*; 'Take a pair of sparkling eyes' from *The Gondoliers*; '*Elle ne croyait pas*' from *Mignon*; 'All hail thou dwelling' from *Faust* and 'When other lips' from *The Bohemian Girl*.

Those recordings would prove to be of vast importance to his career. They would build him a devoted and lasting following. And, of course, it is entirely due to his recordings that successive generations, right down to the present day (aided by expert digital re-mastering, especially by the Dutton and Pearl Laboratories) have had the opportunity to hear and appreciate him. (All the above recordings are still available on CD and still delightful.)

1926 was a year of doom and gloom for the country at large, going down in history as the year of the General Strike, when workers went on strike for nine days in May to support the miners who were heinously facing not only wage cuts of 13% but an extension of their shifts from seven to eight hours. But at that moment Heddle himself was actually bucking the trend. In

the spring, on 30 March, his son John was born and christened John Dennis
Heddle. Later in life, much to his father's great pride, he would become a
fine singer himself – the baritone John Heddle Nash.* For Heddle, who
took the responsibilities of fatherhood very seriously indeed, having a son
to provide for added an extra impetus to his already deep-rooted desire to
carve out and secure a lasting niche for himself amongst the leading British
tenors of his day. There just happened to be an extraordinarily fine crop of

---

*According to John's widow, the former soprano Joan Smalley, Violet was told, while
pregnant in Italy, that if she listened to opera with one hand on her stomach, the sound
would be transferred to the baby and he or she would become a singer. (On the other
hand, it could have been just the Heddle genes resurfacing again.)

them – Walter Widdop, Frank Titterton, Parry Jones, Webster Booth – all chasing the same contracts. And, furthermore, Lilian Baylis was not the only one squeezing fees; they had shrunk by a truly alarming degree in all musical institutions since before the Great War. Not only was the grave economic downturn affecting everyone, the development of the gramophone industry Heddle was so keen to get into had severely hit the live performance fees of singers and musicians, and they would soon be hit yet again by the radio. In the past, the only way to hear the voice of a great singer had been to pay a vast amount of money to see a live performance, but now great performances were becoming available to all, in their own homes, at the mere cranking of a handle or the twiddling of a knob.

The continual mention of the word 'money' in the same context as 'supreme vocal gifts' and 'vocation' might be raising a few eyebrows, but a singer and his family have to eat. Anthony Boden in his book *The Three Choirs Festival* illustrates just how greatly singers' fees at the Festival had shrunk. He quotes top artists such as Heddle Nash and Isobel Baillie as commanding only eighteen guineas per performance in the 1930s – and agents' fees plus all the considerable expenses incurred (travel; subsistence; dry cleaning – singers perspire a lot) would have to be deducted out of that – whereas in 1886 a top flight Victorian singer named Edward Lloyd had been able to pocket one hundred and eighty guineas! Even further back, in 1848 the 'Swedish Nightingale' Jenny Lind was said to have been offered the temptation of a stupendous five hundred – which she turned down! Yet one hundred years later, by the end of 1940s Heddle's fees would only have risen to a paltry twenty-five guineas.

It must have become clearly established in Heddle's mind, as early as 1926, that, as an English tenor of his day – even if he did succeed in his goal and successfully scale to the very pinnacle of his career, he was probably never going to become fabulously rich, nor find the time to swan around basking in the limelight. He would need to dedicate his life – his entire life – to working very hard indeed.

Fortunately, being of hard-working stock and driven by vocation, Heddle remained undaunted.

On the Road to Covent Garden

Over the next few years Heddle's unique voice would win him the accolade 'the finest British tenor of his era', but not without all the determination and sheer hard graft he had foreseen – and some more. A total dedication to a punishing schedule would send him constantly yo-yoing around the British Isles on trains from one end to another, putting him in line for two more titles in the process: 'Britain's most hard-working tenor' and, in terms of time spent actually on the road, 'most travelled singer'.* Heddle would become an expert at one-night-stands.

Earning a living as a singer in Heddle's day was a complex affair, dependent on building up a large and solid base of bread-and-butter bookings – which is where a spot of regional support would have come in handy.† On the whole, bookings in those days were accepted piecemeal, without too much consideration given as to where they were in relation to each other – north, south, east or west. To complicate matters further, the programme Heddle turned up to perform one night might not only be completely different from the one he had performed the night before: he might even be giving a different type of performance: recital, oratorio, concert... He was also slotting in opera. And even juggling different opera companies!

Following his success at the Old Vic, and with those precious recordings under his belt, bookings were starting to flow in a reassuringly steady

---

*The latter title would be hotly contested by Isobel Baillie and Walter Widdop to name but two.
†Walter Widdop had Yorkshire, Isobel Baillie Lancashire, Parry Jones Wales etc.

stream. But he was so reluctant to turn anything down (they might not ask him again! not to mention, of course, being always desperate for the cash) that very soon he discovered a vast amount of his time was being swallowed up in travelling long and exhausting distances.

After leaving home at the crack of dawn and disembarking hours later at an unfamiliar town, maybe in some far-flung corner of the British Isles, he would have to go dashing around locating digs or hotels, unpacking, tracking down the venue – theatre, hall, church, chapel, cathedral (he wasn't fussy), slotting in a quick rehearsal (if there was time) then changing into costume or evening dress – all leaving him barely a few seconds to snatch a cup of tea and nip to the Gents before he went on stage. In those days hospitality in a private home was frequently offered overnight, as part of the fee. If it was, Heddle generally took it, gratefully. It meant having to programme in some time after a performance for being friendly and communicative to his hosts when he was probably feeling fit to drop, but the point was that he was usually guaranteed a good meal, something not always on offer in provincial hotels at ten o'clock at night, and not likely to be obtainable elsewhere, before the age of fast food outlets.

Such an arduous schedule would have taken its toll on the stamina of even the fittest. So how Heddle, who had never recovered full health since the War, managed to keep going, remains a mystery. He must have been running on a mixture of sheer enthusiasm and adrenalin.

Heddle was living out of a suitcase at this particular point in his career not only because of his dedication to building up a name for himself in recitals, concerts and oratorios, but because he had been fortunate enough, while still continuing to appear occasionally in opera at the Old Vic, to get taken on by another company – Sir Thomas Beecham's British National Opera Company (BNOC) which was dedicated to spending most of the year touring around the country in its mission to bring opera to the provinces. The Company allowed itself only two annual outer London slots, at the Golders Green Hippodrome and the King's Theatre Hammersmith.

Opera was the icing on Heddle's cake but, in earning terms, peanuts. His meagre fees at the BNOC came from an unusual source – the profits from Beecham's Pills (advertised as a cure-all from wind and bloating to cold chills and shortness of breath, carrying the slogan 'Worth a Guinea a Box') because Sir Thomas was funding the entire enterprise out of his own pocket, with proceeds from the family pills empire based up in St Helens, Lancashire. In

1920s Britain there was no state funding whatsoever for opera, unlike in other European countries, most notably, of course, Italy, where Heddle had been so overawed by the lavishness of those live-elephant-studded productions. Opera in Britain depended totally on the deep pockets, fund-raising enterprise and/or enthusiasm and dedication of individuals such as Sir Thomas and Lilian Baylis. Like Miss Baylis, Beecham was positive there really was a market for opera in English, if the price was right (and if the provinces could be encouraged to overcome their 'brass-band playing philistine tendencies'!).[1] But he too encountered constant financial troubles in trying to keep his Company afloat.

Heddle was joining a first-class group: Miriam Licette, Frank Mullings, Harold Williams, May Blyth, Marjorie Parry (Mrs John Barbirolli for a while) and Dennis Noble (described by Alan Blyth as 'the Thomas Allen of his day'). But the threat of disbandment constantly hung over them. And as they were working to a very tight budget, the scenery, costumes and props, like those at the Old Vic, were not always top rate, while rehearsal time was so strictly limited that performances were known to attract the comment 'under-rehearsed'.

It was during his time with the BNOC that Heddle made a first – and memorable – appearance in Gounod's *Romeo and Juliet*, finding himself in the nightmarish/farcical situation of being plunged straight into the role of Romeo not merely under-rehearsed, but not rehearsed at all. With no clue about the stage directions (how he would have hated that) he had to guess his moves either from the words themselves, or the covert nudges, gesticulations, and general facial expressions directed at him by his fellow performers – and improvise like mad. Even so, he managed to struggle through without too much mishap, right up to the very last act. Then he came unstuck. Maybe he was just too eager for the ordeal to end. When he returned to the stage to find Juliet apparently dead in her ancestors' vault, relief, not grief, must have gone to his head. He glugged down his vial of poison and thankfully 'died' himself, completely forgetting the fact that Juliet was merely in a drugged sleep. Not only was she soon about to awaken, she would expect Romeo to join her in a farewell love duet. Heddle later recalled how Juliet glided across the stage to where he lay and hissed urgently and unlovingly into his ear the stomach-clenching words, 'You're not dead yet, you fool! Get up!' He had to 'revive' gracefully in order to die for a second time on the altar steps, which he apparently made a point of doing with great panache, to leave the audience in no doubt that this time, it was 'for real'. But to his great alarm, as he lay there 'dead', he felt something warm dripping on to his hand and

Striking a pose in a BNOC production of 'Manon' with Marguerite Anderson.

took it to be blood. Had he now done himself a nasty injury? He couldn't move to find out and consoled himself with the thought that blood would only add to the authenticity. It was only when the curtain finally came down that he discovered it was hot candle wax. In falling he had nudged a seven branch candelabra on the altar, tilting the candles. His relief, however, was to be short lived. He used to claim that he nearly died a third time that evening – at the hands of the wardrobe master who went completely berserk when he discovered that Heddle had got candle wax all over one of the best costumes in the BNOC's cash-strapped wardrobe.[2]

Later Heddle commented that he was learning to be 'more confidently at home on stage' around this time! And he would continue to gain valuable singing and acting experience, and much praise, with the BNOC for three years, until it finally collapsed, under the weight of an enormous tax bill, in 1929 – a very gloomy moment indeed for the British operatic scene. But there would be even more doom and gloom to come...

Fortunately Heddle had been casting his net wide, also getting his foot in with the Carl Rosa Opera Company, another touring company which aimed at the highest quality productions possible at affordable prices. He was also starting to build up a fine reputation on the concert platform, and in oratorio, and he was fitting in more sessions in the recording studio. He must have woken up in some strange bed in some unfamiliar room each morning in a state of near-schizophrenia, wondering not only Where am I? but Who am I today? and even – cursing as he rummaged through his memory in mounting panic – Can I remember the bloody score?!

Then he would fumble anxiously for his cigarettes or his pipe to create a tobacco haze in the hopes of keeping the dreaded cold and flu germs at bay,[3] and blank out thoughts of the critics swimming around, waiting for him to make an error or under-perform. It was a state of affairs that would continue for Heddle almost up to the time of his death.

What was driving him? Apart from the obvious, ambition-fuelled need to keep himself in the public eye, and scrape a living whenever and wherever the chance offered itself? The sheer pleasure of performing, presumably; sharing with an audience his incredible gift and experiencing the totally intoxicating and irresistible feeling that in the course of communicating, magic occurred. As one of his fans would later rather schmaltzily put it: 'Many singers can be said to sing from the heart. Heddle's was an even greater gift – he sang straight to the heart.'

In March 1927, while performing with the BNOC, Heddle found himself returning to the very place where he had started out – none other than the Scala Theatre in Charlotte Street, an event which must have given rise to a few wry thoughts and memories. But on this occasion he was at the Scala because it had been chosen as the venue for a landmark recording session.

Columbia Records had decided to take the unusual step of making complete recordings of the Company performing both *Cavalleria rusticana* and *Pagliacci*. These were to be the first complete opera recordings ever made in Britain using 'the new electronic process'. Heddle sang the part of Turiddu in 'Cav.' and Peppe in 'Pag.' and the accompanying soloists were Miriam Licette, Frank Mullings, Harold Williams, Dennis Noble, May Blyth and Marjorie Parry. Aylmer Buesst conducted the 'Cav.' and Eugene Goossens the 'Pag.' Both sets of recordings were made on to a series of ten-inch shellac discs, each to be played at Columbia's then prevailing speed of 80 rpm.

In recent years these historic recordings have been lovingly refurbished and re-issued by Divine Art, with what is considered to be a huge success. The English translations strike today's critics (as they did many even in the 1920s) as being a little clunky and unspontaneous, to the point of being comically 'Gilbertian', and some of the pronunciation is picked on as being a little 'period'. But Heddle's performance, especially as Turiddu, has been singled out for much praise. On 'MusicWeb' Jonathan Woolf refers to him as 'ardent, Schipa-like in his beauty of tone' and 'a master of perfect diction'. In this recording, Woolf decides, '…it's Nash who rises to the top by virtue of his virility, his elegant and passionate declamation and his sheer beauty of tone.' Alan Blyth describes Heddle and May Blyth as working themselves into 'a suitable lather' in their duet and points out that: 'He displays all the innate, immediate passion and plangent tone that was to be so much admired in his performances over the next decade or so, and which confine the Edwardian stuffiness of his English predecessors to the archives'.

In the October of 1927, Heddle also took part in a wireless broadcast relayed on the Daventry experimental station (long wave) of the full BNCO's first performance of Jules Massenet's opera *Manon*, from the Theatre Royal, Glasgow, singing the part of the Chevalier des Grieux.[4] And incidentally, in that same week, the BBC transmitted their first-ever live boxing contest when the Baldock v Smith match at the Albert Hall was the subject of a running commentary. Full-length opera and live boxing, both novelties in the same week!

Meanwhile, on 16 August 1927, during this action-packed period, Heddle had also made his first appearance at the Proms. Enormously popular, the success of the Promenade concerts had been based not only on cheap tickets but on the excitingly varied programmes (including doses of the new and unfamiliar) insisted on by Sir Henry Wood. The concerts were already attracting unconventionally casual audiences, described as 'buzzing with enthusiasm' and noted, in that era, for filling the air with thick tobacco smoke! Back then they were always held at the Queen's Hall, a fine and much-loved Art Nouveau edifice, said to have had 'perfect' acoustics. To Maggie Teyte, the atmosphere at the Queen's Hall was 'embracing' while to Gerald Moore, walking through the stage door entrance was like 'calling on an old friend'.[5] Queen's Hall stood next to BBC Broadcasting House in Langham Place, a handsome addition to the street scene, before it was gutted by the Luftwaffe in 1941. Heddle would have been performing there with 'Sir Henry Wood and his Symphony Orchestra' at that time, the BBC, with their newly formed BBC Symphony Orchestra, not formally taking over the Proms until three years later, in 1930. Much to the delight and enthusiasm of the audience, he sang '*Il mio tesoro*' on this first occasion, thrilling them by singing the long run in the middle on a single breath, something which very few tenors have ever achieved. Heddle would go on to establish himself as a great favourite with the lively Proms audiences and would continue to appear there – an 'aristocrat' among performers – almost every year until 1952, performing mostly single arias or lieder.

Just how far and how wide Heddle travelled in those early career-building years, with what degree of success he was establishing his reputation, and in what a rich variety of roles, can perhaps best be gleaned from examining a small selection of his reviews for the year 1928:

Yorkshire Post, January 1928 *La Bohème*
Mr Heddle Nash was at his best as Rudolpho; he looked the part, and it suited his voice perfectly.

Manchester City News, January 1928 Halle Concerts, *Fidelio*
Mr Heddle Nash was a dramatic Florestan, and his fine voice should be heard oftener.

Yorkshire Post, February 1928, *The Mastersingers*
Mr Heddle Nash is an unfamiliar representative of David, but he is made for the part, his light, flexible voice suits it, and he enters into the spirit of the apprentices' games. It was an admirable performance in all respects.

Manchester Evening News, March 1928, *Rigoletto*
Heddle Nash's fine voice and debonair manner fitted him perfectly for this role.

Liverpool Express, March 1928, *The Barber of Seville*
Heddle Nash, as Count Almaviva, gives a performance in this character the equal of any predecessor. The singing lesson scene is one of his greatest successes.

Irish Independent, June 1928, *Faust*
Mr Nash's voice is admirably suited to Gounod's music. He sang the cavatina with rare artistry, showing a perfect command of its vocal technique.

Edinburgh Dispatch, October 1928, Massenet's *Manon*
Mr Heddle Nash as the Chevalier des Grieux maintained the role with
a fine free method, singing with touching beauty of tone and acting
with really convincing force and sincerity.

Liverpool Courier, December 1928 (Welsh Choral Union), *The Messiah*
Mr Heddle Nash sang with fine resonance and purity of tone.

The Times, November 1928 (Lincoln Musical Society), *Alexander's Feast*
Mr Heddle Nash's florid tenor solos, beautifully sung, gave brilliance.

Yet, like all artists, Heddle occasionally suffered when a critic was feeling
a bit dyspeptic:

The Manchester Guardian, February 1928, regarding a solo with the
Co-operative Wholesale Male Voice Choir
Mr Heddle Nash sang one or two airs. He lifted 'Sally In Our Alley' up
to the regions of rhetorical statement; we could scarcely hear the old
tune – there was so much tenor voice about. It is, of course, one of the
best tenor voices in the country; still, it ought to know its place.

However, the poor contralto, Miss Gwladys Garside, fared even worse:

She phrases in a short-winded way and does not put a deal of light and
shade into her work. And now and then she is capable of flatness. One of
her songs last night was a bombastic setting of Tennyson's 'Break, Break,
Break' by Easthope Martin. It is as well that the musical critic is not
permitted to utter all the thoughts that arise in him.

Traditional songs, like 'Sally in our Alley', and drawing room ballads, like
'Come into the garden, Maud', were so popular with audiences in the 1920s
that for Heddle, like other top artists including Caruso and McCormack,
they formed part of the stock in trade, often included in recitals, when
Heddle would lavish on them just as much of his artistry as on an operatic
aria. He had recorded 'Sally in our Alley', with a superb anonymous accompanist, just a few months earlier, and the late critic and Nash fan Alan Blyth
regarded it as 'an absolute winner' and 'one of the most desirable of his early
recordings.' To Blyth, 'Nash lives every word and bar of the song'. Which just
goes to prove that one critic's 'relish and enthusiasm' is another critic's idea of

'showing off' (unless Heddle had indeed got carried away by the adulation of the audience on that occasion with the Co-op, but being always a thorough professional, that seems unlikely).

Yet despite all the plaudits he was winning in that hard-working, career-building year of 1928, when one would have imagined he had not a single free slot, it comes as a surprise to learn that in May Heddle was overcome by an urgent need to dash back to Italy for a few refresher lessons – 'my singing wants lots of hard work to get it into proper shape,' he declared![6]

Throughout his career on the concert platform, Heddle's Mozart arias were always especially popular. But Mozart is notoriously difficult to sing, as the soprano Maggie Teyte was at pains to point out:

> ...what a hair-splitting business it is, and how infinitesimal the margin must be between perfection and something quite unacceptable to the ears of a connoisseur of good singing.
>
> With Mozart, that infinitesimal margin is fined down still further... 'Learn to sing Mozart well, and the rest will take care of itself.'[7]

Yet Mozart was Heddle's preferred composer – 'good for the human voice' he used to say (unlike Bach who 'treated it like a trumpet').[8] Don Ottavio in *Don Giovanni* was a role his unique voice and Italian training made him entirely suited to. But he must have been quakingly aware of that 'infinitesimal margin' when he was finally paid the honour of being invited to make his debut at the Royal Opera House Covent Garden, on 27 May 1929 during the Summer International Season, and the invitation was to sing that very role. The largely international cast was impressive, made up of Mariano Stabile, Anne Roselle, Elisabeth Schumann and Miriam Licette with Sir John Barbirolli conducting.

Though thrilled to have been offered this ultimate honour, the signs are that Heddle was acutely anxious and sweaty-palmed about his debut at Covent Garden. How well would he be received by an urbane, evening-dressed and bejewelled audience? – so unlike the enthusiastic Old Vic, outer London, and provincial audiences with their affordable tickets, who were easily won over by his fine voice, his charm, and his determination to give them an unforgettable night at the opera. Maybe some often-quoted words from his stingingly no-nonsense employer Miss Lilian Baylis were preying on his mind: she is said to have informed one of her debut performers bluntly, 'Well dear, you've had your chance: and you missed it.'[9]

What if he 'missed it' at Covent Garden? What then?

According to Violet's own account, Heddle insisted that she should watch the performance not from the comfort of the stalls, but from the gallery – where the acoustics were good and where he had often sat himself in his impoverished days – so that she could tell him how well his voice had carried.

Afterwards she dashed round to his dressing room bursting with eagerness to report that he needn't have worried! Not about how well his voice would resonate, nor about his overall performance, nor the audience's reception – far from it! He had received *nine* ovations! In an ecstasy of excitement Violet must have counted them all. *NINE* ovations![10] It was the sort of reception rarely seen at Covent Garden.

In the words of *The Daily Express*, Heddle's singing had 'brought the house down'!

The Daily Express
Mr Heddle Nash, an English tenor, twice brought down the house with some glorious singing, especially in '*Il mio tesoro.*'

The Evening Standard
Another and even greater success was the Don Ottavio of Heddle Nash, who is that rare thing, an English tenor with an absolutely genuine Italian production and quality. His flexibility is wonderful – I have never heard '*Della sua*' sound better – he has no 'tightness' of tone, and his singing on this occasion was quite one of Covent Garden's big events.

The Times
Mr Heddle Nash too, with a supple style and a lyrical tone made the arias of Don Ottavio stand out as events of remarkable beauty and gave more significance to the part than it often has.

The Daily Mail
His tone was liquid. He rose like a bird to the demands of the music which, with all its sweetness, is really so stern, so difficult to approach – music which pitilessly betrays the least fault of execution. The young singer (whose career we have followed with interest ever since his first appearance at the Old Vic) proved himself as good a lyric tenor as there is in the world today.

'As good a lyric tenor as there is in the world today' – what more could
he have wished for? – it was enough to turn his head! But Heddle couldn't
afford to sit around on his laurels, gloating. He must straight away have been
asking himself the nail-biting question, now how the hell do I follow a success
like that?

Fortunately the very next month provided an answer. He was invited to
take over the part of Rodolfo in *La Bohème* at Covent Garden, from the
great Italian tenor Aureliano Pertile, the very same tenor whose performance
he had admired so much at La Scala during his student days: a stimulating

yet at the same time highly daunting prospect. Heddle was of an altogether different cut from Pertile – his voice decidedly wasn't the size of Pertile's – but then neither was his physique! A fact that was not lost on the appreciative audience, who, on the whole, found the contrast quite refreshing and wonderful. Grenville Eves did, for one:

> Of all the many Rodolfos I have heard since 1919, whether in English or Italian, in the opera house or on record, that of Heddle Nash has pleased me most. Rodolfo is primarily a young poet living in poverty, and ardently in love, not only with Mimi, but with life. So often is he presented in the image of a stocky, middle-aged 'international tenor'... his (Heddle's) approach presented his character, and indeed all the romantic young lovers he portrayed, as a living human being.

> *Morning Post*
> Last night he advanced his reputation considerably by singing the Puccini role with a real sense of musical phrasing and without the slightest trace of exaggeration – which is as much as to say with no touch of vulgarity. Without endowing the highest notes with the vibrant tone we associate with Italian tenors, he lifted his voice with ease and without ever forcing the quality beyond its natural bounds. In addition, he lived and moved and had his stage being convincingly.

With those two performances in 1929 Heddle established himself in the first rank of Covent Garden opera stars, much to the delight of opera enthusiasts, because here – at last – was an English tenor capable of holding his own amongst all the foreigners. Which was exactly what Heddle had in mind when he had left Milan.

Yet with his growing reputation Heddle would soon find himself having to resist attempts to push him into heavier roles – tempted as he might have been, because heavier roles, particularly the Wagner ones, were in fashion and would have offered him far more opportunities. But, as he pointed out: 'People do not seem to understand that operas are of many different kinds. And a lyric singer cannot manage dramatic roles, although he may be able to act them.'[11] On this point Heddle rarely gave way, though that did not stop him constantly trying to lower his timbre.[12]

A month or two later, in October 1929, at the invitation of Beecham, Heddle contributed to the London Delius Festival programme, singing 'A Late Lark', a piece never previously performed, because only recently completed by the blind and infirm composer, assisted by the young Eric Fenby. Delius had been brought over from France especially for the occasion. Described as 'wraith-like', he was wheeled into the Queen's Hall in a bath chair to hear the concert in which Heddle took part. But the festival is said to have lost money, and it may be that Heddle was never actually paid. In his biography of Sir Thomas Beecham, John Lucas[13] tells how the soprano Miriam Licette, who had herself sung a solo piece, bumped into Eric Fenby in Bond Street a year or two later and told him 'with amused resignation' that she was still waiting for her fee.

The fact that Licette showed 'resignation' and not 'ire' or 'resentment' about the non-payment of fees was probably due to the fact that such disappointments were not uncommon in 1929. It was the year of the Wall Street Crash which plunged the world economy into the Great Depression.

Despite all sorts of valiant, fund-raising efforts on the part of Sir Thomas Beecham, the Royal Opera House itself – so recently the scene of Heddle's greatest ambitions, hopes and fears, but always vulnerably dependent on the financial support of private individuals, found itself – not for the first time, nor, indeed, the last! – teetering on the edge of insolvency. It was even being threatened, briefly, with demolition. The British middle classes were becoming increasingly unwilling to put their hands in their pockets at a time of financial uncertainty, even to save such a great institution. Imagine all the frantic and complex behind-the-scene machinations and shenanigans going on, including lengthy negotiations with the BBC who were keen to acquire broadcasting rights.

Eventually it was the Labour government of Ramsay MacDonald that stepped in and, at long last, tendered a subsidy to help keep the place afloat. An annual sum was set for the following five years, to be paid out of wireless licence fees and passed on by the BBC, who would be given broadcasting rights. But finalising the subsidy, even though it was by no means a huge one, was apparently very touch and go, because serious objections were naturally raised about the appropriateness of the state subsidising 'the exclusive pleasure house of the few' at a time of industrial decline and growing unemployment. (*Plus ça change.*)[14] Yet if the government had not stepped in and offered a financial life-line, the whole future for opera in Britain would have looked very bleak indeed, leaving just the Carl Rosa scrabbling to keep opera alive, in English, in the provinces, and Lilian Baylis, having resorted to ingenious methods in her struggle to raise the cash, still in the throes of amalgamating the Old Vic with Sadler's Wells.[5]

Ironically, just when Heddle was starting to achieve his burning ambition

to become a brilliant success on the British operatic stage, on a par with other European singers, he almost saw his opportunity snatched away. There could so easily have been no international-calibre opera house for him to sing in; it could have been turned into a pile of rubble. Had it not been for the government subsidy, Britain's finest inter-war lyric tenor would have had to concentrate his talents on those recitals, concerts and oratorios. That's if he remained determined to continue pursuing a singing career in his own country. And Heddle most emphatically did.

Perhaps it was the pressing need to diversify that was at the forefront of his mind when Heddle agreed to take part in such a glamorously glitzy event as the grand opening of the Brixton Astoria, on 19 August 1929.[6] Despite the behind-the-scenes precariousness still pervading his career, the fact that he had been invited to sing at such an event highlights the extent to which he was starting to become a 'name' with the British public at large.

While the Royal Opera House and Lilian Baylis had their begging bowls out, there were private funds aplenty being pumped into brand new, atmospheric 'picture palaces' like the Astoria.[15] Built at the whacking cost of £250,000, with a lavish use of marble, a cascading fountain and *trompe l'oeil* effects, no expense had been spared, the idea being that the new picture-going clientele would be unable to resist such a magical escape from the economic depression. And, as was the norm in picture palaces of that period, there was also a stage for live variety performances, which still remained hugely popular; at the Astoria it was an immense 100' by 40' and it was this stage that Heddle was invited to inaugurate.

Heddle would certainly have felt in his element in the auditorium, which was designed to give the audience the impression that they were sitting in an Italian garden, shaded by cypress trees, with special effects machines delivering soft moonlight and twinkling stars by night or scudding clouds and sunshine by day. But he was probably grinding his teeth when comparing it with his threadbare operatic haunts. His reputation for rendering arias in Italian, which would suit the surroundings, whilst at the same time looking dashingly romantic, was obviously what had led to the booking. And being the latest singing sensation at Covent Garden could only have dignified the proceedings.

After an opening ceremony, performed by the local MP, came the 'lavish' variety show, followed by the main attraction on the big screen – the Al Jolson talkie *The Singing Fool*. Appearing with Heddle in the variety show were the husband and wife operetta stars Winnie Melville and Derek Oldham (of Ivor Novello and Gilbert and Sullivan fame) and a popular music hall comedian and singer named Fred Kitchen, to add a bit of grit. VIPs in the audience included Alfred Hitchcock and two female stars of the silent screen, the glamorous 'wildcat' Pola Negri, famous for her black and white outfits and scarlet finger-nails, and 'the British Mary Pickford' Betty Balfour. The second half of the concert was thought enough of a 'happening' to be broadcast live to the nation by the BBC. The event generated the sort of mass enthusiasm later to be seen at pop concerts – excited crowds began queuing for tickets at 8.45 a.m. and by noon the queue was stretching twice round the block. It was all a rip-roaring success.

Headlining at Covent Garden one month, crowd-pulling at Brixton Astoria the next – no doubt about Heddle's versatility. Should he, despite the prevailing economic climate, perhaps have been managing his career with an eye to a little more artistic exclusivity? Maybe, but his agents never advised him, nor indeed any of their artists in those days: they just took the bookings. And having such 'minstrel-like' tendencies, an audience was an audience to Heddle. So just as he did at the Old Vic, or Covent Garden, or some music club in the back of beyond, you can bet he gave the Brixton Astoria audience his best, and doubtless thoroughly enjoyed all the excitement and splendour of the evening just as much as they did.

Okay – it probably paid well too.

8

Meistersinger and Gerontius

In 1930, despite all the doom and gloom in the economy, Heddle must have felt sufficiently confident that the reputation he was building up would be strong enough to keep on pulling in the bread-and-butter contracts that he decided to take a big risk: he took out a mortgage on a house. It was a place he would call home for the rest of his life – just over thirty years. On first impression the house, which now bears a commemorative blue plaque bearing the inscription 'International Opera Singer Lived Here' seems like an odd choice: a suburban mock-Tudor three-bed detached, of a style to be seen in countless middle class English suburbs. It stands in Towncourt Crescent,* a trim but unassuming road in Petts Wood, near Chislehurst in Kent. Heddle even permitted his wife Vi, after the fashion of the times, to bestow on it the name 'Vycot'.† ('Take a pretty little cot, quite a min-ia-ture affair' which he'd recorded in 1926?)

Having been raised in the streets of South East London, 'the countryside' to both Heddle and Violet meant Kent. And the brochure for the Petts Wood Estate boasted of its peaceful setting, with 'green vistas of woodland' and 'birds, trees and flowers – a real country home.' Heddle had recently become father to a second boy, born in February 1930 and christened David Leonard Heddle (David after Heddle's part in *The Mastersingers*). Remembering his own early childhood on the busy Lewisham High Road, Heddle was

---

*Town Court Crescent in Heddle's day.
†George Formby allowed his wife Beryl to name their house near Blackpool Beryldene.

particularly keen, like many young London fathers right down to the present day, that his own children should grow up surrounded by trees.[1] What is more, the much-advertised newly opened Petts Wood railway station, within only a short walking distance from the house, had a regular train service which could speed him into London Bridge or Cannon Street in just over twenty minutes. From there he could easily access lines to north, south, east or west, as well as being in reach of all the central London venues and there was also a valuable late-night service to get him back, when possible. The houses were well built, brand new and attractive to a safe, middle-class type of buyer. They must have seemed excitingly modern, in contrast to the second-hand digs the young family had been occupying up to that point. Heddle would have taken out a mortgage in the region of £800-£900 for his, which was a bit higher than in certain other areas, and represented a substantial risk for a family man relying on the fickle, irregular earnings of a tenor. But then Petts Wood was a ' high class district'.[2]

It's not so surprising that Heddle wanted to buy 'Vycot', given all the advantages. But what might seem surprising, is that he remained there and never up-graded to a property and area that might be judged more stylish and stimulating once he became firmly established as 'Britain's leading tenor'. Would he have wanted to upgrade? The impression is that he was quite comfortable where he was and a lack of flamboyance never bothered him. He had experienced a hollow-centred flamboyance in Wickham Road and perhaps he thought a home-base that provided cosy comfort was preferable. And money would always continue to be tight. Violet, like the vast majority

Vycot (hedge precision-clipped by Heddle).

of middle class women in those days, would never have dreamt of going out to work, later going so far as to describe her position as the wife of a famous opera singer as 'a hundred percent job',[3] as well as displaying a penchant for being adorned with all the personal trappings. Heddle would take great delight in being able to equip both his sons with the sort of expensive boarding school education and opportunities he had so often felt the lack of himself. If he travelled to an interesting venue for any length of time, Heddle would pay for the family to accompany him. In fact David remembers his father being at all times and in all ways unstinting in his generosity.

With all these other demands on his resources, money for a housing up-grade was perhaps never seriously available. Soon part of the extended family moved out to Petts Wood to join them, including Violet's sister Gladys, who married Bob Jones and moved in right next door; followed by his Pearce in-laws and Violet's brother and his wife – all a comfort for Violet to have around in his absences as well as a source of useful child and house minders if she wanted to attend Heddle's performances. He had his singing, which by then was absorbing all his energies and totally fulfilling him, as well as taking him away so frequently – so why not indulge his wife on the home front? In later years there is some suggestion that he felt the need of a bit more personal space, and in time-honoured fashion he solved it by erecting a shed at the bottom of the garden, ostensibly for woodwork, but which his sons recall being used as a bolt-hole.

The blue plaque on his house, however, bearing the wording 'International

The blue plaque has his date of birth wrong.

Opera Singer Lived Here' might strike passers-by as a bit incongruous. 'Britain's Best-loved Between-the-wars Opera Singer' is too clunky, but it has a fitting Betjemanesque, suburban man-of-his-time appropriateness to it. And it's unfortunate – yet somehow inevitable – that the plaque has Heddle's date of birth wrong.

Interestingly, the bass Sir Geraint Evans also chose to make his home in Petts Wood for a time in the 1950s, but his former house is set back behind a wide lawn on the premier residential road and is roughly twice the size of Heddle's; the status of his house, together with his knighthood, perhaps pointing to the fact that Sir Geraint belonged to a more fortunate generation of singers? And that he had the support of the Welsh?

In the same year that Heddle moved to Petts Wood there came the exciting opportunity to sing at the newly government-subsidised Covent Garden, in a role that had always been one of his favourites: David in Wagner's only comic opera *Die Meistersinger*. He would become the first Englishman to perform the role in 'near perfect' German and he would always look upon this performance as one of the highlights (if not the highlight) of his career.

> Although he was a born Mozartian his David in *Die Meistersinger* was quite out of this world: I do not ever recall seeing or hearing a more beautiful portrayal of this role. His actions were so convincingly boyish, a remarkable contrast to the stillness and repose he achieved when on the oratorio platform. [4]

The highest praise must always come from a member of one's own profession and it could not get much higher than that, handed out by Isobel Baillie who sang so often with Heddle on the concert platform. She went on to repeat a bit of gossip, circulating around the time he first performed the role of David at Covent Garden. It was being said that he had actually gone so far as to waylay the great conductor Toscanini in the street, cheekily telling him that he – Heddle – was the best David he could ever have! And that as a result Toscanini had actually offered him the part in the Summer International Season of 1930. Whether there was any truth in his buttonholing Toscanini nobody knows, but we certainly shouldn't rule it out, knowing how impetuous and how go-it-alone Heddle felt he had to be. And as for his being the best David, that was certainly true, as he proved.

It was on this occasion that an often-repeated heckling incident took place. Heddle had been singing his heart out, and keeping the audience thoroughly entertained with a scintillating and 'impishly' amusing acting performance. But the German tenor singing the part of Walther had been having an off night and apparently was so lack-lustre by comparison that when the victor's crown in a singing contest was about to be placed on his head, a voice from the gallery was heard to shout out the instruction, 'Give the crown to Heddle Nash!' an incident one might have thought smacked more of the Hackney Empire, but was by no means unusual at Covent Garden in the 1930s, and illustrates just how warmly audiences reacted to Heddle. He would go on to repeat the role of David with great success and much enjoyment a number of times at Covent Garden, including the very last occasion he appeared there.

Though she is unspecific as to time and place, other than that it was some time around 1930, Maggie Teyte described her first-hand experience of appearing with Heddle on one occasion in *Die Meistersinger*. She felt that, for her, singing the part of Eva was a big and never to be repeated mistake, but she had nothing but praise for Heddle, who joined the cast for her last performance, and that night, in the quintet, made her realise what it meant, particularly in Wagner, to have the support of really experienced musicians. With Heddle Nash she felt there was 'a guide who would not falter, and who gave me fresh confidence.'[5]

Praise indeed from a singer who was a bit stingy in her references to other singers in her autobiography. But it is ironic that this accolade happened to come within a chapter headed 'Failures'!

It was also in 1930 that Heddle was invited to sing for the first time at the Three Choirs Festival. Held annually since Victorian times, and rotating between the cities of Worcester, Gloucester and Hereford, it was to become a regular venue for Heddle. His appearances there would last throughout the 1930s and, apart from the war years, right down to 1950. He would become a great favourite with audiences, especially when performing in such works as *The Dream of Gerontius*, *The Messiah*, *Elijah* and *The Apostles*. The fees might have been slashed since Victorian times, but the Festival would still become a valuable source of income for Heddle and most years he would take his

family along to make a little holiday for them. Not that it would have been an entirely reliable source for him, despite his success, because, like all classical music institutions in the early 1930s, it too was undergoing financial strains and stresses – of such magnitude that, after an existence of over two hundred years, its organisers were suffering real fears that its demise might be near.

Yet despite all the doom and gloom and balancing of accounts going on behind the scenes,[6] the Three Choirs Festivals clung to their reputation as great social events, attended by the local big-wigs and still attracting some of the leading lights from London society and the Arts world. In those days the solo artists themselves were not only expected to perform, but to hob-nob at the official receptions and the grand lunches given at each venue by wealthy

private patrons in their own homes – occasions when they were required to be on their best behaviour, and exercise their social graces. Heddle complied because it went with the booking. But not, one gathers, with the utmost relish. Attired in morning dress and up on the platform he was famous for cutting a splendid figure, described as 'compelling attention'. But off-stage he was never one for putting on airs and was even known to attract, in an assembly of more thrusting colleagues and socialites, the put-down description 'quite ordinary'. At one particular Three Choirs luncheon party he recalled committing an embarrassing gaffe concerning a very tasty jelly dish they had served up. He had enjoyed it so much that he had made a point of finding the chef afterwards and enthusiastically enquiring, 'Would you mind

telling me what brand it was?' The chef's expression, he winced ruefully, was a picture![7] One gets the impression that certain more self-regarding soloists, less averse to strutting their celebrity stuff and adding a discreet dash of off-stage razzmatazz, probably ingratiated themselves more with the grand patrons of Worcester, Gloucester and Hereford.

Heddle's impressive on-stage performance, however, would acquire him a very influential fan indeed in Mr George Bernard Shaw, who was a friend of Elgar's and a regular Festival attender in those days. Shaw's accolade: 'I have heard all the great tenors (except Guiglini) from Mario to Heddle Nash,'[8] would eventually touch and delight Heddle very much.

At the 1930 Hereford Festival Heddle was booked to perform in *The Apostles*, with Elsie Suddaby, Astra Desmond, Roy Henderson, Norman Allin and Keith Falkner – all singers with whom he would perform on numerous occasions. Elgar, scheduled to conduct, went ahead, even though he was suffering very badly from sciatica. He was suffering so badly in fact, that not only did he have to be helped on and off the platform, he had to conduct sitting down. Later that week, during a performance of *The Messiah*, it was reported that 'Mr Heddle Nash earned very generally expressed admiration for his touching delivery of the recitative "Comfort ye". Mr Nash boldly took a long note without the leaning note usually prescribed.'[9] It may have been this particular performance that impressed another of Heddle's new and influential fans – Sir Edward Elgar himself.

At a luncheon party the following year, during the 1931 Gloucester

Festival, Sir Keith Falkner recalled hearing Heddle, seated further down the table, make what proved to be a momentous and conversation-stopping announcement:[10]

'It's alright! Gerontius is mine! Elgar has told me I'm the one!'

Their hostess, a grand dame named as Mrs Gwyn Holford, a lady who apparently had strong convictions regarding her Anglo-Catholic religion, appeared to be having trouble believing her ears – to her *The Dream of Gerontius* was such a strongly Catholic piece. Elgar had set to music an epic poem, written by Cardinal Newman in 1865, which portrayed, with great fervour, the death of an ageing knight named Gerontius, and his temptation to despair as his death became imminent. Heddle Nash claiming he had been invited to undertake a part so dripping in Catholic sentiment? Young Mr Heddle Nash to sing the part of an ageing knight? Into the pregnant silence which followed Heddle's exclamation, Mrs Gwyn Holford's imperious voice was heard demanding very loudly that Mr Nash should be so good as to repeat what he had just said. When he did so, she brusquely and very rudely informed him that he didn't have the slightest idea what Gerontius was about! According to Falkner, Heddle managed to defuse the situation with aplomb, by politely offering to go and talk with her about it afterwards.

Yet despite the incredulity shown by Mrs Gwyn Holford, not to mention countless others when they heard the news, what Heddle had just announced in such a casual fashion was indeed a fact – Elgar in person had chosen him to be a successor to the great tenors Gervase Elwes and John Coates by singing the part of Gerontius.

The idea had first been mooted by Elgar in a letter written several months earlier, dated 29 April 1930, in reply to one from Heddle asking for advice.

In truth Heddle was full of doubt himself about whether he could, and should, perform the part of Gerontius. 'I can't sing that! – it's too difficult!'[11] had been his immediate reaction. And he was only too well aware of how the part had previously been sung to such tremendous acclaim by those other two great English tenors, Elwes and Coates. Gervase Elwes was himself a staunch Roman Catholic, said to have been capable of bringing a 'cathedral atmosphere'[12] into the most secular of concert halls. Both he and John Coates, who had originally trained as a baritone, had possessed not only the voice but the stature ideally suited to that of the elderly, dying knight of Newman's poem. But Heddle's greatest acclaim so far had been for his boyish, joyful humour in *Die Meistersinger*, his elegant, Italianate singing in Don Giovanni, and his youthful, passionate interpretation of the young lover in *La Bohème*!

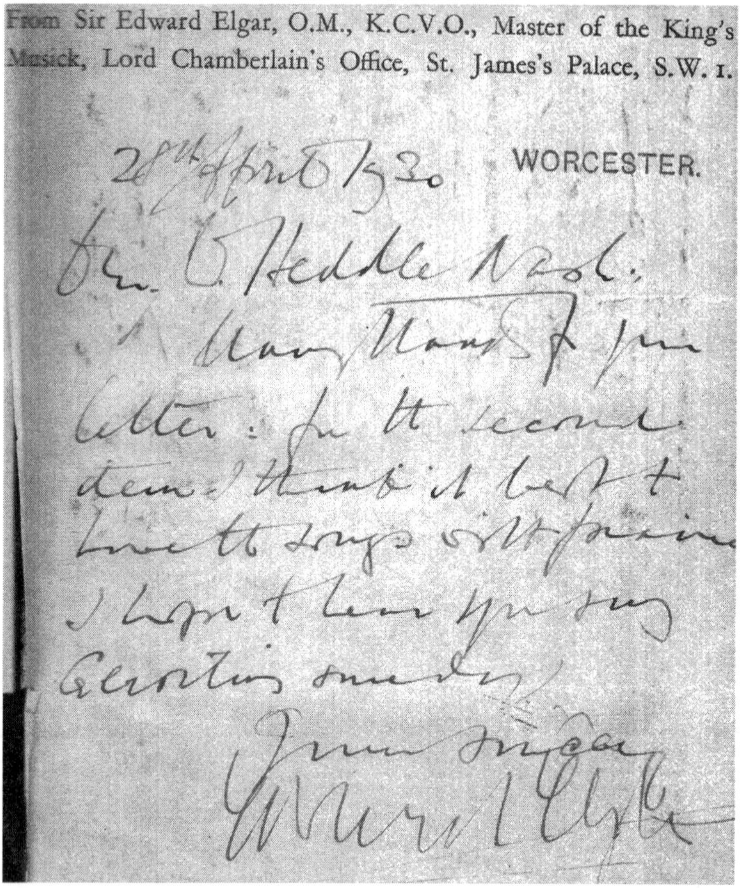
From Sir Edward Elgar, O.M., K.C.V.O., Master of the King's Musick, Lord Chamberlain's Office, St. James's Palace, S.W. 1.

28th April 1930 WORCESTER.

Dear Heddle Nash:

Many thanks for your letter: for the second item I think it best to leave the songs with piano.

I hope to hear you sing Gerontius some day.

Yours sincerely
Edward Elgar

Nevertheless, Elgar must have witnessed first hand the transformation that occurred when Heddle was on the oratorio platform performing, and he must have judged him well capable of achieving the profound depth of spiritual intensity demanded by the role.

Over a period of time, Heddle succeeded in wrestling away his doubts, though reactions like the one he had encountered at the Three Choirs luncheon party can't have helped his self-confidence.

He would finally make his debut in the role of Gerontius several months later, at Croydon, on 10 November 1931, with the seventy-four-year-old Sir Edward Elgar himself conducting.

The performance obviously did not disappoint Elgar because, satisfied that he had indeed made a good choice in Heddle, he made a point of inscribing in his score the words:

Heddle proudly pasted the letter, along with the inscription, inside his score. And later, on the inscription, he added the words 'First performance from memory September 24 1936. Heathcote Statham'.*

From that point onwards Heddle would sing the role from memory, as he generally did in oratorio, studying his part in an oratorio in the same way as for opera until he was note and word perfect. 'I can then feel as free on the concert platform as on the stage of the opera house,' he declared. To other oratorio artists Heddle threw down a challenge, which many were quick to follow. Soon a new fashion would be set, though of course not all oratorio singers would find the courage, or feel the inclination to sail free of the score. And neither would Heddle himself always be memory perfect.[13]

But at first the critics were not so convinced by Heddle's performance. Perhaps inevitably, in view of his previous experience, they found his interpretation to be somewhat 'operatic', compared with those of his predecessors, and for a number of years they persisted in dragging out the names 'Puccini' and 'Gounod' whenever he performed Gerontius. Even Sir Henry Wood was so tickled by the following criticism that he thought it worth repeating it in his autobiography:

> Some of them [critics], fortunately, have a sense of humour – always to be desired. I was highly amused with a criticism (I think it was in the *Daily Telegraph* or *Morning Post*) the day after Heddle Nash had sung

---

*Heathcote Statham had been the conductor.

Gerontius so splendidly at the Albert Hall in 1936. Nash had been singing *La Bohème* frequently, and the writer said he feared that at any moment Gerontius would tell the Angel that 'her tiny hand was frozen'. [14]

Yet, as a critic in *The Manchester Guardian* pointed out, 'It should be remembered that, even after the first and now historic interpretations of the part, Elgar is said to have expressed a wish for "a more Italian style of performance".' And after a time the critics began to concede that Heddle had mellowed and refined his interpretation:

> Mr Heddle Nash is a new Gerontius of the first order. One thinks of Mr Nash chiefly in connection with other sorts of music and as a somewhat Italianate singer, but his sympathies and his range of style have become enlarged, so that his voice, always beautiful, takes on the subtlest nuances of mingled ardour and restraint which Elgar demands; the line was maintained, the tone unforced, and the special character of this music fully realised in a very remarkable and deeply satisfying performance. [15]

> From end to end of the part of Gerontius Heddle Nash gave us melodious singing without a tonal inequality or flaw. His pure lyrical quality made for a certain suggestion of youthfulness – of a Gerontius somewhat more ingenuous than the, so to say, travel-worn spiritual adventurer of the famous characterisations of a generation ago. But there is nothing incongruous in the idea of a young Gerontius, and it is safe to assert that the part has never been more beautifully sung. [16]

> Heddle Nash sang Gerontius. He had to survive severe comparisons. We remember – and shall never forget – Gervase Elwes and John Coates. Writing with knowledge that I must at all costs maintain proportion, I am bound to say that Mr Nash came through his ordeal superbly and, in his own way, penetrated to the heart of his music as passionately as any of his great forerunners. His voice is not, 'before the event' the voice one would choose for the part; its quality can too readily become lyrical in a familiarly romantic or operatic way. He brought intelligence and feeling to his singing: the tone acquired the spiritual stress and pain for Part One, and more remarkable still, it acquired the right rapt simplicity, the note of release and of faith, which is absolutely necessary for the interpretation of Gerontius's music in Part Two. His platform manner as moving in its dignity and the sense of utter absorption in a searching sudden swelling of the heart; it was so expressive in an unselfconscious way – for example, the enunciation of the poignant passage: 'My soul is in my

hand: I have no fear'. No living singer, I am certain, can challenge Mr Nash's realisation of one of the most difficult, because one of the most spiritually intense, parts in all vocal music.[17]

But Isobel Baillie is the one who captures a moment which perhaps best encapsulates what was so special about Heddle's oratorio performances, and his Gerontius in particular:

> One Three Choirs Festival performance of Gerontius will stay with me all my life. I sat in the back stalls, the entire length of the cathedral away, and heard a truly inspired performance. I have only to close my eyes to hear his highly individual voice ringing out in '*Sanctis fortis*' or achieving an exquisite pianissimo in 'I went to sleep'.[18]

The International Opera Season of 1931 had found Heddle back at Covent Garden again, appearing as Rinuccio in *Gianni Schicchi*. In the autumn he was engaged in a season of opera in English, performing as Almaviva, Rodolfo and David, and displaying his versatility as an elegant Eisenstein in *Die Fledermaus*. But the Royal Opera House was still going through a rickety time, the summer season of 1931 being described as 'financially depressing' and the autumn season as 'disastrous'.[19]

In between times Heddle was fitting in not only Gerontius at Croydon, but concerts, recitals and oratorios here there and everywhere, and fulfilling his heavy broadcasting and recording commitments.

During that period Heddle repeated his recording of '*Il mio tesoro*' (following his sensational debut at Covent Garden); arias from *Il barbiere di Siviglia*, and Rossini's *La danza* – sung in Italian and full of his famous youthful gaiety; various pieces of operetta (of which more in the next chapter); 'Deeper and deeper still Waft her, angels' from Handel's *Jephtha*, and last, though anything but least, a selection of Art and traditional English songs accompanied by Gerald Moore at the piano.

Heddle Nash and the accompanist Gerald Moore were a dream team. Yet, as is often the way with two huge talents, the same level of harmony was not always achieved on a personal level. Maggie Teyte, who also recorded and performed recitals with Gerald Moore, gives a few clues as to why a partnership with him might have been a bit edgy.[20] If a singer did not know how to keep his end up, she points out, he would soon find himself 'eclipsed'. And she musingly ascribes his unmistakable quality on disc to his mastery of the necessary weight of arm, according to its distance from the microphone (one would love to have heard Heddle's theory). Generally, she observes, any little disagreements would end to the satisfaction of both parties, though there would always be a degree of mystery about which one had given way.

In his autobiography *Am I too Loud?*, Gerald Moore describes Heddle as the most prominent English tenor of his era, magnificent in opera, oratorio, and in concert, but adds that his 'egocentricity was bewildering', though not 'provoking' because 'one could repay him in his own coin without arousing his resentment.' And he goes on to recount the tale about Heddle claiming to be 'the best bloody Messiah in the country!'*

Heddle kept his end up by nicknaming Gerald Moore (within his family circle at any rate) 'the man they could never hang', on account of the way his head appeared to be attached to his body without the benefit of a neck.

Yet when Heddle Nash and Gerald Moore performed together, some rare alchemy occurred, especially in their interpretation of the traditional English and Art song. In Ralph Vaughan Williams's 'Linden Lea', Jack Moeran's 'Diaphenia', Elgar's 'Shepherd's Song' and Quilter's 'Go Lovely Rose' in particular, their exquisite interpretation at times comes close to perfection.

In the opinion of many, Heddle Nash can be heard at his quintessential best in the Art and traditional songs he recorded with Gerald Moore. Entwined with supreme vocal artistry is such a green-shoot spontaneity and a sheer joy in word-painting.

If any other nation had produced such definitive accounts of its traditional and Art songs, one can't help feeling that both they and their interpreters might have been more keenly treasured and revered.

---

*HN apparently made this comment casually, and in private, to an acquaintance at a time when *Messiah* festivals were taking place at venues around the country and he, for some reason, found he had not been engaged. One can understand his dismay. JHN described it as 'not a boast' but 'a cry from the heart'.

9

'If I am dreaming...'

While Heddle was winning plaudits for his operatic, oratorio and concert performances, his occasional forays into lighter music had likewise not gone unappreciated. The D'Oyly Carte Opera Company had been quick to spot a potentially winning package – a superb lyric tenor voice combined with youthfully handsome looks, elusive charm, and the ability to play the ardent lover convincingly, while at the same time performing with a manly sense of style and comedy. Such a rare, audience-wooing combination had tempted Rupert D'Oyly Carte to stake a claim with the sort of offer that would have provided Heddle with the financial stability he craved.* He had already demonstrated a connection with the Gilbert and Sullivan idiom back in 1926 with his recording of 'Take a pair of sparkling eyes' from *The Gondoliers*, full of such joy and elegant spontaneity one wonders why he never recorded 'A Wandering Minstrel I' from the *Mikado*. It was undoubtedly a sad loss to Gilbert and Sullivan fans when Heddle unhesitatingly turned down Carte's offer, but to have let himself become type-cast in Gilbert and Sullivan at that point in his career could only have been perceived one way: squandering the richness of his talents.

Nevertheless, Heddle was about to raise eyebrows by suddenly announcing his intention to take a whole year out from classical music. Between March

---

*The Company's leading tenor at the time was Derek Oldham, who also enjoyed success in musical comedy though his voice nowadays seems heavily tinged with period flavour. Heddle would have made a lively contrast.

1932 and April 1933, he would appear on the West End stage as a leading man, performing the tenor role of the love-sick poet René Lavallery in *The Dubarry*, an operetta by the Viennese composer Karl Millöcker. So how come?

First staged back in 1879, *The Dubarry* had undergone a thorough re-vamp. Now, with its juicily rich and melodious score, and a plot set against the colourful backdrop of Paris in the reign of Louis XV, it packed just the right ingredients to appeal to audiences looking to escape the miserable grey pall of the Depression. London audiences were already flocking in their thousands to indulge in the escapist, feel-good factor stirred up by a night of spectacle and nostalgia, at lavish shows like *The Whitehorse Inn* and *Waltzes From Vienna*. Small wonder that *The Dubarry*, already up and running and proving a huge box-office success in Berlin, had attracted the attention of a go-getting young British impresario by the name of Stanley Scott who was planning to stage his own production at His Majesty's Theatre in The Haymarket (renamed Her Majesty's).

Scott was thinking big. His Majesty's had recently hosted Noel Coward's hit musical *Bitter Sweet*, and he had lined up the American producer Felix Edwardes, whose CV boasted a whole string of glamorous hits on Broadway and in the West End: George and Ira Gershwin's *Lady Be Good* on Broadway in 1924–5, starring Fred and Adele Astaire; the Astaires again in the Gershwins' *Funny Face* at the Prince's Theatre London in 1928 and Jerome Kern's fabulous *Showboat* at Drury Lane, with Paul Robeson (of 'Ol' Man River' fame), in 1928–9. After *The Dubarry* he would go on to produce *The Gay Divorce* with Fred Astaire and Claire Luce at The Palace Theatre London in 1933. Producers did not come any bigger than Edwardes at that time. Ernest Irving[1] was signed up to conduct, and with such corner stones for success in place, the management's eye – directed, it is said, by Irving – soon came to rest on Heddle Nash for the part of René.

Hadn't Nash already demonstrated his ability to pluck at the heart strings – when singing the part of a romantic lover scribbling verses in a garret in *La Bohème*? and as the jilted lover Des Grieux in *Manon*? Not forgetting those charming and popular operetta recordings for Columbia: 'When other lips' from Balfe's *The Bohemian Girl* in 1926; 'O Maiden, my Maiden' and 'Wayside Rose' from Lehár's *Frederica* and 'Come with me' from Strauss's *Die Fledermaus*, in 1930 – thereby proving his ability to make the most of a

lively score and romantic sentiments and, as the critic Alan Blyth so exactly put it, 'caress a pleasing melody with the utmost care for word and note'. His rising popularity with the public was calculated to be such a potentially strong draw for the show, that the management decided to offer an attractive sum to tempt him – say, £50 a week? (An agricultural labourer could still subsist on £3 a week in 1932 and you could buy an Austin 7 de luxe for £125, so they were talking seriously fat cheques.)

£50 a week – guaranteed. Heddle wasn't going to turn down that offer in a hurry. And there was an added perk: he would be able to return home and sleep in his own bed every night... Now that *was* very tempting...

Furthermore, Stanley Scott was renowned for having introduced the Austrian tenor Richard Tauber to Britain the previous year in Franz Lehár's *Land of Smiles*. Heddle must have been only too well aware that Tauber was managing to combine grand opera with stage appearances in operetta, especially the popular operettas of Lehár, with huge success.

Heddle felt flattered by the offer – even enjoyed flirting with the idea. But he remained adamantly against undertaking operetta. A West End show could tie him up for at least a year, just when it was crucial he should be building on his reputation as a serious artist.

'Well if you're really sure you don't want to do it,' Violet claimed to have advised, 'ring and tell them you want double the amount! – that should settle it.' Heddle did just that, only to find himself reeling at the end of the line – the offer had indeed been doubled. £100 a week, incredible![2] Now, for his family's sake, it had become an offer he felt he couldn't afford to turn down. Son David sums it up (aged only two at the time so speaking with hindsight): 'It paid off the mortgage! Bought a car! and gave the family a sort of financial stability – took away the fear of, oh dear, where's the next penny coming from?'

But where was Heddle's famed second sight? Bedazzled by the triple digits, maybe? It failed to forewarn him that *The Dubarry* would turn out to be a notoriously 'unlucky' play which would eventually involve him in one of the biggest personal tragedies ever to hit the West End musical stage.

But the black clouds were still over the horizon and in the meantime, things were looking rather rosy...

The book of the operetta was based, loosely, on the real life rise of a little Parisienne milliner, Jeanne, to become first the wife of the Count Dubarry then ultimately the mistress of King Louis XV, after he had tired of Madame de Pompadour (the subject of another operetta). Cue the opportunity for lavish eighteenth-century sets, powdered wigs and sensational costumes, all giving the audience plenty to feast their eyes on, plus some pretty ballet sequences, to be choreographed by Anton Dolin. The story of Jeanne, however, 'the shop girl, who came, was seen, and conquered'[3] was considered quite 'meaty' for operetta material.

For the lead soprano role of Jeanne, Scott hit on the idea of poaching the glamorous star Gitta Alpar, noted for her slinky, Dietrich-like delivery, from the Berlin production. (The words 'slinky' and 'Dietrich' linked with 'eighteenth-century France' will already be giving a strong hint that certain liberties were to be taken with historical accuracy.) But, frustratingly, when Scott arrived in Berlin, he soon learned that not even his wily negotiating skills could release Alpar from her contract. He remained undaunted: a Continental leading lady was what he had set his mind on, and he had no intention of returning home empty handed. He began to search around all the Continental operetta theatres for a replacement (or so the publicity story went) but without success, until one night just for 'relaxation', he went back to Berlin to hear Richard Tauber singing in *The Song Of Love* at the Metropol Theatre in Nollendorfplatz. There and then he 'unexpectedly' struck lucky.

Singing opposite the star was a discovery of Tauber's own: a gorgeous twenty-five-year-old German soprano and former prima ballerina, blessed with the additional attribute of naturally flaming red hair. Her name was Anny Ahlers. Scott professed himself so blown away by Ahlers that in true 1930s style, he dashed straight round to her dressing room waving a contract, and signed her up on the spot. Whatever the truth of the matter, Scott had found his Jeanne – the star of the show – and he engaged her, it was rumoured, for £300 a week! Scott immediately set about turning *The Dubarry* into a vehicle for Anny Ahlers.

By comparison Heddle's part as Jeanne's first and true love, the poor poet René Lavallery, was turning out to be a tad smaller than he had envisaged, given the hefty size of his pay cheque. He was to spend a lot of time languishing off stage, while Ahlers would scarcely leave the stage at all. But he had a couple of audience-pleasing duets with her, which were never recorded (unfortunately Anny was with Parlaphone; Heddle with Columbia) and a solo, 'If I am dreaming', which fortunately was.

Heddle's hauntingly romantic solo would become one of the hits of the show, along with Anny's 'I give my heart', a defiant, show-stopping number, performed in 'the notorious salon of Madame Sauterelle' for a group of lascivious eighteenth-century roués in powdered wigs, while herself scantily costumed in an outfit of black lace which unashamedly shrieked '1930s Berlin nightclub'. Nobody appears to have been complaining though – Anny's performance in that particular scene alone was 100% guaranteed to put bums on seats.

Combined with an excellent sense of humour, Anny was reputed to be highly intelligent and even keen on grand opera. As a *Manchester Guardian* reporter was impressed to discover, here was a musical comedy star capable of discussing the rival merits of Kraus as a conductor in Vienna and Bruno Walter in Charlottenburg, and whether Walter was really a Beethoven or a

WILDING
Bond St W.1.

Wagner conductor! Hardly surprising that on a personal level Heddle and Anny should immediately have hit it off. As for the all-important on-stage chemistry, it was destined to send a pleasurably romantic tingle through the audience. Heddle never made any secret of his admiration for Anny.

(Opposite)
*Anny putting
bums on seats.*

One potential problem was speedily taken in hand: when the young German star first arrived in the West End, she hardly spoke a word of English. Undeterred, Scott cleverly turned this into a publicity hook: 'When Anny Ahlers agreed to come to London she could not say as much as "How do you do?"' he boasted.[4] He straight away set her to work learning the whole part of Jeanne parrot-fashion while cramming in English lessons – two solid hours every morning before rehearsals, more in 'rest periods' between rehearsals, and even late into the night (2 a.m. said to be not unknown) with an 'indefatigable coach', who went by the delightfully period name of Miss Flossie Freedman.

Reports would later describe the young German star as 'lonely' and 'isolated' in a foreign capital, unable to speak the language and with no friends. An exaggeration, according to Heddle. Along with other members of the cast, he soon became a friend off-stage as well as on. He would invite her down to Petts Wood on a Sunday, where the extended Nash family found her refreshingly untheatrical and likeable. Several times she visited young John at his prep-school near Brighton – a never-to-be-forgotten perk for male members of staff.[5] Apart from her sweet nature, Anny soon became noted for boundless generosity to her theatre colleagues – all the money she was earning was said to be 'not important' to her. To celebrate the 100th performance of the show, she rejected a personal present in favour of a party for the entire cast and crew. And when Christmas came round she took 'immense pleasure' in buying presents for everybody at His Majesty's – nobody got left out.[6] All too good to be true? Scott's clever publicity machine at work? Apparently not, as the staunch loyalty of her colleagues would later demonstrate.

But – his pleasure in performing with Anny Ahlers apart – Heddle's own behind-the-scenes experiences in rehearsals for *The Dubarry* were rapidly tarnishing. He and the director were not hitting it off. The ultimate professional, Heddle Nash was spoken of with high esteem throughout his career for his ability to get along well with colleagues, and he would seem to have been a perfect choice for the role of René, On this occasion, however, he anxiously confided to the family his belief that his problems all boiled down to the fact that the director, who was gay, happened to have a tenor boyfriend whose career he desperately wanted to promote in that particular role; an opportunity of which Heddle had unwittingly deprived him. During rehearsals, to his mounting discomfort, Heddle got the impression that the director was going out of his way to needle him – griping, criticising and generally making life unpleasant – hoping, maybe, he would grow so sick and fed up he would pull out and hot-foot it back to the operatic stage. He nearly did. One day the situation reached a climax. In front of the entire cast, he was taunted with the words, 'Know what? – your performance will stand out like a chalk mark on a white wall.' Deliberate provocation to throw a punch and storm out of the show? Heddle struggled with both reactions. (Maybe the director had learned about the whip incident and thought he had form?) But Heddle kept his cool and determinedly hung on to the part.[7]

The Dubarry eventually premiered to rave reviews and turned out to be the big, glittering success of the 1932/3 season. London went crazy over Anny Ahlers, just as Stanley Scott had craftily foreseen:

> *The Manchester Guardian*
> Commendably direct in its speech and sentiment; there is no greasy pretence that professional workers in the industry of love are really amateurs with hearts of gold... the play has a real acting part instead of an excuse for pretty poses, and the part is really acted by Miss Anny Ahlers, a German player who is a tremendous acquisition... Her performance would be magnetic and arresting on any stage; in a musical piece it had the added bouquet of surprise.

> *The Observer*
> The triumph of Anny Ahlers, auburn-haired heroine of *The Dubarry* at His Majesty's, has now become unique among the successes of all Continental artists in post-war London. What is the secret of this 'personality'?

> *Theatre World*
> A performance of the utmost brilliance that has brought all London to her feet.

The critic James Agate had fun describing Anny as 'the complete Amazon, militant Valkyrie, and Germanic fury, all three at maximum pressure... There is no question of liking or disliking Fräulein Ahlers; the liking is compulsory, and complete when you get used to it, like a plunge into the German Ocean.'[8] And he couldn't resist making what he thought were clever references to Heddle spending 'limitless periods dropping furtive *lagrime* off stage', adding that though he sang 'beautifully' he acted 'as tenors act'. Perhaps Heddle was letting the 'chalk mark' insult get to him?

A tender moment in The Dubarry, *Heddle as René with Anny as Jeanne.*

But it was *The Daily Herald* which came up with a statement soon to prove full of tragic irony: 'Anny Ahlers beats the screen sirens at their own game, for she has all the lure of a Garbo or a Dietrich without their somnambulism...'

Overnight Anny found herself the darling of English society, expected to fit in fashionable tea parties with the aristocracy, as well as charitable events and after-show hand-kissing visits to her dressing room. All that on top of giving press interviews in English and continuing her lessons with the relentless Miss Flossie Freedman. No wonder that, only one month into the production, she was already reported to be 'feeling tired'.[9]

And Heddle himself? He had to be content with taking a back seat generally with the critics – *The Manchester Guardian*'s: 'There are no great acting parts for the men, but Mr Heddle Nash has a fine vocal chance, and naturally takes it', was fairly typical.

But the public loved him. Along with a glamour unknown in the threadbare world of classical music, he suddenly experienced the thrill of finding himself not only a big West End heart-throb, but temporarily possessed of a healthy bank balance. When he recorded the hit song 'If I am dreaming' for Columbia, 'sung with just the right amount of passion and brio',[5] it brought him to the notice of an even wider audience. His performance in *The Dubarry* secured 'Heddle Nash' as a household name and it would draw him legions of fans, both male and female, with ego-boosting fan letters in abundance.

Heddle would notch up an incredible 398 performances in the role of René – eight performances a week, including two matinees – and not miss a single one. If he found it boringly repetitive after the demands of concert, oratorio and opera, he never let it show. Gossip columns started to take an interest in him. When not actually performing, the *Daily Mirror* revealed, he spent all his spare time learning foreign languages. They informed the public that, already fluent in Italian and French, he was now concentrating on German: 'A fearful grind' but he recognised that 'no singer, with English alone, can hope to compete with the foreigner'! Heddle was already proficient enough in the German language for his part of David in *Die Meistersinger* to have been described as 'sung in impeccable German'. So one wonders if this was a subtle hint that he was sighing over Anny Ahlers off-stage as well as on. (Few would have been surprised.) Or perhaps he was aware of an article by Stanley Scott in *Theatre World* in which the impresario mentioned having several British players in mind whom he believed would be 'tremendous hits' in Berlin if only they would 'learn a bit of the language'.

But if Heddle was anticipating a call from the Continent, it never came. His voice was far too light for Continental operetta taste. No 'Britisher' was ever likely to have wrung any worthwhile reciprocal arrangement for the likes of Tauber and Ahlers out of the Continental world of operetta. In the international 1930s mind-set, any British singer in operetta, just as in opera, attracted the label 'lightweight'. Furthermore, given the events lurking just around the corner, the following declaration of Scott's looks remarkably naive: 'a free interchange of artistic ideas helps the peoples of the world to avoid friction and misunderstandings and to collaborate with each other for the common weal.' (Following *The Dubarry*, when Scott put on Gerhardt Hauptmann's play *Before Sunrise*, in September 1933, starring the famous

German actor Werner Krauss, there were riotous scenes on opening night, with stink bombs, anti-Hitler pamphlets and cries of 'Britain for the British' being flung from the gallery. Once the demonstrators had been evicted, the audience did, however, have the grace to give Krauss a standing ovation.)

Meanwhile, *The Dubarry* had been set up to hinge so completely on the young leading lady's tremendously famed 'personality' that by June her nerves were reported to be 'in a screaming fatigue' and she had played two performances with the understudy 'ready to take her place at any moment'.[10] Her doctor had resorted to giving her an injection during the evening to combat the strain. By 22 September she was not only exhausted: her voice was showing signs of giving out. Newspapers were reporting how she had broken down and collapsed in the wings, suffering from laryngitis, during the second scene of one of those gruelling evening performances following on top of a matinée.[11] She had gamely returned to the stage, but doctors had ordered her to take a rest.

Now, belatedly, it dawned on everybody that Stanley Scott should never have thrown his leading lady into such a major role on the West End stage on top of performing for over two years (including making five 'talkies' in Germany, one with the director Max Ophuls[12]) without taking a proper rest and with scarcely any preparation or advice about how to pace herself. But audiences had booked up and paid their money to see her, not an understudy, so Scott (who seems to have been constantly wheeler-dealing abroad at the time) found himself with no option but to close the theatre down for a day or two, while she went off to Folkestone (a fashionable seaside resort back then) to recuperate.

Although Anny was back again and apparently 'completely recovered' from her 'brief indisposition' and playing again to enthusiastic and crowded houses a week or so later, it was a fragile time for Heddle, as well as the rest of the cast, constantly wondering whether the leading lady might crack up.

Not only did she totally immerse herself in the part, Anny was on stage for the entire performance, except for about four minutes and the two very short intervals, which were taken up by rapid costume changes. And as she threw herself around the stage night after night with the 'tremendous vitality' expected of her, she was wearing huge crinoline gowns supported by a wood and steel frame, said to weigh forty pounds, plus thick make-up, hats and wigs.[13] According to her actress friend Miss Margaret Yarde, who played the part of the Parisian hat-shop owner Madame Labille: 'She had not so much the technique of an actress, but on stage she actually became the person of her part. I have seen her almost too ill to crawl about become a different being before the footlights – a laughing, vivacious, magnetic thing.'

With a callous eye on the profits, rather than the wellbeing of their young star, the management got the doctor to keep up the injections on a regular basis. They also had miniature brandies 'kindly' placed in her dressing room for an added fillip.

Inevitably gossip started to circulate about the German sensation. There were hints that she was suffering from unrequited love for the constantly absent (and married) Stanley Scott. One person who was in love with her, and had no hesitation in saying so, was a recently divorced member of the aristocracy, Sir Merrick Burrell, who was so smitten that he commissioned a painting of her by the highly fashionable society portrait painter of the time, Philip de László. László himself fell under Anny's spell and followed his urge to paint her full-length, though portrait-size had been requested. It turned out to be one of the most arresting examples of de László's work, said to be amazingly life-like, though the finished canvas eventually proved too large to fit comfortably into Sir Merrick's house.

But, in March 1933, shortly before the end of *The Dubarry*'s run, and before the portrait was quite complete (due to frequently missed sittings) – the tragedy (which might be perceived as having long been lurking in the wings) finally struck. Anny Ahlers died – under sensational circumstances.

A brief but chilling announcement came on 15 March, almost a year after *The Dubarry* had opened. According to the first reports, she had passed away in a nursing home in fashionable Dorset Square, Marylebone, aged only twenty-six, following a fall downstairs at her 'luxurious' first-floor flat on the corner of Duchess Street, off Portland Place.

But the following day this was followed by a further shock announcement.

Anny had died as a result of injuries sustained two days earlier, not in a fall downstairs as originally thought, but in a mysterious fall from a small balcony outside her bedroom window.

The following facts would later emerge at the inquest.

After going for an afternoon drive with her maid, Maud Farace, she had drunk champagne, then gone to bed, hoping to catch up on some sleep. Later that evening the doctor had called round to check how she was (she had been ill and off work for several days), but when the maid had ushered him into the bedroom, they had found Anny's bed and the room mysteriously empty. Farace's eye had then been caught by a curious thing – a curtain was billowing and behind it one of the narrow French windows opening on to the little balcony – always kept firmly closed – was standing open...

Farace had flown across to the window, looked down, and had her worst fears confirmed. Anny, still in her nightdress, was lying unconscious on the pavement below. She would never recover consciousness.

1 Duchess Street. Anny fell from a balcony on the first floor.

Heddle, along with the cast and crew and all her numerous fans, was utterly devastated. Immediately on hearing news of the fall, he and Violet had hurried over to the nursing home, but one glance at Anny had prepared them for the worst.[14] 'She was the nicest person I have ever acted with,' was his initial gut reaction to the *Evening Standard*. 'I have heard that she was a somnambulist. She told us once that she had been found sleepwalking somewhere, but I never took it seriously.

'However, she was very highly-strung and may have relived her part in her sleep.

'She was very charming and greatly beloved,' he added.

Newspapers were only too eager to promote the big debate: did the star Anny Ahlers accidentally fall – while sleepwalking?... while befuddled by champagne?... under the influence of the controversial sleep-inducing drug Quadronox? – or – quite likely – a combination of all three? Or did she deliberately jump, with suicidal intent? (Pushed was never an option, the incident having occurred while both the doctor and maid were in the sitting room.)

A nerve-fraying time ensued for everybody concerned. The following day Heddle gave the journalists still crowding round his door short shrift.

With no doubt in his mind that Anny's fall was the result of a tragic accident, he later referred to her excitement at being inundated with offers of work following her success in *The Dubarry*. He was convinced – and would never change that conviction – that she had always behaved like a girl who had everything to live for.

His attitude was endorsed by all those closest to her. They were keen to point out that she had been prone to sleep-walking for some years – the result of an over-active brain, and that she had been doing so frequently of late. Stanley Scott, who rushed back from Berlin only to learn of Anny's death at Dover, seems to have been equally keen to promote the sleepwalking theory, giving the *Daily Mirror* some interesting evidence:

> On one occasion a porter, hearing singing at four o'clock in the morning, went to investigate and found Anny singing a Dubarry song in German on the fourth floor. She was then fast asleep. Her flat was on the first floor.

She had been twice caught by her maid at the open window of her bedroom still sleeping. As a precaution the windows were tied up, and chairs set to form a barricade.

The actress Margaret Yarde commented that the maid had found Anny on point of climbing through the window only a few days earlier. 'In the opening scene of *The Dubarry* she makes her escape by climbing from a window and over a balcony,' she added, personally believing that Anny must have been re-enacting her part in her sleep, an explanation widely held by her colleagues, who felt that a combination of a highly-strung nature, over-work and prescription drugs had caused her to sleep-walk. As she said herself, 'I live my part' – maybe she dreamed it too.

The controversy continued to snowball. The popular press chose to sensationalise evidence given by the maid, with headings such as 'Champagne every day'. And sly references were made to the miniature brandies between acts, hinting at alcoholism. Also a phial, which Farace claimed should have contained twelve drugs, was found to be empty. Although the maid added a full account of how she had found her mistress several times playing the piano and singing in her sleep, and that at around 3 a.m. on the very Sunday of the tragic fall, she had discovered her wandering upstairs at the apartment block in her nightie and bare feet – still fast asleep – the jury eventually brought in a shock majority verdict 7:2 of 'suicide while of unsound mind'.

The verdict caused outrage. It was hotly contested by all those who knew Anny, including Heddle. Certainly the geography of the apartment block (now offices) on the corner of Duchess Street, with its deep, narrow basement area surrounded in those days by serious, spiked, cast iron railings, combined with the fact that Anny's apartment was only on the first floor, makes it an unlikely location for anybody seriously contemplating suicide, messy injury seeming the more likely outcome. The fact that Anny didn't just fracture her arm and suffer nasty bruising, but also sustained the concussion that killed her, appears to have been downright unlucky. Yet the suicide verdict was upheld and the stark wording on her death certificate would be: 'Injuries. Fall from Window. Suicide. Unsound Mind.'[15]

The outrage escalated. Staff at His Majesty's Theatre next took the highly unusual action of issuing a combined statement of protest to the press:

> We wish to protest against the inquest verdict on our dear Anny Ahlers; also against articles about her which we think give the British public a false impression.
>
> We who were her friends knew her well and loved her as a woman who lived to make others happy.
>
> It is our wish that the public should know the real truth of her beautiful nature.

It was an extraordinarily difficult time for Heddle. The show, nearing the end of its run anyway, staggered on for a further six weeks. And though grieving, and caught up in all the controversy, he not only had to continue performing, he was also being called upon to give his constant support and encouragement to an understudy, Miss Sylvia Welling, who was struggling to fill Anny's shoes in the part of Jeanne, after taking over from another understudy, Miss Kathlyn Hilliard.

But at least the management spared him the ordeal of having to perform on the day of the funeral, by taking the dramatic decision to close the theatre, leaving it to stand dark and silent in tribute, while at Golders Green Crematorium 'amid the most astonishing scenes the chapel has ever known', crowds of women onlookers stormed the doors to catch a glimpse of the coffin.[16]

And still the controversy rumbled on.

Anny's mother and sister took half the ashes to be interred in the cemetery of her home town of Hamburg in Germany. But the other half were retained, it was claimed, at the request of Stanley Scott, who then failed to make any arrangements for them. Eventually the embarrassed undertaker was advised to approach Sir Merrick Burrell for instructions. Sir Merrick immediately took over the responsibility, collected the ashes and had them interred at the little country churchyard of Shipley in West Sussex, close to his family seat at Knepp Castle. And on the north aisle of St Mary the Virgin, he set up a plaque to Anny – 'renowned in her generation for genius in dramatic art and beloved for her virtues and grace of charity to all around her' – the full inscription composed by the poet Hilaire Belloc who lived close by.

By then it was well over a year since the tragedy, yet on the day in June 1934 when the plaque was dedicated, the former cast and crew of His Majesty's Theatre gave Anny a final, full theatrical send-off, travelling down 'en masse' from London and crowding into the little church. 'Stage hands and scene-shifters,' gushed *The Daily Mirror*, 'most of them wearing black ties, dressers and beautiful young actresses from His Majesty's Theatre, had made the journey to this lovely village set in the smiling Sussex countryside.' After a short and dignified ceremony, the deep hush was shattered by the orchestra of His Majesty's, massed on either side of the chancel, who 'crashed into' the opening chords of Wagner's Valkyrie. And then it was the turn of Heddle himself to face the congregation and sing. He had chosen the deeply moving aria 'Waft her, angels', from Handel's *Jephtha*, the words by Thomas Morell:

Waft her, angels, through the skies,
Far above yon azure plain,
Glorious there, like you, to rise,
There, like you, for ever reign.

As the *Manchester Guardian* pointed out, 'Later she might have done anything. Even when her singing voice was worn to ribbons by the strain of a year's performances, as an actress and a comedienne she remained magnificent.'[17]

For Heddle Nash, it should have been a light-hearted and lucrative year out, acquitting himself in sparkling form and becoming idolised in a big West End hit operetta. He had certainly revelled in the glamour, but the experience had been far from joy galore, marred as it had been by behind-the-scenes power struggles, anxieties, understudies and theatre closures, all culminating in what must surely be an unprecedented nightmare for any leading man: having his leading lady defenestrate herself in mysterious circumstances.

The mystery surrounding the death of Anny Ahlers would engender newspaper articles and speculation for years to come.[18] As for the show itself, and eventually also the Hollywood film based on it, they came to be regarded in superstitious theatrical circles as 'unlucky', even 'cursed'. Only a month or two after Anny's death, her understudy Kathlyn Hilliard also suddenly died, aged only thirty-seven, and was cremated at Golders Green. Then the star Mary Ellis turned down the film part on the grounds that she did not want

The ambitious Mr Stanley Scott.

to be associated with such a 'bad luck' play. And when, after many delays, the film's director was injured in a car crash, just as production was finally due to start, the film earned the nicknames 'Over-du Barry' and 'Hoodoo Barry'.[19] It would eventually be released in 1935, as *I Give My Heart* with Gitta Alpar in the lead role. (An excerpt can currently be seen on the internet.) But Alpar herself, despite her enormous popularity, found herself forced to flee Nazi Germany that very same year and had her marriage annulled, because she was Jewish. She would settle, eventually, in the USA, where her career soon fizzled out.

Even the ambitious and rather dastardly-sounding impresario Stanley Scott himself, still aged only thirty-four, would not be immune. It seems he had way over-stretched himself and would crash spectacularly to earth, also in the year 1935. A mere two years after the 'unlucky' play had completed its London run, he was putting in a few public appearances of his own: unravelling within a matter of months, in the bankruptcy court,[20] the divorce court[21] and the Marlborough Street Magistrate's Police Court, ignominiously accused of wilfully damaging two public telephones in Piccadilly Circus by slamming down the receivers in a fit of frustration 'after trying in vain to get a number for three-quarters of an hour'![22] His place of abode had notably slipped downhill, from Hampstead to Acton.

Nowadays both the stage and film versions of the *The Dubarry* are largely forgotten. But the tragic tale of Anny Ahlers still throbs with interest and speculation, its overtones of stress, sleep-walking, drink and prescription drugs giving it a chillingly modern ring.

Heddle himself, thankfully, survived *The Dubarry* professionally unscathed. An evocative memory-shot of him during his Dubarry year shows him travelling home on the late night train back to Petts Wood, after a performance, along with his friend, one of the most popular radio announcers of the era, Stuart Hibberd, who lived one stop away, at Chislehurst. Hibberd would have just completed one of his late-night stints at the BBC newsdesk (he was held in great public affection for saying, 'Good night everybody,' then allowing four beats – one, two, three, four – to give listeners the time to respond out loud – which many actually did – before repeating, 'good night').

'Our friendship was renewed,' Hibberd recalled, 'when he was singing the lead in *The Dubarry* at His Majesty's Theatre. Often we would meet at Charing Cross Station and come home to Chislehurst on the same train, and always we spoke – and sometimes sang – about songs, singers and the art of singing, for singing was his life.'[23]

It's a nostalgic picture: the incredibly tall and imposing newsreader and the handsome tenor, possessors of two of the best known voices in Britain, chin-wagging and holding forth in the moquette-upholstered compartment of a late-night suburban steam train...

The recording of 'If I am dreaming' is still available on CD, along with recordings by Anny Ahlers, and it demonstrates clearly how, in spite of everything, Heddle could apparently still pour his heart into the part of René. In fact, 9 September 1932, when he recorded 'If I am dreaming' turned out to be an exceptional day for operetta fans, even though Heddle was suffering from a slight cold. He also recorded another charming operetta title for the 'B' side, 'The Shepherd's Song', composed for a Charles Cochran adaptation of Offenbach's *La belle Hélène*, running in London at the time, under the title *Helen!*

And still Heddle had not finished for the day. He also managed to squeeze in an operatic aria – 'The Serenade' (Hear the voice of one who adores thee) from Bizet's opera *The Fair Maid of Perth*. Based on a novel by Sir Walter Scott, which tells the adventurous tale of Catherine Glover, an honest burgher's daughter, the opera (first premiered in Britain in Manchester, 1917, when it was conducted by Sir Thomas Beecham) has only rarely been performed. 'Serenade' itself was not an especially well-known piece before

Advert for Heddle's Columbia recordings (from programme)

Heddle recorded it that day. Yet the aria rapidly became Heddle Nash's most famous, best-selling and most enduringly popular recording; one totally associated with him; his passionate word painting generally thought to be at its most spine-tinglingly effective. Perhaps it's hardly surprising that in the late 1940s and early 1950s it went on to have a new lease of enormous popularity, even becoming one of the most frequently requested records on the Light Programme's 'Housewives Choice'! Floating out over the breakfast dishes, his love-sick, midnight tones from the dark shadows of a lonely garden, would bring a much-needed frisson of colour and romance to lonely housewives chained to the nation's utility and ration-strapped kitchens. They would roll his name on their tongues like a rationed sweet. Even in today's more cynical world, his impassioned, plea to 'open thou thy window, as in days of yore' doesn't fall on deaf ears, and visitors to what is reputed to be the site of the Fair Maid's house in Perth are still drawn there as much by Heddle Nash as by Sir Walter Scott.

On 28 October 1932 Heddle recorded 'Tell me tonight' by Eyton and Spoliansky, the theme song from a film of that title, directed by Anatole Litvak, and 'Wild Violets' by Robert Stolz, both characteristically Heddle, but rather slight in contrast with other pieces, and never released on CD. They were to be his last pieces of operetta available on record.

Operetta for Heddle had so far run an unexpectedly stormy course. He would go on to sing Eisenstein in *Die Fledermaus* again at Covent Garden, and Sir Walter Raleigh in *Merrie England* at the Princes Theatre, both roles winning him great acclaim; but for the moment, and much to the satisfaction of his more high-brow followers, he announced that he was keen to return to the world of opera and oratorio.

If another equally lucrative operetta part, or a film opportunity, had been on offer at that particular moment – who knows? It would certainly have been a matter of now, or never: being such a late starter, 'young' Heddle, seemingly all of a sudden, was by then aged thirty-eight. But as far as we know, no such temptations were either being courted or extended – there was plenty of fierce competition around, and a superb tenor voice is not the first essential for success in operetta, as Heddle was by then wise enough to know. And in the world of operetta maybe he had been too over-shadowed by Anny Ahlers, in life and in death.

In May 1933, fortunate to have escaped the jinx of *The Dubarry*, Heddle was invited to return to Covent Garden for the Summer International Season to perform in a run of three performances of Richard Strauss's *Der Rosenkavalier*, conducted by Sir Thomas Beecham. Singing the role of the

Italian singer, he was singled out for praise by the critics from a glittering international cast of Alexander Kipnis, Lotte Lehmann, Eva Hadrabova and Adele Kern. Operetta hadn't blunted him. A huge sigh of relief must have accompanied such a smooth and triumphant return to the operatic stage, drawing a curtain across what he must by then have viewed as a dangerous and heady excursion into the mad, glitzy world of 1930s West End operetta.

10

Goings on at Glyndebourne and Portland Place

Curious happenings were afoot in deepest Sussex in the early years of the 1930s...

Not only did the cast and company of *The Dubarry* descend on sleepy Shipley – thereby linking the little church for evermore with the glamorous world of the West End stage – the author Stella Gibbons was sending her feisty heroine Flora Poste Sussexward to stir things up on the Starkadders' farm, and poke her nose into 'something naarsty in the woodshed'.[1] Meanwhile, in a favoured spot on the edge of the Downs, a member of the landed gentry was strolling around in lederhosen, singing Wagner, and plotting to dig up the vegetable plot to build an opera house for his wife...

Heddle's services were not required at Cold Comfort Farm, but since singing was involved in the other events, he was, quite naturally, down in Sussex too ...

In his comings and goings with the Carl Rosa Opera Company, Heddle had met an attractive, well-connected young soprano named Audrey Mildmay. She, in turn, had gone on to meet, through an intense, shared love of opera, a former Eton schoolmaster named John Christie, who had not only been fortunate enough to inherit a large fortune, but along with it a beautiful Tudor manor house named Glyndebourne, near Lewes in East Sussex. In 1931 Audrey Mildmay had married John Christie, and within months of the ceremony, due largely to Audrey's influence and encouragement, the pair had embarked on the scheme of building an opera house in the grounds of Glydebourne, on the site of their erstwhile kitchen garden.

The plans had started out reassuringly small-scale – just a little place in which to entertain their friends. But not for long. Once the idea took root in Christie's mind, as fertile as the Sussex soil, it had started to blossom and grow, until eventually the 'little, private' enterprise had turned into a full-scale, full-blown opera house. Then Christie, with mind-blowing enthusiasm and optimism, went a step further still, declaring that he intended to turn it into a 'world-class venue', and 'a touchstone for operatic excellence' – to challenge even Salzburg and Bayreuth! In view of all the shrivelled and blackened shoots of private operatic enterprise in Britain, had he perhaps turned a trifle bonkers?

When the building work actually started and people began to see the full scale of it, the 'bonkers' theory became almost universal. (Sir Thomas Beecham didn't even bother to reply when Christie wrote to him on the subject – hardly surprising.) For starters, had the 'crazy man in Sussex' as the newspapers dubbed Christie, any idea of the sheer cost of such an enterprise which, did he realise, would have to be met entirely out of his own pocket? Not to mention the Expert Skill and Expert Knowledge that would be required to bring such an elaborate operatic scheme to fruition. As for keeping it up and running...

Fortunately, once John Christie had got an idea in his head, like all truly inspired people, there was no talking common sense; no stopping him. He managed to persuade the highly regarded German conductor, Fritz Busch (at a loose end after the last minute collapse of his annual season conducting in Buenos Aires), followed by a German producer, Carl Ebert, to join him in his enterprise. They only agreed to do so on condition that 'the last word in such matters as the engagement of singers, the planning of the repertoire and the number of rehearsals needed, was to rest with them.'[2] John Christie readily and sensibly agreed – it saved his project.

By the spring of 1934 the building works on his opera house were almost complete. Now they could get down to the fun part of planning an inaugural programme. At first Christie (a devotee of all things German like many of the English upper classes at the time, and not only given to wandering around in lederhosen, but to using German words where possible, for instance labelling the loos *Damen* and *Herren*) – had been desperately keen to put on Wagner opera. But eventually he was persuaded by Busch and Ebert to drop over-ambitious Wagner in favour of the then lesser known, and less popular Mozart.

Le nozze di Figaro and *Così fan tutte* were the two operas finally selected. In a desire to achieve the most excellent, European standards, each opera was to be performed in the language in which it was written – Italian, rather than in that inferior sort of English translation prevailing at the time. For many in the audience, it would be the very first time they had heard either opera sung in the language in which it was originally composed! What is more, the artists engaged to perform were to be only those who were deemed to be the very best and most suited to their particular role, no matter what nationality they were. (Apart, of course from Audrey Mildmay herself who – fair enough – was guaranteed a part; though in order to win a leading part, even she, apparently, had to audition for Busch.)

This is the point at which Heddle himself comes in. How very fortunate he was that there had been a change of heart from Wagner to Mozart. The Mozart, of course, suited him completely, and he soon found himself being invited down to Sussex to sing two roles: Ferrando in *Così fan tutte* and Basilio in *Le nozze di Figaro*.

The Glyndebourne operatic experience would prove totally different from anything Heddle had known before. In the quest for perfection, the artists soon learned they were expected to attend many rehearsals, as well as the actual performances. Like his fellow artists Heddle found it necessary to rent a place nearby for the duration of the Festival (apart from especially honoured foreign singers, who were invited to stay in the house itself – a sore point). Many rented in the local village of Ringmer, but Heddle found a cottage, 'The Little Bat' (as in bat and ball, an ancient Sussex game), about five miles away where his family joined him.[3]

All the artists and their families had the beautiful Glyndebourne estate at their disposal. And (as can well be imagined) Heddle was soon taking a keen interest in all the creative activities going on in the busy scenery and props workshops which were situated on site in the early days.

Sometimes the performers and their families went off on relaxing excursions as a big jolly group to the nearby seaside town of Seaford to swim and picnic on the beach. But one such outing nearly ended in tragedy. David Nash recalls how, aged six or seven, he paddled out too far in his inflatable dinghy, found himself being carried out to sea by the tide and was lucky to be rescued by the strong swimming skills of the conductor Fritz Busch. The paddle he had been striking out with to such bold effect had been specially made for him by none other than his father, who had pronounced the bought one 'substandard'!

The artists found all sorts of original touches at Glyndebourne. Money had to be spent in the first instance on providing comforts for the audience, so initially there were only two communal dressing rooms for the principals,

*Studying
a score at
Glyndebourne.*

one for the men and one for the women. It helped, of course, to foster a community spirit and Heddle wasn't complaining. One very thoughtful touch (Miss Mildmay's, obviously, and brought about by her own back-stage experiences) – the door to the ladies' loo was made wide enough to be accessed in a crinoline. On the first night of a performance, again at Miss Mildmay's suggestion, the artists found not the usual good luck telegram or flowers on their dressing tables, but a half bottle of champagne – appreciated far more. Heddle also spoke gratefully of the chaise-longues introduced, at some later date, for moments of relaxation, though he also commented that such moments were always few and far between.

But the Sussex country life for Heddle Nash, as for Flora Poste, was not destined to be a total rural idyll. Heddle was prone to hay-fever, and the performances took place just when the pollen count was at its highest, in

June, from timothy grass in the meadows surrounding Glyndebourne, not to mention the may-buds and, on the estate itself, the grand herbaceous borders. It became so bad that he started consulting specialists, trying to find a cure, and spending lavishly in the process. All to no avail. When one particular medical expert proceeded to inform him that his allergy was, 'all in the mind, Mr Nash, all in the mind,' he reached the end of his tether and was seized by one of those 'Heddle moments' when confronted by what he perceived to be pompous authority: the toe of his shoe made sharp impact with the consultant's shin, producing a satisfactory yelp. 'Was that all in the mind?' Heddle enquired, with a charming smile of satisfaction.[4]

The price of a ticket to Glyndebourne in those early days was reckoned 'pretty pricey' at £2 or 30/- (£1.50), especially since there was the extra expense of having to take a train down from London and purchase a dinner. Dinner was reckoned on the whole to be not good value, at around 5/- (picnicking did not come in until the following year) and many grumbled that you could get a far superior opera supper at the Waldorf, only one minute from Covent Garden, for the same price. It is hardly surprising that the audience for the inaugural performance of *Figaro* was full of titled names – 'Lords' 'Ladies' and 'Capts.' predominating. But for the second evening's *Così* performance, reckoned an even bigger success than *Figaro*, the audience was pretty sparse.

Nevertheless, the whole enterprise, of which many had justifiably been so dubious, was reckoned, apart from some teething troubles with the much-vaunted acoustics,[5] as having been a remarkably huge success. Most of those who had undergone the novel experience of donning evening dress in the afternoon to take a train and venture down to deepest Sussex seem to have gone away with the feeling that they had 'enjoyed a truly unique experience'; not only sampling the finest in opera, but being permitted the added pleasure of wandering about the beautiful Glyndebourne grounds, where they could imagine themselves to be the private and privileged guests of the Christie family.

Heddle won plaudits for both his performances, though according to Spike Hughes[6] he had to endure being 'ruthlessly deprived' of two of Ferrando's three arias. But in what was described as his 'outstandingly comic' Don Basilio, he was given an extra solo scene in the last act where he was really able to shine. In that same last act came another unexpected bonus, when a number of live bats flew on to the garden set, adding greatly to the enjoyment of the audience, who cheered heartily as the final curtain fell.[7]

Being Heddle, of course his first appearance at Glyndebourne had not been without its last-minute personal drama. Just one month beforehand

he had had his tonsils removed by Mr Cyril Horsford, his Harley Street throat specialist. It had been touch and go whether his voice would have recovered in time. Or, indeed, whether he would still have a voice to sing with! His concerns were compounded by the fact that, only shortly beforehand, David's tonsils had been removed using the new 'guillotine procedure', which had accidentally sliced off part of the soft palate along with the tonsils. Not surprisingly, Heddle opted for supreme caution, insisting on having the old-fashioned 'scalpel method', and demanding in addition a local rather than a general anaesthetic, because he intended to keep a wary eye on the proceedings![8]

Christie made a huge personal financial loss that year, but he was so encouraged by the enthusiastic reactions that there was now no stopping him – he decided he wanted to go ahead and do the whole thing all over again the following year. And even to extend the programme to include Mozart's two German operas, *Die Zauberflöte* and *Die Entführung aus dem Serail*. It was just taken for granted that Heddle Nash would want to repeat his big success as Basilio and Ferrando, and it was now decided to offer him the two extra parts of Monostatos and Pedrillo.

Heddle, however, along with certain other outstanding soloists, in particular the American-born Ina Souez, who had been a great hit as Fiordiligi, had apparently not been sent a contract. So since the whole enterprise had always seemed in doubt anyway, they had naturally gone ahead and fixed themselves up with engagements elsewhere. Heddle had contracted to sing in *Il barbiere di Siviglia* at Covent Garden, and in any case, he made it clear when he was finally approached, he would rather sing Tamino (a part in which he had always had such a huge success) and Belmonte. So it looked for a time in the spring of 1935 as though Heddle's association with Glyndebourne was about to to be short-lived. According to Spike Hughes's account, however, Busch was determined to have him back – 'a better Basilio I do not know', he's quoted as having said. He despatched Bing (his managerial assistant) and Oppenheimer (chief of musical staff) to sort it out, so 'like a couple of Canadian Mounties... they set out to get their man.'[9] And succeeded, somehow arranging matters so that Heddle could manage to juggle both Covent Garden and Glyndebourne.

But Heddle did not get what he wanted in the way of parts – he got Basilio and Ferrando again, no Tamino (so he turned down Monostatos), but he agreed to Pedrillo, and won great praise in the part: 'a superfine achievement alike in character and in delicacy of vocal art. Mr Heddle Nash as Pedrillo once more makes his serenade the loveliest thing in the whole opera'; '...it was left to Heddle Nash (Pedrillo) to give us in his serenade the best singing of the evening.'[10]

On the morning of 25 June 1935 Heddle would sing the part of Ferrando for an HMV recording of *Così fan tutte* which was made in the theatre.

Again Heddle greatly impressed the critics with his excellent Italian, though even *The Manchester Guardian* could show a surprisingly patronising attitude towards English singers:

we expect Continental artists to feel at home in any language; but it is a different matter amongst artists of a land where opera is virtually unknown these days, even in English... Mr Heddle Nash as Basilio and Miss Constance Willis as Marcellina also were instances of the little known truth that, given the opportunity and the coaching, English singers can enter the regions of opera skillfully and naturally.

Yet only the month before that review was written, Heddle had been singing, and more than holding his own, in Italian at Covent Garden as Almaviva in *Il barbiere di Siviglia* with an otherwise almost exclusively international cast. This prejudiced attitude was always highly frustrating for him.

The whole Glyndebourne experience was once again greeted with enthusiasm in the press however:

> The Glyndebourne production of *Le nozze di Figaro* is one of the most beautiful that can be seen at the present day anywhere. And it is being done this summer not in a country where opera enjoys a long tradition; it is not even being done in the one and only opera house which we have usually regarded as our only real opera house. This exquisite production can be heard in the theatre of Mr John Christie at his home on the Sussex Downs; out of nothing he has created a school of opera that already is in some points comparable with the best which Salzburg and Munich can show.[11]

A 1936 season followed, with Christie digging deep into his pockets yet again. Heddle was signed up for Basilio, Ferrando and Pedrillo once more. But *Don Giovanni* was being added to the programme that year, and in view of the huge success he had achieved in the part of Don Ottavio, with his amazing debut at Covent Garden, it must have been particularly galling for him when he learned that he was being passed over for the part – in favour of a foreign tenor by the name of Koloman von Pataky. Especially when it later turned out that von Pataky 'didn't make much of an impression'![12] On the other hand, one wouldn't blame Heddle if he felt quietly relieved and smug about that. And according to Alan Blyth, Heddle did, in actual fact, get to take over from von Pataky for three performances of Ottavio in the 1936 season, though this fact was 'for long unlisted in the Festival's annals.'

When the 1937 season came round, a row blew up, which affected Heddle, over the use of British singers. Both Christie and his wife wanted to include as many English singers as possible (it was their theatre and their money, after all). Busch, Ebert and Bing, however, insisted that they already went out of their way to use British artists, where possible, and argued that their first consideration must be 'not just to maintain the Glyndebourne standards, but to improve on them'. The Christies were particularly keen that Heddle should sing Don Ottavio in all performances that season, which seems reasonable in view of the fact that the last foreign import had not exactly shone. But Busch, always on the look out for fresh, foreign talent to 'up' the standards, had heard that a tenor named Dino Borgioli had just had a big success in the part at Salzburg and set his sights firmly in that direction. (Borgioli had also alternated with Heddle for two or three performances of *Il barbiere di Siviglia* at Covent Garden in 1935 and had recorded *Il barbiere* for Columbia with the Chorus of La Scala.)

On getting wind of what was afoot, Heddle apparently took matters into his own hands. He is reported to have leapt into his car and motored full speed down to Glyndebourne where he confronted Christie. One wonders what exactly was said, because Christie ended up – despite having promised Busch the last word in the engagement of singers – offering Heddle, in addition to the Pedrillo and Basilio he was already engaged for, two performances of Ottavio, with Borgioli to get the rest;[13] a decision which apparently landed Christie in serious hot water with his management team.

Borgioli's Don Ottavio is said to have been sung with 'an instinctive intelligence', but according to Spike Hughes 'John Christie remained unconvinced that he could "beat" Nash in the part'. And Heddle was said to be 'furious' – and who could blame him – when the aria '*Il mio tesoro*', for which he was so famous, and which he was so often requested to sing at the Proms, was cut out by the producer Janni Strasser, who despite the evidence to the contrary, maintained that no English singer could ever perform it satisfactorily![14]

Heddle's last appearances at Glyndebourne were as Ferrando and Basilio again in 1938. Singing in the chorus that season happened to be an up and coming, impressively tall, fair-haired young tenor named Peter Pears. In a letter to Benjamin Britten,[15] written from The Old Cottage, Laughton, Lewes, in June of that year, Pears put his own slant on life at Glyndebourne. He complains of having, 'a bloody cold that won't go' due to having a lot of running about and changing to do in *Macbeth* and being 'always in drafts [draughts?], so colds stick'. He adds, 'I'm running mildly after a sweet tough Stage Hand but as usual I can't come to the point!!' And then: 'I've been playing the piano for Heddle Nash, which is rather funny.' Pears doesn't elaborate, but there was certainly a camaraderie between the two tenors, one at the top of his profession, the other just starting out, because Pears apparently approached Heddle on the matter of coaching. Unfortunately Heddle was far too busy even to think about giving lessons at that point in his career, even to such an exceptional young man. Years later, when he had made his name, Pears would recall, with wry amusement, turning up to perform in a Celebrity Concert somewhere in South Wales, only to be warned by one of the promoters, by way of a greeting, 'I hope you're in good voice. We had Heddle Nash last year and he was *marvellous*'.[16]

Heddle is said to have been hugely popular with all his fellow performers, as well as with the audiences. It is gratifying to hear the comment that he went out of his way to be 'especially kind and welcoming to nervous newcomers', always ready with a relaxing joke or two before performances. And he made some firm personal friendships, in particular with the German baritone Willi Domgraf-Fassbaender, the first Glyndebourne Figaro, who had encountered a few problems initially in reigning in his tremendous voice to suit the Glyndebourne acoustics. He and Heddle had plenty in common, since Fassbaender had also been a pupil of Giuseppe Borgatti in Milan and both had talented children who would eventually follow them into the singing profession, in Fassbaender's case a daughter, the mezzo-soprano Brigitte Fassbaender.

Despite all the behind-the-scenes goings-on and all the frustrations he had faced yet again, Heddle nevertheless loved performing at Glyndebourne. He always claimed that being a part of the Glyndebourne scene, and establishing its traditions from the very outset, was a supremely fulfilling period in his life. And when he performed there among so many top foreign artists, he was genuinely proud to believe that he was 'doing something for the honour of England.'[17]

Though only a very few people know it, on 6 July 1934, following his first season at Glyndebourne, Heddle Nash helped to make minor television and opera history by performing in the first-ever, experimental, BBC performance of opera, along with the Canadian soprano Sarah Fischer and a Spanish dancer who was much in vogue in London at the time, named Elsa Brunelleschi.

Exactly how Heddle came to be the tenor involved isn't known, because the opera was *Carmen*, which he normally regarded as being too heavy, but Sarah Fischer used the word 'chosen' in her case. Heddle, who was, of course, pretty busy at the time, seems to have had a rather throw-away attitude towards this event, because he personally didn't bother to leave any mention of it whatsoever. Perhaps he regarded the happening as just a bit of fun.

Fischer, however, seems to have been more astutely tuned-in to the performance's possible historical significance because she took care to leave a careful account, now preserved in the Canadian National Archives, along with an impressive photo of herself wearing the very costume.

Obviously it wasn't a full-scale version of *Carmen* they were performing – an all-round impossibility, given that the studio, converted from a first-floor drawing room in a former private residence in Portland Place, was a mere 28' long by about 14' wide – this was a potted version with a cast of just the three. According to a write-up in a magazine named *Television*: 'Drastic cuts were necessary to the score which had to be compressed into 40 minutes' yet 'still was easy to follow.' A reporter in the *Daily Telegraph*, however, apparently estimated it would take place: 'in the space of half-an-hour. This feat of compression ... will occur in the television period from 11 to 11.30 this morning', when he forecast that the cast of three would give a 'colourable [*sic*] representation' of the complete opera.

These early broadcasts seem to have had a remarkably wide reception area, stretching as far as the Channel Islands and Dublin. How many viewers, or 'lookers-in' as they were then termed, might have been tuning in to watch Heddle in *Carmen* that morning is a matter for conjecture, but the viewing audience at that point remained small. Television sets, nicknamed 'Tin Box' sets, were being marketed by the Baird Company at 25 guineas each in the early 1930s. But apparently there were a number of enterprising amateur enthusiasts who had preferred to get their hands on a Baird Television do-it-yourself kit – on sale at around 16 guineas and offering the opportunity for hours of blissful tinkering. In 1933 it seems that the *Sunday Dispatch*, by including a rough estimate of those do-it-yourselfers who might have actually managed to follow the instructions and get theirs up and running (and those who did were said to be so delighted with the results they would sit and watch anything at all) settled on the vague figure of between 3000 and 5000 fully functioning sets. The BBC are said at one point to have tried to arrive at a closer figure by putting out an announcement asking all those watching at that particular moment to please send them a postcard, marked Z, to Broadcasting House, so they could tot them up! Unfortunately the result was never published – perhaps the response was disappointingly lame. [18]

In the stuffy, overcrowded Portland Place studio, with all its sound, lighting and vision equipment, props, engineers, musicians, backdrop painter and other personnel, there would only have been just enough flickering light for Heddle and his two fellow artists to see where they were going – not that they would have been moving very far – once in position, they would have been confined almost to the spot. Sarah Fischer was keen to point out that a 'chosen' artist would have to be 'an accomplished musician and most reliable, as the conductor was not visible'. The reason being that he and the musicians were tucked away behind a heavy black curtain where they could have light to read their music by. Also the curtain helped to balance their sound volume with that of the performers.

'Faces were not clearly defined as there were no "close-ups"', Fischer explains, and 'the make-up was green for the lips, red when black was needed, and yellow for white'. Heddle would doubtless have had a laugh over the make-up – apparently the performers' comic-looking faces usually caused hilarity. Not that the clown-like faces would have bothered the lookers-in, who, due to the poor quality of the picture, would only have seen shadowy figures and not been able to recognise the artists taking part anyway.

According to Fischer, the singers would also have needed 'a sound stage technique ... as the stage setting was no higher or broader than a large mantel shelf'. But her next comment suggests that a contortionist's technique, combined with a sound sense of humour might have come in more useful: 'This special schooling required knowledge of how high to raise the arms, or where to place a limb, for the height of the knee had to fit in with the position of the tenor playing Don José, when kneeling at Carmen's feet with his head in her lap at the end of his aria "The Flower Song".'[19] One sincerely hopes that Heddle was up to speed on all that!

The whole event, in fact, rather smacks of The Reduced Shakespeare Company's comic productions over sixty years later, especially when readers are chattily informed by *Television* that: 'behind the curtain there was the usual rush to get changed in time, which (ominously) was not always achieved.' And yet the publication claims it was 'a realistic scene when Carmen (Sarah Fischer) was stabbed by Don José (Heddle Nash).'

Constantly on hand for each experimental broadcast was a nimble-fingered lady, stitching away in a corner all day, adjusting the costumes to the needs of the small screen. But seeing Fischer in her outfit, one can't help wondering how Heddle coped – duetting in such a confined space alongside such an exuberant-looking soprano, not only wearing an intimidatingly large mantilla, but also wielding a fan!

Yet *Television* gushed, *HELLO!* style, that Heddle Nash 'was delighted with the role and resolved to sing it on the operatic stage.' Ever the gentleman! Of course, he never did sing the heavier role of Don José on stage, only excerpts from *Carmen*, particularly 'The Flower Song', on the concert platform. As for his appearing on television again, that would not happen until near the end

*The ebullient
Sarah Fischer
in the Carmen
costume she
wore on TV.*

of his career in the 1950s; the opportunity simply never arose.

It is at this appropriately light-hearted point in Heddle's life in 1934 that the ebullient showman Vittorio Podrecca (by mere coincidence?) crops up again. The very same August edition of *Television* that carries the report on *Carmen* also contains a glowing report on how the Teatro dei Piccoli had been putting in their own appearance on experimental television.

Fresh from his triumph in America, Podrecca and the marionettes were back in England. After opening again at the Scala Theatre, they were enjoying an extended season at the Fortune Theatre when they too were invited to go along to the studio in Portland Place, the search for novel and interesting acts to entertain the lookers-in being a constant one – Bruce Norman records how, on one occasion, even a performing seal was brought into the studio – a huge hit. The programme the marionettes took part in was called 'The Cocktail Club' and it was described by *Television* as 'a bright and spontaneous effort to raise the spirits of the forenoon',[20] which has a ring of Breakfast Television about it.

Scaffolding with planks placed on top apparently had to be 'raised to the ceiling to enable the operators to work from above. Though the ceiling was lofty, there was barely room.' Worth all the effort though, because the 'wit and charm' of the Little Ones turned out to be perfectly suited to the small screen, the lack of detail in the picture actually working in their favour, by hiding their imperfections! (In fact the second transmission of 'The Cocktail Club' in which Podrecca was a guest, was judged by some lookers-in to be the best they had seen. A gentleman from Eastbourne even felt impressed enough to fire off a telegram of congratulations. He claimed that the programme had amused him more than any other. What's more, he gleefully pointed out, he could even see the rims of glasses standing on the bar!)

'In transmission the puppets occupied the whole screen,' readers were told, 'so lookers were not conscious of their size. Before the scanner their diminutive stature gives an advantage over human artists because they are able to move and dance close to the lens in a focus which would take only the head and shoulders of an actor. There were moments when their movements became uncannily perfect.' It was possible to forget that they were mere 'dolls' – especially, one imagines, when the shimmyingly life-like 'Josephine Baker' was brought on.

Could it be that Heddle, despite the valiant effort he had obviously put into promoting televised Grand Opera in July of 1934, had been up-staged yet again (or out-televisualised?) by a brilliantly entertaining team of puppets, who were still, ten years after he had first dubbed for them, managing to be excitingly avant-garde?

11

Prima Donnas, Scares and Serenades

That Glyndebourne had problems securing Heddle's services in 1935 is hardly surprising. We already know that he was pre-booked to sing in *Il barbiere di Siviglia* at Covent Garden at the end of May, so he must somehow have worked in the Glyndebourne rehearsals around it. That would have meant making sorties down to Sussex to be either Ferrando, Basilio or Pedrillo then speeding back to London to be Almaviva. No wonder he was reported on 25 May in a performance of *Il barbiere* as having a 'frog in his throat that gave him a lot of trouble in the first act'.[1] Once again he was the only English star in a superb international cast, which included the sensational French soprano and star of the Metropolitan Opera House, New York, Lily Pons, then at the height of her fame, as well as Ezio Pinza and the vibrant baritone Giovanni Inghilleri. Lily Pons, a beautiful twenty-seven-year-old coloratura soprano who was eagerly dubbed by the press (like Maggie Teyte before her) a 'Pocket Prima Donna' (she was 5' 2"), had arrived in England in a blaze of publicity, her photograph splashed across the front pages. She was quoted as being worried about how the 'stolid' Covent Garden opera-goers might receive her, and told the press that she was 'very nervous' in case they did not applaud her.[2] Naturally, therefore, they made a special point of doing so. When the 'diminutive' star had completed her 'big' aria at the beginning of the second act, 'sailing up to the high notes' the audience clapped and cheered and stopped the performance for two whole minutes while she graciously took her bows.[3]

Yet Heddle himself was far from being out-shone by this glamorous

media-savvy French/American star. His Almaviva won a hugely enthusiastic response all round, most notably from the future impresario and record producer Walter Legge who commented in the *Manchester Guardian* the following day that, once he had conquered the frog, Heddle Nash 'sang better than any tenor at Covent Garden this year'. Legge would later prove to be an influential fan, eventually signing Heddle up as a recording artist for HMV.

This production of *Il barbiere* had the honour of being chosen for a royal command performance, attended by the Duke and Duchess of York (the future King George VI and Queen Elizabeth) on 29 May. The glittering event was also shared with the nation, the first act being made the highlight of the broadcasting schedule that day, put out at the peak listening time, between eight o'clock and nine in the evening, when Heddle's unique voice, ringing out amongst this fine international cast, brought pride and pleasure to millions who were experiencing the thrill of being able to enjoy in their own homes what had previously been the exclusive province of the rich.

'Opera broadcasts' enthused the *Daily Mirror*, 'have now reached a high stage of perfection'. Now that the BBC had finally got their microphones into the Royal Opera House as part of the subsidy deal, they were employing six – two in the wings, two in the footlights, one in the orchestra pit, and a 'floating' one for moving around to pick up a particular artist. The gallery had been considered the best position for the microphones, because of the good acoustics, but it was very soon found to be unsatisfactory, because what was discreetly referred to as the 'atmosphere' created by the audience proved too much of a distracting 'background'. Even back in 1929 'Beachcomber', in his column in the *Daily Express*, had been drawing attention to the chattering audience: 'Nobody seemed to notice last night that *Rosenkavalier* was the opera being played. The conversation was carried on at a pitch usually reserved for *Valkyrie*.' Sir Thomas Beecham is reputed to have got into such a strop with the rude cackling of upper-crust audiences at Covent Garden on one occasion in 1934 that he whipped round and bellowed at them – 'Stop talking!'[4] and 'Shut up you!' – as well as adamantly refusing entrance to late-comers.

Following the high-profile production of *Il barbiere* Heddle spent June at Glyndebourne and recorded *Così fan tutte*. He popped up in a radio broadcast again in *The Love of the Three Oranges* on 6 July, followed, after a slight, unaccounted-for gap (when he was probably off serenading holiday makers at The Pier, Llandudno), by an appearance at the Proms. 1935 was an exciting year for Proms audiences, other legendary performers including Elisabeth Schumann, Maggie Teyte and Eva Turner (Turner being another who, in the words of Sir Henry Wood, had 'taken up the cudgels for England' by singing in the heart of Italian opera, at La Scala under the baton of Toscanini).

From 1 to 6 September Heddle was appearing at the Three Choirs Festival in Worcester, performing in *Elijah*, *The Apostles* and *The Messiah* with his old friends Isobel Baillie, Mary Jarred and Harold Williams. A week later, on 13 September, he was dashing off a letter to Columbia Records apologising for the delay in sending a publicity photo they had requested for the *Così fan tutte* recording because he had been working hard at *La Cenerentola* for Covent Garden for five days (so he must have gone straight there from the Three Choirs) 'and as you will have heard, it is now all off,' he grumbled. 'This has usurped my time.'[5] He fitted in two more *Il barbiere* appearances during September, but by 26 September he had rehearsed and switched to

a short Covent Garden season under the auspices of the Imperial League of Opera, opening as Rodolfo in *La Bohème*. No wonder his wife claimed that her parting words to him as he raced out of the house to catch a train were always: 'Music? Money? Handkerchief?' Yet he was hardly funding a champagne lifestyle, boarding school fees for his two boys appearing to be his top spending priority, now that the nice little earner *The Dubarry* had paid off the mortgage.

Perhaps we should pause to draw breath for a while and pin down Britain's 'most hard working tenor' – then at the supreme height of his talents – at the 1935 Covent Garden production of *La Bohème*. It was at the première of *La Bohème* on 28 September that one of the 'greatest hoaxes in London's operatic history' took place.[6] Though Heddle was not involved in planning it, he became a party to it, and he could be said to have suffered as a result: it involved him being up-staged by an attractive soprano – yet again!

The soprano in question was the beautiful young dark-haired Dora Labbette, well respected on the concert and oratorio platforms and noted also for her down-to-earth sense of humour. She also happened at the time to be the mistress of Sir Thomas Beecham. The story goes that Dora longed to appear in opera, but she was nervous about how the public would react to her switching roles. Beecham understood her anxiety all too well and one day came up with a suggestion: why not appear on the opera stage incognito?[7] And, since he was of the commonly held opinion that if you happened to be an Italian soprano, so much the better, he cynically added that she should pass herself off as a little-known Italian artist who was making her English debut on the Covent Garden stage. Dora mulled over the idea, liked it, and decided to go along with it (unlike Heddle who had personally rejected such a course). As a pseudonym she selected the Italian-sounding name Lisa Perli (Perli adding to the joke because she had been born at Purley in Surrey, though Labbette itself sounds foreign enough). A big publicity campaign was then set rolling to whet the opera-going public's appetite for this 'sensational' 'new' soprano, who was about to undertake the part of Mimi to Heddle Nash's Rodolfo. The cast were all sworn to secrecy by Beecham, who had convinced them that it was all good publicity for the performance anyway, so there wasn't much that Heddle could have done but cynically play along.

On the opening night, the public and critics, of course, flocked along full of curiosity to hear 'Lisa Perli', the critics sharpening their pencils in anticipation, though the secret is said to have been out already and they were just keeping up the pretence for the sake of a good story.

Beecham, who was conducting that evening, had handed Perli/Labbette her big moment and she was a singer who knew how to seize it. The critics gave her rave reviews – though it was perfectly obvious that few were deceived, despite the blonde wig: '... her phrasing revealed an experienced singer behind the clear, almost girlish, tones ... she had at her disposal a richer and more powerful quality when it was needed', coyly hinted *The Times* reviewer, though remaining mum. But Walter Legge, reviewing for the *Manchester Guardian*, while heaping praise, and stating that Lisa Perli was beyond question the most natural and convincing Mimi he had ever seen,

was happy to let the cat out of the bag, by adding, with a flourish of youthful-sounding rhetoric:

> considerable interest naturally centred in the identity of this artist, whose voice has a curiously familiar ring but who surpassed the achievements of the person who in colour of voice and shape of face she so strikingly resembled. But although no statement has been made, I am prepared to wager that Signorina Lisa Perli bears the same relation to Dora Labbette that Tantris bore to Tristan.

The novelty of Perli/Labbette's Mimi generated so much interest that Heddle's Rodolfo (although there is no reason to believe he gave any other than his usual ardent and involved performance) was seen as nothing more than a reprise, being thoroughly eclipsed in the press and covered by such unexciting comments as, 'he seemed as much at home in Puccini as in Mozart or Rossini'. *The Times* managed the comment that he 'revelled in the Italian cantilena'. Heddle had found himself out-publicised by a soprano with powerful male backing, yet again!

As for Beecham, though it was familiar gossip in inner circles that he had hatched the thing, he ruthlessly disclaimed all knowledge of it. But the wily conductor had done exactly what he had intended to do: set his mistress firmly on the road to a new career, while at the same time proving, what Heddle Nash already knew to his cost, that the possession of a foreign name, especially an Italian-sounding name, was still, without doubt, an asset to anybody hoping for a successful operatic career in 1930s Britain.

It was around this time that Violet Nash bumped into Sir Thomas Beecham in New Bond Street and added her own personal anecdote to the pile that had already accumulated, concerning the conductor's flamboyance, wit and idiosyncrasies. They had fallen into conversation and he had begun to stroll along the pavement beside her. The day having turned unexpectedly warm, she noticed that he had stripped off his overcoat and was carrying it draped over his arm. But all of a sudden he stopped walking and hailed a passing taxi, giving Violet the impression that the conversation must be over and he was about, albeit rather abruptly, to take his leave. No such thing: the great man flung his overcoat on to the back seat and casually instructed the cab driver to crawl along behind them, carrying it for him!

In November and December 1936, Heddle rounded off this extraordinarily busy time in his career by recording parts of *La Bohème* in Italian, with Perli, Beecham, the London Philharmonic Orchestra and the original cast. Regarding this recording, his son John Heddle Nash would later pay this tribute:

> My own feeling is that one of his unique gifts was his vivid appreciation of *words*, allied to a sense of the poetic. It so happens that I sang the opera *La Bohème* for six years, with a number of good tenors, before I heard my father's recording of it – and suddenly there was poetry in the air! Rodolfo had often sounded romantic before – but never *poetic* as well.

Heddle also managed to fit in a performance of *The Dream of Gerontius* at the Free Trade Hall in Manchester with Dr Malcolm Sargent, the Hallé Orchestra and choir, Astra Desmond and Keith Falkner. An engineer and composer by the name of K H Leech had the enterprise to make a live recording of the performance off the radio at home, on his own equipment and purely for his own pleasure. It precedes the famous Nash/Sargent recording for HMV by a whole ten years and in the enthusiastic words of Alan Blyth, reveals 'a youthful intensity, on a live occasion, hard to repeat in a studio. His interpretation undoubtedly matured later, but here it is in its raw prime.'[8]

And so the hectic 1930s continued. There was an invitation by Bruno Walter to sing in Prague; another by Fritz Busch to sing in Buenos Aires, and a number of other invitations to sing abroad, including one from Australia. All of which Heddle turned down. The reason usually given is that he was reluctant to spend even more time away from his family, but the truth is likely to have been more complex. Perhaps he feared that his light, English tenor voice might not be fully appreciated abroad, amongst all the heavier competition, and that while he was away, certain other English tenors would be only too eager to step in and snaffle up his regular bookings. As long as the work and the appreciation were here for him in England, that appears to have been what he really coveted most: to be an English tenor at the top of the tree, in England. So there was more touring with Covent Garden; seasons at Glyndebourne; bookings at the Proms and the Three Choirs Festival; appearances with the Hallé and the usual round of provincial concerts, oratorios and broadcasts squeezed in, as well as further performances at the Royal Opera House Covent Garden; *Die Meistersinger* in the Summer Season, starting in April 1936; *Der Rosenkavalier* on 1 June; a performance of *Bohème* on 4 June, and *Il barbiere* again in December, in the Winter Opera Season – a workload so varied it becomes difficult to get one's head round it.

Was Heddle driving himself too hard? The answer is probably 'yes' because in one of the Summer Season performances of *Die Meistersinger* he gave himself a nasty health scare. It began when he was struck down by influenza, found by his doctor to be running a temperature of 104 degrees, and was ordered to bed. But, being Heddle, he did not remain there for very long.

The Covent Garden management set off frantically phoning round all the opera houses of Europe, trying to find a replacement. But a replacement David at short notice does not come easy. In triumph, they at last announced that they had secured one and named him as Valentin Haller from Berlin. Only to be wired, virtually at the eleventh hour, that another engagement would prevent Herr Haller making it after all. The hair-tearing stage had been reached. It was then that someone came up with the bottom-of-the-barrel suggestion of the aging tenor Octave Dua, who happened to be conveniently to hand, but had not actually sung the part since 1914... However, if the choice lay between engaging him, or cancelling the performance altogether, we-ll ...

This proved too much for Heddle![9]

When he heard the news (he was obviously following events closely from his sick-bed), he reacted in true valiant and dramatic style – though incredibly rashly. He hauled himself out of bed, demanded his clothes, and rang through to the Royal Opera House to say forget Dua! – Nash was on his way!

He got Violet to drive him up to London, where he installed himself in a hotel in Covent Garden. From there he staggered into the theatre:

'BRITISH SINGER LEAVES HIS SICK BED TO SAVE OPERA' reported the *Daily Mirror* on Saturday 2 May 1936.

> Only two people in the audience at Covent Garden last night knew the drama that was being played out behind the scenes – the drama of a British singer who left his sickbed to save the opera, *Die Meistersinger*.
>
> They were Mrs Heddle Nash, the singer's wife, and Mr Cyril Horsford, Harley Street throat specialist...
>
> In the interval they went round to his dressing room. Mr Horsford sprayed Mr Nash's throat, he was massaged, and a train of attendants went to and fro with bottles of liniment and raw eggs. [!] ...
>
> 'They have fixed my throat for to-night. What it will be like tomorrow I dread to think! But I will carry on,' Mr Nash told me.
>
> Mr Nash had to sing for a quarter of an hour practically without stopping. Despite his illness, he gave a spirited performance.

Sir Thomas Beecham, who was conducting that evening, was reported as commenting afterwards, 'Mr Nash's performance was an extraordinary effort of fortitude and endurance.' It's said that some members of the audience, having heard that Heddle was suffering from influenza and would be replaced by a certain Herr X, failed to read the correction slip in the programme and sat through the whole performance thinking how well the mystery singer was doing!

Heddle had saved the opera, but he was to pay a serious price. According to David Nash, 'He returned to his Covent Garden hotel afterwards, where he was cosseted. But he probably had a slight stroke as a result, because half of his face was paralysed. It took a whole day's massaging even to get a slight twitch back.'

Obviously Heddle did recover full feeling eventually, but the incident had shocked him. Ever afterwards he took precautions to protect that side of his face, because he still felt it to be vulnerable, especially from draughts. He even had a special baffle fitted to his car for occasions when he drove with the window down.[10]

A mishap in a lighter vein nearly put Heddle out of action once again during the 1936–7 Winter Concert Season at Covent Garden. He was singing Eisenstein in *Die Fledermaus* with Dennis Noble as Falke and the beautiful Austrian soprano Irene Eisinger (with whom he had performed and recorded *Così fan tutte* at Glyndebourne) in a sparkling production full of gay lightheartedness and charm. The part called for him to be lively and nimble on his feet so he was already resorting to supporting them with elasticated bandages, due to his War legacy. One morning before a performance he took little David for a walk in the woods near their home and, noticing that some late leaves were falling, he felt inspired to invent a game. He called it 'Capture a contract for Father' – (he must have had contracts on the brain, even at the height of his success). 'It was great fun. If you could catch a leaf before it hit the ground, you would 'capture another contract for father,' David recalls. But the game nearly had the adverse effect: 'In rushing to catch one himself, my father tripped over a root and badly sprained his ankle! Agony!'

Heddle got the ankle strapped up, gritted his teeth, and went on to perform that evening – exercising mind over matter (another War legacy?) As he bubbled with Eisenstein's customary verve and vitality he somehow managed to wring the illusion of 'twinkle' out of a pair of flat, knackered-out feet and a twisted ankle.

It was also in the 1936–7 season at Covent Garden, after more performances as Rodolfo, that Heddle achieved an ambition he had been harbouring ever since the days when he had sat mesmerised up in the gallery in 1922 – he finally got to sing the part of Lieutenant Pinkerton to Maggie Teyte's Butterfly. This other 'Pocket Prima Donna' was aged forty-eight by then, six years older than Heddle, yet the ubiquitous Grenville Eves was far from disappointed: 'I again heard Maggie Teyte as Butterfly, the Pinkerton was Heddle Nash and the Sharpless Percy Heming – for me the most perfect "Butterfly" cast. What a well-matched pair Teyte and Nash were...'

The *Times* critic, however, had a few reservations:

Mr Heddle Nash as Pinkerton sang very pleasantly and acted the ungrateful part with a winning simplicity, though the note of passion was not to be found in his performance.' As for Maggie Teyte, who had already sung the part of Hansel that afternoon: 'The small, semi-recitative phrases were especially well done and so, indeed, was all the music which lay in the middle of her voice; in this there was compensation for a certain lack of richness of the full thrilling tone that is demanded, at the climax especially. Her voice, not unnaturally, sounded a little tired.

To Heddle an American lieutenant's uniform ranked as serious business. So important was it to him to feel unassailably 'in character' as Pinkerton that he had gone to the lengths of having his own uniform especially tailored. He had taken the same trouble over the leather apron he wore for the part of David in *Die Meistersinger*, having had that designed and made for him in Germany using traditional methods and materials.[11] (Italian legacy? or BNOC?) His fan Frank Stokes, who was working behind the scenes in Leeds when he was once on tour there, was amazed to witness how, when a prop (believed to have been a shepherd's harp sent up from the London theatrical costumiers) didn't meet with Heddle's approval, he immediately rolled up his sleeves, set to work and knocked up a replacement: 'Typical of him!' chortled Mr Stokes in admiration. 'His attention to detail. A top operatic star! Making his own prop! Can you believe it?' When a role called on him to carry a sword, it comes as no surprise to learn that Heddle would not be armed with a mere replica, courtesy of the props department – he had purchased a fine authentic one and that was the one he preferred to carry. And for a year or two after lighter forms of stage makeup became available, Heddle still went on using the heavier and messier grease paint, for the simple reason that applying it took longer and required more skill, allowing him extra time to dig himself deeper into the character. His wife complained that that was all very well, but it messed up his collars.[12] (One wonders what effect the old thespian trick he adopted for a while in later life, of applying a slick of black boot polish to his hair, might have had on the laundry.)

In 1938 Heddle would partner Maggie Teyte again, this time in a radio performance of Massenet's *Manon* conducted by Stanford Robinson, which listeners greeted with such enthusiastic delight, it was given no less than four repeats. Fortunately a recording of some excerpts from this broadcast is still in existence, so Heddle can still be heard singing one of his most famous roles, accompanied by one of his most perfect partners – but only by chance! According to Alan Blyth,[13] this precious recording was rediscovered and rescued only a few years ago from the back of a cupboard at the BBC where it had lain forgotten, gathering dust and in grave danger of being binned.

In October of that same year Heddle not only sang in *Faust* and *Rigoletto* at Covent Garden, on 5 October he took part in another landmark event. He was one of the eminent group of British singers who were invited to perform in the *Serenade to Music*, a composition for sixteen soloists and orchestra commissioned from Ralph Vaughan Williams to celebrate Sir Henry Wood's fifty years as a conductor. It was to be performed at the Albert Hall as part of

The 'heavyweights' of British choral music. Serenade to Music solosits, Abbey Road Studios, October 1938. **Front row:** Isobel Baillie, Elsie Suddaby, Eva Turner, Stiles Allen, Sir Henry Wood, Margaret Balfour, Astra Desmond, Muriel Brunskill, Mary Jarred. **Back row:** Walter Widdop, Parry Jones, Frank Titterton, Heddle Nash, Vaughan Williams, Roy Henderson, Harold Williams, Robert Easton, Norman Allin.

a special concert 'for and dedicated to Sir Henry Wood on the occasion of his jubilee, in grateful recognition of his services to music'. Vaughan Williams had chosen a setting of lines from Lorenzo's speech in Act V of Shakespeare's *The Merchant of Venice* which begins:

> How sweet the moonlight sleeps upon this bank!
> Here will we sit and let the sounds of music
> Creep in our ears; soft stillness and the night
> Become the touches of sweet harmony.

He had composed the piece with the individual vocal qualities of each singer in mind, carefully inserting their initials into the score to mark their solos. To HN he had of course allotted the line into which he could best inject his famous lyrical ardour: 'Look how the floor of heaven Is thick inlaid with patines of bright gold.'

On the night of the concert, performed before a vast audience, the piece was declared a triumph. The combination of such beautiful words with such beautiful music moved many to tears, including, according to the composer's wife, Rachmaninov who was at the concert to play his Second Piano Concerto. A few days later the importance of this occasion was reinforced when the artists were invited to put on a repeat performance in order that Pathé News might film it for posterity, with Vaughan Williams himself sitting on the steps of the stage, looking on.

Dear Heddle Nash,

I have pleasure in enclosing herewith a copy of the group photograph taken last Saturday and should like to express our thanks to you for your kindly cooperation in this recording.

Sir Henry Wood and Dr Vaughan Williams have heard the records and are delighted with them. I shall be sending you copies as soon as they are in production.

The Pathé film has also turned out very well and when it has been cut, I hope to arrange for a private showing at the Pathé Studio, 111, Wardour Street, W.1. and will ask you to come and see it.

With kindest regards,

Yours sincerely,[14]

The glimpses we get of Heddle on the platform with the other singers in this bit of archive film footage are rare moving images of him. Yet frustratingly, it's not possible to get more than a fleeting glance, the tenors and baritones all being positioned on the second row, behind the sopranos and contraltos. When the same group, apart from one or two changes, was reassembled to repeat the performance ten years later, at the newly opened Festival Hall, the big concern was apparently not whether they would all still be able to hit the right notes, but whether the platform would be able to bear their considerably increased combined weight![15]

Gaiety Theatre Dublin. Left to right: Arthur Hammond (conductor), Richard Tauber, Lucia Danieli, Heddle Nash.

In May 1938, towards the end of his magnificent 1930s run of performances at Covent Garden, Heddle performed with yet another singing legend of the twentieth century – Richard Tauber. In a performance of *Die Entführung* with Beecham conducting, he undertook his Glyndebourne part as Pedrillo, with the greatly-loved Austrian tenor, a supreme Mozartian, singing Belmonte. The British public had fallen so heavily for the Viennese charms and broken English of Tauber, who, during those days of Depression encapsulated the British idea of 'romance', that one might have excused Heddle if that fact had rankled a bit. (Tauber was nowhere near so good looking as Heddle.) But on the contrary, the pair are said to have shared a mutual admiration, and to have got on rather well. Heddle was quoted as saying to his wife, 'Richard Tauber is a wonderful chap. He can sit down at the piano and play like anything. I wish I could do that.'[16] (Heddle himself played with one finger only.)

Heddle would perform again with Tauber at the Dublin Opera House in

1939, a place where he had sung with much enjoyment on other occasions. But at that particular point in his life he was so extremely busy that he had been rather reluctant to take up their invitation. (Even though he claimed they resorted to tempting him with a blank cheque!) But when he eventually did make the trip over, he could not have been more delighted with the warmth of the reception he received. Near the Opera House the IRA had pasted up a huge poster saying: 'Lousy English Go Home' (or words to that effect) but across it someone had stuck another sign proclaiming, 'Dublin Welcomes Heddle Nash'! Heddle was so proud and amused that he had a photo taken of it (disappointingly now gone astray). He was also presented with a silver cigarette box to commemorate the occasion, inscribed: 'To Heddle Nash – a real trooper [sic] as a token of thanks from Dublin Operatic Society'.

He treasured it.[17]

But at this point, just when things were going so well for Heddle, when his career was flourishing, when he was thoroughly enjoying being at the pinnacle of his hard-won success and his position as Britain's most well-loved leading tenor looked unassailable, war broke out again and temporarily scuppered him.

On 3 September 1939, when Britain went to war with Germany for the second time in just over twenty years, it would come as an enormous blow to Heddle and all the others of his generation who had been led to believe they were fighting the 'War to end wars' in 1914–18. They had already sacrificed a huge chunk of their late teens and early twenties. Now, after all their huge efforts to make up ground and finally arrive, belatedly, at the height of their powers in their mid-forties, they were about to have their lives blown apart all over again. And all those carefully submerged memories from twenty years ago were about to be dredged up and all the old mental scars and sores picked open.

In the opening days of the war Heddle immediately switched from gala performances to entertaining at army camps and hospitals throughout the British Isles. But as early as November 1939 it was already a very different Heddle from the witty, ebullient one, chatting and singing on the late night train after performances of *The Dubarry*, that Stuart Hibberd described in his diary, when they travelled up to London together:

He was full of woes, lamenting lost work and opportunities because of the war, in particular a cancelled tour of New Zealand. I had not realised how much artists had been hit in this way. It must make life very difficult for them.[18]

Only two months after the declaration of war, Heddle was living in fear that all his good times, so abruptly snatched away, might conceivably never return. His career – and with it his means of livelihood – was already in jeopardy. Paid work, even for a tenor of his calibre, had for the time being virtually dried up.

12

Down Under and Back Over:
1940–1941

The plight of musicians at the present time is so serious that it is most desirable that the whole amount of the collection should be handed to the [Artists' Benevolent] Fund.[1]

One of those lost contracts that Heddle would have been bemoaning to Stuart Hibberd was his regular little earner at the Three Choirs Festival. In 1939 it had been due to take place in Hereford, and Heddle and his family had already travelled up there in readiness. Heddle heard the announcement of the outbreak of war on his father-in-law's costly new gadget – his car radio – on 3 September. It changed everything. He had been booked to sing Elgar's *The Kingdom* on 5 September and on the 7th to take part in the premiere of Sir George Dyson's *Quo Vadis* with one of the usual teams – Isobel Baillie, Astra Desmond and Roy Henderson. But the whole programme was immediately cancelled. The Nashes found themselves returning home without Heddle having sung a single note, and Dyson himself would have to wait until the Festival resumed in 1946 to hear his composition finally aired.

Patriotic sentiment, as in 1914, had led to the immediate closure of theatres and concert halls, but hard on its heels came the risk factor – concern about the demoralisingly high casualty figures that would result from a direct hit on a crowded entertainment venue. Bombing was known to be inevitable and in September 1939, the nation was all keyed up for it.

Yet during the opening months those bombing raids failed to materialise; nor were there any major land or sea hostilities; things went so eerily quiet that they took to calling it 'the phoney war'. With a dismissive shrug at the empty skies, entertainment establishments set about exploring ways of re-opening for business – theatres and concert halls being pretty quick to work out a way of getting round the Health and Safety regulations by simply closing down the gallery and circle areas and restricting audiences to the stalls. Blackout restrictions were side-stepped by putting on performances early in the afternoons; an awkward time travel-wise for performers, but audiences were able to travel home during daylight hours.

Artists fortunate enough to be offered work in those opening months soon discovered, however, that their earnings were being undercut. When Heddle was invited to sing at a concert in the Winter Programme of the Friends of Worcester Cathedral in February 1940, it was typically announced that: 'The artists are giving their services at fees which do little more than cover expenses.' Which rather poses the question of what the artists only 'covering expenses', were expected to live on? Heddle was finding his fees were so regularly being under-cut that earning a living as a singer during the war was soon not only looking precarious, he was harbouring serious worries that it might eventually prove impossible.

One venue that certainly wouldn't be ringing with the sound of Heddle's top Cs for the duration of the war was the Royal Opera House Covent Garden. During the First World War the building had been requisitioned as a furniture repository; this time round the sound of grand opera was about to be replaced by shrieking saxophones: it had been transformed into a Mecca Dance Hall for the entertainment of on-leave troops, complete with a make-shift dance floor thriftily knocked together on a base of Morrison Shelter frames. This handily-placed venue was destined to become especially popular with American GIs who would introduce into its august portals both the jitterbug craze and the dropped-gum menace. Sadler's Wells was commandeered for a less flashy role – as a refuge for bombed-out families.

Life had turned both frustrating and demoralising for a man who lived to sing and who was still at the height of his powers. Heddle knew he had an invaluable gift to contribute to the war effort; his singing could raise morale in a unique and unforgettable way, but for the time being, his gift was being virtually ignored.* The fact that colleagues were suffering in the same way

---

*Though there is a tale, said to have emanated from Violet, that early in the war HN was spirited away to a secret venue – a country house in deepest Gloucestershire – where he was set to work recording a number of English folk songs to be 'banked' in case Britain got overrun by the Nazis. He was asked to record each one several times, putting emphasis on different words: a code which could be broadcast to agents on the Continent. Unfortunately extensive research has failed to unearth any corroborative

can't have afforded him much solace.

Then, in the spring of 1940, came some unexpectedly cheering news. Those Centenary Celebrations, hastily cancelled by the New Zealand Government at the outbreak of war, were to go ahead after all, albeit in a modified form. Heddle's official invitation to take part – the cause of much excitement when initially issued a year earlier, in the spring of 1939, was now being renewed: provided he was prepared to take the risk of travelling. Obviously there were risks involved, as he was soon to discover. But at that point the Allies appeared to have control of the war at sea, so the risks must have seemed small, compared with his need to be singing, which was large, insatiable and necessary for his livelihood. Heddle gratefully opted to go.

Isobel Baillie and the contralto Gladys Ripley, both good friends, as well as close colleagues, also had their invitations renewed, and Heddle must have been delighted when they too decided to take the risk. Violet, always reluctant to be left out on an exciting adventure, decided to travel with them, though how Heddle managed to scrape together the necessary to fund her travel expenses at such a precarious time remains unknown. Isobel and Gladys would doubtless have kept a womanly eye on Heddle during the tour, but maybe Violet wasn't taking any chances?*John and David were to be left at their boarding schools, Violet explaining the decision thus: 'the boys are better looked after at their schools than I could do for them, so everyone tells me,'[3] and she must have reasoned that there were plenty of relations around to keep an eye on things. Isobel and Gladys were both leaving a child behind in England, but in the care of their husbands. It appears somewhat out of character for Heddle to separate himself from his sons in time of war, but opting to go must have seemed like the right decision to make at a difficult time. For him this tour of New Zealand was not only a big career opportunity; it was also an honour to be representing his country, and that meant a great deal to him.

So on a cold day in March 1940, Heddle and his three lady companions set sail from Liverpool to cross the Atlantic on a ship crowded with refugees

---

evidence – but HN being famous for his clear diction, it seems a possibility. In the possession of the Nash family are four of these delightful recordings: "Phyllis hath such charming graces", "My lovely Celia", "Linden Lea" and "Have you seen but a whyte lily grow".'

*Violet need not have worried, apparently – the soprano Megan Thomas is reported by Eric Rees as having told him that she considered Heddle to be not only the 'best' tenor she had ever sung with but also the nicest. 'He never showed off and never tried to out-do the rest of us. He was lovely to work with and always the gentleman. Never any hanky-panky with him – not like some of the others.'

Dressed to impress on the New Zealand tour. Left to right: Violet, Heddle, Isobel Baillie, Gladys Ripley.

from Europe. The sea was rough – no such thing as a calm, luxury cruise was on the cards for Heddle. And memories of his nightmare journey on board the troopship *Ivernia* back in 1916 must soon have come flooding back, because once again it transpired that German U-boats were lurking.

On the journey in 1916 the *Ivernia* had zig-zagged her way out of trouble. But in 1940, despite being better equipped, somewhere out in the vast, grey waters of the mid-Atlantic, their ship took a hit from a torpedo. Strangely, Heddle is not known to have made any comment about this potentially disastrous incident – maybe he preferred to keep it secret from the boys? Again it is left to Isobel Baillie to recount how the ship managed to escape being sunk by putting on a sufficient spurt of speed to get out of range. But the seriousness of the incident was underlined by the fact that two of their seamen had been killed. Isobel reckoned that the whole thing was kept as low-key as possible for propaganda purposes and admitted that even thirty years later she knew very little about what actually happened, though, with a cautious display of understatement, she recalled that when they reached Halifax, Nova Scotia, the sight of a submarine came as a 'most unpleasant reminder'.[4]

This narrow escape was not quite the end of the story, however, because it turned out that for a second time Heddle had found himself aboard an ill-fated ship. Her name was the *Lancastria*, and anybody with any knowledge of disasters at sea will know that her sinking, only three months later, would involve the worst single loss of life in British maritime history, estimated at around 4000 and surpassing that of the *Titanic* and the *Lusitania* combined. After returning from this Atlantic crossing with the British singers on board, the *Lancastria* was refitted as a troop carrier, made a voyage to Norway to pick up refugees, and was then despatched to the Bay of Biscay off St Nazaire to evacuate troops and refugees still stranded in western France, two weeks after Dunkirk. There, severely overcrowded with 6000 on board (her usual complement being around 2000) she was bombed by German planes and sank within twenty horrific minutes, the surrounding sea ablaze with leaked fuel oil; enemy planes were said to have been machine-gunning rescue vessels and survivors in the water, while many troops who couldn't swim were reported as clinging to the sides and courageously singing 'Rule Britannia' and 'Roll Out the Barrel' as she went down. Churchill at first slapped a D-notice on the press, afraid that the huge loss of life would damage morale, but the facts soon leaked out and must have sent a few chill shivers through Heddle and his lady travelling companions.[5]

Meanwhile, having disembarked at New York, the party made the four day train journey across America, fitting in a quick visit to the Hollywood Bowl before boarding the Matson Line luxury cruiser *Mariposa*, bound for New Zealand. Scheduled to stop at Fiji and Hawaii, the voyage promised to be much calmer and more enjoyable all round. And who should also turn out to be on board but three other famous figures from the musical world – the violinist Yehudi Menuhin and his accomplished pianist sisters Hepzibah and Yaltah, *en route* for Australia.

This thrown-together-by-chance group of gifted musicians did just what fellow passengers might have hoped for – they got together and put on an impromptu concert, making heavenly music right there, in the middle of the exotic Pacific Ocean. Hepzibah accompanied Heddle on the piano but, tantalisingly, all the other little details, such as which pieces he or any of the others performed, have been lost in time. Heddle did comment afterwards on the fact that Yehudi refused to expose his precious Stradivarius to the ravages of the salt air, and insisted on playing on a borrowed instrument – not that that would have detracted too much from the magic. It sounds like just the sort of informal musical happening that Heddle would have thoroughly relished.[6]

The music festival was part of New Zealand's celebration of a hundred years of organised British settlement. A Centennial orchestra, made up of around thirty players, had been specially formed for the occasion, under the baton of the British-born Andersen Tyrer. Joining the English guest singers would be Raymond Beatty, a popular and robust Australian bass-baritone and, from time to time, Oscar Natzke, a young, English-trained New Zealand bass with a huge and glorious voice and a face and physique to complement it (he had started out earning a living as a blacksmith).[7] Natzke and Heddle already knew each other, having performed together in the 1938 *Faust* at Covent Garden when Natzke, then aged only twenty-six, had made his debut. The pair seemed to get on well at that point. But the normally kind and tolerant Isobel Baillie found it difficult to stomach what she saw as Natzke's egocentricity, to such an extent that she made a point of highlighting how, in her opinion, he did not always commit fully to those New Zealand performances, preferring, she suspected, to save himself for Covent Garden and the New York Met.[8]

Wherever they toured, the singers were joined by local choirs and music societies, all specially rehearsed and augmented to take part in what was planned, and turned out to be, a grand and memorable occasion. But it would be quite a punishing schedule with little time off. Here is just a taste, taken from the itinerary of Isobel Baillie:[9]

1 July	Fly to Nelson. Concert at Nelson
2 July	Travel 203 miles by road
3 July	Greymouth
4 July	Stay Christchurch
5 July	Timaru
6 July	Oamaru
7 July	Stay Dunedin
8 July	Leave Dunedin 8.33 am. Arrive Invercargill etc. etc.

One potential hitch: only shortly before leaving England, Isobel had discovered that she was not only contracted to join her fellow singers in such choral works as Elgar's *King Olaf* and *Gerontius* and Mendelssohn's *Elijah*, she was also signed up to perform in *Faust* – and opera absolutely was not her cup of tea. In deep concern she had tried to beg a few tips from Dora Labbette, but it would be Heddle, her 'handsome Faust' who would gallantly come to the rescue. He was so experienced in the part, she found him 'a tower of strength,' so ceaselessly encouraging, boosting her confidence by paying little compliments, that in the end her excursion into opera would even prove to be 'a happy and rewarding experience...'. In fact, after the sixteen scheduled performances of *Faust*, Isobel was declaring that she could have 'repeated the entire exercise all over again'.[10]

> Mr Heddle Nash's sense of style and fullness of tone were conspicuous in his handling of Faust. He infused the part with great passion, especially in 'All hail thou dwelling' and imparted an air of freshness and gaiety to 'Be mine the delight'. He handled his part in the great love duet with

appropriate tenderness, and was powerfully dramatic in the Prison Scene. Not only the beauty of his voice and what he did with it, but his understanding of the part fully confirmed the high repute in which Mr Nash is held on the stage in grand opera, as well as on the platform in arias and ballads.[11]

On 7 June, when they were performing *Faust* at His Majesty's Theatre in Auckland, Sir Thomas Beecham turned up, passing through on his way to Australia with Dora Labbette. When Andersen Tyrer, an old acquaintance, invited him to take over the baton, it seems he was unable to resist. But after announcing that he hadn't conducted the opera for a while, he amused the audience by telling them he had chosen to confine himself to the Garden Scene because, he claimed, it was 'the easiest'. Nevertheless the *Auckland Star* was proud to report that the performance Beecham produced was 'electrifying'.

New Zealand audiences everywhere packed in for a one-off chance to hear these top-notch performers and, of course, the performers themselves fed off such 'heartwarming appreciation'. They were treated to a marvellous VIP reception and revelled in the luxury of being expertly chaperoned by government officials, whose job it was to ensure that all their touring arrangements went 'like clockwork' – in sharp contrast to their own do-it-yourself travel arrangements back home. Heddle experienced flying for the first time, between locations, and reported that he 'loved it'. In return for all the cosseting, the singers made little official speeches everywhere they went and, needless to say, they sang unstintingly.

Wellington Town Hall 27 April 1940:

The singers from overseas, without exception, scored an immediate and deserved triumph. Mr Heddle Nash was the first to appear. A lyric tenor of pleasing strength and quality and consummate artistry, he sang the recitative and aria, 'Waft her Angels' from Handel's *Jeptha*, a beautiful number, which has not been heard in Wellington for many years. Handel's music is a good test for any singer, not only for vocal quality, but also breathing and phrasing in the long runs. These Mr Nash invested with a new beauty. His second number was the familiar aria 'Sound an alarm' from Handel's *Judas Maccabaeus*, which he sang with clarion effect. There was voluptuousness in the tenor's reading of the serenade from *Don Pasquale* (Donizetti), sung as an encore, and it is a long time since Wellington audiences have heard 'Come into the garden, Maud'

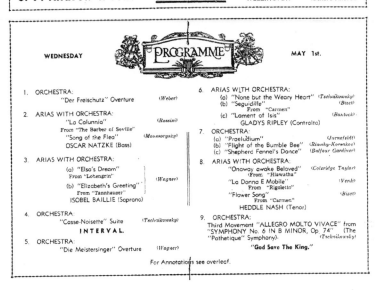

WEDNESDAY ☙ PROGRAMME ❧ **MAY 1st.**

1. ORCHESTRA:
   "Der Freischutz" Overture   *(Weber)*

2. ARIAS WITH ORCHESTRA:
   "La Calunnia"   *(Rossini)*
   From "The Barber of Seville"
   "Song of the Flea"   *(Moussorgsky)*
   OSCAR NATZKE (Bass)

3. ARIAS WITH ORCHESTRA:
   (a) "Elsa's Dream"
   From "Lohengrin"
   (b) "Elizabeth's Greeting"   *(Wagner)*
   From "Tannhäuser"
   ISOBEL BAILLIE (Soprano)

4. ORCHESTRA:
   "Casse-Noisette" Suite   *(Tschaikowsky)*

   INTERVAL.

5. ORCHESTRA:
   "Die Meistersinger" Overture   *(Wagner)*

6. ARIAS WITH ORCHESTRA:
   (a) "None but the Weary Heart"   *(Tschaikowsky)*
   (b) "Seguidille"   *(Bizet)*
   From "Carmen"
   (c) "Lament of Isis"   *(Bantock)*
   GLADYS RIPLEY (Contralto)

7. ORCHESTRA:
   (a) "Praeludium"   *(Jarnefeldt)*
   (b) "Flight of the Bumble Bee"   *(Rimsky-Korsakov)*
   (c) "Shepherd Fennel's Dance"   *(Balfour Gardiner)*

8. ARIAS WITH ORCHESTRA:
   "Onaway awake Beloved"   *(Coleridge Taylor)*
   From "Hiawatha"
   "La Donna E Mobile"   *(Verdi)*
   From "Rigoletto"
   "Flower Song"   *(Bizet)*
   From "Carmen"
   HEDDLE NASH (Tenor)

9. ORCHESTRA:
   Third Movement "ALLEGRO MOLTO VIVACE" from "SYMPHONY No. 6 IN B MINOR, Op. 74" (The "Pathetique" Symphony).   *(Tschaikowsky)*

   "God Save The King."

For Annotations see overleaf.

sung with such romantic conviction.

The admiration was mutual: 'things and places we have seen impressed us very much...' Heddle reported to his brother-in-law Bob Jones and sister-in-law Gladys on 28 May.

Christchurch [which reminded him of Cambridge] is the capital of Canterbury Province – where the lamb comes from – which you get up the road. This is a flat plain rich in farm and grazing lands with a great range of snow-covered mountains 50 miles away, running the length of South Island. The air is soft and rather dreamy...

In that letter home he goes so far as to enthuse that 'New Zealand is the most attractive country I have ever visited.' He would always retain a soft spot for New Zealand and its people.

An indication of just how individually popular Heddle had become with the New Zealand audiences comes across in the actions of the government finance minister, whose name happened to be Walter Nash. Finding himself having to make a speech on the sticky business of increasing income tax, he addressed the New Zealand Parliament with the opening words, 'On a day like this, I wish my name was *Heddle* Nash!'[12]

But halfway through this successful and hectic tour, Heddle received an unexpected blow from England in the form of a cable announcing the death of his father at a nursing home in Falmouth, Cornwall, where he was being treated for a heart condition combined with dropsy (oedema). William had actually written to them,[13] c/o the National Broadcasting Service in New Zealand, just two days before he died so his final letter would have reached them only after the news of his death. Writing in reply to a letter and photograph from Violet, and sounding lonely, he congratulates them both on looking 'so young and handsome' and 'in the pink', hopes they 'will be able to get other engagements out there, as the latest war news seems to cut down the kind of work useful to Billie'. He worries about whether John and David will be safe from bombing, and with great irony reassures them, 'We are all keeping our peckers up, feeling sure that in the end we shall win!'

He makes no mention of Heddle's mother Harriette, from whom he was estranged by that time – hardly surprising, since for many years he had been noted for pursuing other women, latterly on cruise ships, his overtures generally prefaced by the giving of the rather Edwardian-sounding gift of a pair of gloves. But it was not until his actual funeral service (which Heddle, of course, was unable to attend) that the family suffered the additional shock of discovering the existence of a long-term mistress and illegitimate daughter whom he had been maintaining for years in a separate establishment.[14] Yet despite the difficult relationship which had existed between them, Heddle was nevertheless deeply affected by his father's death:

> I realised that I could do so little 14,000 miles away, but went to Christchurch Cathedral and they arranged evensong at 5.15 as a memorial Service with the Archbishop. There I sang in the choir, also solos from Passion music in *Messiah* and Berg's *Faithful unto Death*. It was the best tribute I could pay.[15]

Such was the visiting singers' success and popularity in New Zealand that when the six-month tour officially came to an end in July, they found themselves being urged to extend their stay for a short while longer, with tempting offers of a few extra engagements.

But the war news from home had turned dire on a scale they had not envisaged. The 'phoney war' had ended with a vengeance in their absence – the Germans had roared through Denmark and Norway and isolated Sweden. By mid-June, France herself had surrendered, Italy had entered the war on Germany's side and Britain had been left standing alone. From 10

July she had been threatened with invasion and fighting the Battle of Britain. Both Isobel Baillie and Gladys Ripley, each with a husband and a daughter left behind in England, were achingly anxious to get back, despite the risks. German U-boats had secured Atlantic bases following the fall of France and, reinforced by Italian submarines, they were now hunting in the Atlantic in packs, with ever increasing success. Mesdames Baillie and Ripley would feel it was only by some miracle that 'nothing untoward happened' on their journey home.

Matters, however, were different for Heddle and Violet. For them, the shores of Australia beckoned.

Just how, or when, it came about, is unclear, but certainly as early as 15 May, the Australian press[16] had been reporting that three 'noted' singers, namely Peter Dawson,[17] Heddle Nash and Oscar Natzke had been signed up by the Australian Broadcasting Association for a series of studio broadcasts, and that Nash and Natzke, who would be giving joint performances, would be arriving in Australia just as soon as their New Zealand tour came to a close at the end of July.

Contrary to some thinking, Heddle's voice was already well known and much appreciated in Australia, due to his recordings for Columbia. ABC had, in fact, 'endeavoured to secure'[18] him as far back as 1936 – a time when he had been far too busy career-building in England. But the fact that Heddle had set out from England with only the music he required for the New Zealand tour – a matter that would cause him problems later – points to the fact that he had not initially planned to cross over to Australia and that his decision must have been made 'on the hoof'. In addition to the broadcasts, Heddle mentions being booked to perform in four concerts with Beecham in Australia (his old friend the Australian baritone Harold Williams had also been booked) but yet again it remains unclear at which point that arrangement was entered into.

The broadcasting tour was arranged as follows:

4 August to 25 August	Sydney
27 August to 7 September	Adelaide
9 September to 23 September	Perth
25 September to 6 October	Sydney
7 October to 26 October	Melbourne[19]

Somewhat surprisingly, on first arriving in Australia, Heddle and Violet bunked-up in a small flat in Manley Beach, Sydney, with Oscar Natzke. It's not easy to picture the meticulous tenor and his wife attempting to cohabit in cramped surroundings with the larger-than-life and temperamental young bass, even if they were all hard up and it was a wartime expediency. Though Nash and Natzke would go ahead and make the scheduled series of broadcasts together for ABC throughout August, September and October, accompanied by the pianist Henri Penn, it wasn't long before they were no longer hitting it off.

Natzke was apparently indulging in what Heddle and Violet considered to be a 'wild and dissolute' lifestyle – he was only twenty-nine and unmarried at the time – and that soon caused friction. They thought that he was 'squandering his talents' and tried to caution him to take more care.[20] Later that year Natzke (later changed to Natzka) would marry a New Zealand soprano and go off with her to the USA. Eventually he would join the Entertainments section of the Canadian Navy and after the war, following more performances in England, sing with the New York Opera Company. Natzke is generally considered to have been one of the most brilliantly gifted singers of the twentieth century, but as Heddle had predicted, his career was unfortunately to be a short one. He collapsed on stage in New York in 1951, while performing in *Die Meistersinger*, suffering from a cerebral haemorrhage. Two weeks later he died, aged only thirty-nine. Perhaps this time Heddle's second sight had foreseen a tragic end?

By 13 September, exactly in the middle of the schedule, Heddle is writing home from Perth that he has been doing so much travelling and singing he has had no time to put pen to paper for a month. And he adds a reminder that he has undertaken this Australian tour – travelling vast distances between locations – straight on top of his hectic months in New Zealand, with no rest in between. 'But I must keep going...' he reminds himself. He knew he had no option by then – he was well and truly stranded in the southern hemisphere.

A return home was impossible on two counts: not only due to U-boat domination of the Atlantic, but also to a decision that he and Violet had made, not long after signing the contract with ABC. For although the radio bookings promised him work in Australia only until 26 October, it appears that Heddle had taken a huge gamble: he had sent for the boys to come out and join them, in the optimistic hope that he would be able to pick up extra bookings and earn sufficient to extend his stay indefinitely.

Facing the threat of invasion, the British Government had been persuading parents to send their children to safety overseas in Canada, Australia, New Zealand, South Africa or the USA and this might well have fuelled Heddle and Violet's decision to arrange for John and David, then aged fourteen and ten, to be evacuated over to join them in Australia. Early in July, while Heddle and Violet were still on tour in New Zealand and movement by sea was still possible, the boys had already set sail, on a voyage across the world that would take them a whole three months.

'...the boys will soon arrive,' Heddle continues on 13 September, sounding an anxious note about whether, work-wise, his gamble will pay off. He is only too well aware that 'there must be a follow-through' once the ABC broadcasts have come to an end. Although he can see 'signs of more work to come' and has the consolation of knowing that he will always be welcome back in New Zealand, he nevertheless confesses, 'It's like planning a new life all over again...'[21]

The Australian gamble seems to have been an example of Heddle listening to his head (and perhaps the advice of others) rather than his heart, but in the world of 1940, no decision was straightforward. Having already sacrificed so much for his country in World War I, it would be understandable if he had been telling himself, 'I've done enough!' and feeling determined to seize the opportunity to distance himself – and his sons – from the horrors of World War II. Yet for an enduringly patriotic man, whose his heart would always belong on a concert platform in the British Isles, sitting out the war in Australia was never destined to work out successfully, even had there proved to be work opportunities galore.

Along with his broadcasting slot for ABC in Perth in September, Heddle had been booked to take part in a Beecham performance of *The Messiah* at the Capitol Theatre with Dora Labette, so the trio undertook the 1680-mile, two-day, journey over to Western Australia together on the Trans-Australian Railway. Controversy, however, rumbled in their wake, stirred up by a rather touchy press, who had taken offence at certain forthright comments Beecham had been making on topics ranging from Australia's attitude towards the war to the bad manners of her audiences – with a perceived insult to Prime Minister Robert Menzies thrown in. The controversy thundered on in Perth, so Heddle found himself in the thick of it, but his loyalties are said to have always lain firmly with Beecham, of whom he thought very highly indeed – 'grand chap' was how he would refer to him. According to Heddle, Beecham relieved the boredom of the train journey across the vast Nullarbor Plain by playing a grand piano they were transporting on board!

From newspaper reports we gather that *The Messiah* performance was, nevertheless, a huge success, and that the 'enraptured' Perth audience called upon the principals to take repeated encores. It was a fittingly sparkling end to Beecham's final conducting assignment on his 1940 tour of Australia, before he went on to tour Canada and the USA. A highly gratifying moment for Heddle too.

From a sheet of notes hastily jotted down in his room at the Hotel Esplanade, we learn that Heddle treated his radio audience in Perth to a few nostalgically Scottish airs – 'Mary Morison', 'The Road to the Isles', 'Turn ye to Me', and 'Johnny Drum'. He found Perth the most pleasant of the Australian cities and waxed lyrical in a letter home to the Jones (knowing that with their Pearce Signs connections this would interest them) about the 'beautiful panorama of coloured signs and lights' to be seen from the High Commissioner's house, built on a hill overlooking the Swan River – in such stark contrast to the blackout back home. 'It is the same everywhere,' he adds, 'and at last we have grown accustomed to lights at night, though at first it seemed all wrong.'[22]

He indulges in no details about the *Messiah* performance, nor his singing successes in general, but writes about what he feels might interest the Jones, going on to describe the flora and fauna of Australia and showing an almost poetic appreciation, despite his obvious weariness:

> The trees and palms are varied and gorgeous. One type of tree – coral tree, having flame coloured flowers like small bunches of bananas and hardly any leaves – just a blaze of flame. The strangest is the bottle tree – like a huge pear with a tuft of leaves at the top... There was an African tree with arms like Pop-Eye's arms and leaves like bunches of bananas. The gum trees are often beautiful, being white and smooth in the trunks and very tall. And we went to the quaintest zoo for an hour yesterday... the gardens like a jungle of canes and palms. It was late... and all the animals woke up and did their stuff...'

But then guilt – about maybe sounding too up-beat – seeps in, combined with an underlying anxiety and uncertainty: 'All this must seem like another world to you. I am glad you have the dugout... I hope Grandma and Mrs Jones can negotiate the dugout iron ladder...' And he then reveals that he is feeling tired and has discovered that he has a tendency towards diabetes.

Their first two months in Australia must have proved an extremely anxious time all round for Heddle and Violet because the welfare of the boys at sea could never have been far from their minds. In September, while John and David were still on their voyage, a ship named the *City of Benares*, carrying among its passengers around a hundred evacuee British children to 'safety' in Canada, was torpedoed and sunk in the Atlantic, with the loss of all the children, apart from six. As a result of that appalling tragedy, the government had cut short its official resettlement scheme.

Heddle's boys were travelling – a scary-seeming arrangement today – completely unaccompanied, though in such confused and panicky times, when imminent invasion and unimaginable atrocities loomed large, it was by no means such an unusual arrangement. David remembers how he and his brother were put on the boat train by Grandpa Pearce, and that their grandpa, spotting a likely-looking young woman also bound for Australia, gave her some money to keep an eye on them. The young woman took the money, but maybe Grandpa Pearce's notorious eye for a pretty face had put his judgement at fault – once they set sail, the boys never saw her again![23]

When John and David eventually turned up on Australian shores safe and sound and the family were reunited, on 10 October, their arrival attracted newspaper coverage in Australia, along with Heddle's comment, made in a fit of euphoria, or diplomacy, that the family hoped to settle down there.

Heddle made his debut on the Melbourne concert platform at around the same time, taking part in a Saturday celebrity orchestral concert with the Melbourne Symphony Orchestra and the Finnish conductor Georg Schnéevoigt, followed by another in the Brighton Town Hall only a few days later, again with the Melbourne Symphony Orchestra.[24]

By this time Heddle had decided to look for accommodation for his family in Melbourne, and in doing so he was able to call on the help of a singing colleague. At Glyndebourne he had sung, and become friends with, the renowned Australian baritone John Brownlee, whose career had by then taken him to the Met. in New York. He and Heddle had kept in touch, and Brownlee was able to give him an introduction to his 'plump and jolly' sister Jessie, who lived in Melbourne, where she managed a residential park named Ardoch. She was able to fix them up with a bungalow to rent in St Kilda Road, and there the family would live for just over a year.[25]

In Melbourne Heddle managed to drum up some additional work teaching singing at the Conservatoire and he also picked up a few bits of private coaching. After a time, to add to the radio broadcasts (which he was now making alone, in the prime evening slot of around nine o'clock) more concert engagements were coming his way. Reviews prove that he need not have feared about finding a good reception on the Australian concert and oratorio platforms. Melbourne was very soon alert to the fact that the War had temporarily washed ashore a highly valuable commodity. Coming from reviewers who were discovering Heddle Nash in the flesh for the first time, the following reviews make interesting reading:

Mystical conviction and emotion far transcending former experiences in Melbourne's performances of *The Dream of Gerontius* made its singing at the Town Hall on Saturday night one of the momentous events in Philharmonic history.

At last, in Heddle Nash, a tenor was permeated with the spiritual agonies and ecstasies of the transfiguration of Gerontius...[26]

The Dream of Gerontius
Heddle Nash's extraordinarily impressive interpretation of the name part gave great distinction to the performance in this beautiful oratorio on Saturday night. Never in Melbourne has there been a Gerontius with the intuitive understanding and extreme sensitiveness of this English tenor.[27]

Those spiritual tinges and agonies of both mind and soul by means of which Heddle Nash so identified himself with Elgar's *Dream of Gerontius* were also discoverable yesterday when he sang in the Vaughan Williams song cycle *On Wenlock Edge* at the chamber concert in the Union Theatre...[28]

But just when it was really beginning to look as though things were not going too badly for Heddle in Australia, other, unexpected problems suddenly kicked in to plague him. Of all things – tax problems!

David explains: 'Being a property owner in England he had to pay not only English tax but Australian federal and state taxes as well, with the result he discovered that when he sang professionally, there was no profit left.'

He decided to seek professional help on such a thorny matter. And unexpectedly, in the course of doing so, he ended up making a very valuable and lifelong friendship. It was in the Melbourne Tax Office that Heddle first encountered Frank Menzies, the Crown Solicitor, and elder brother of the then prime minister of Australia, Robert Menzies (who, after losing office in 1941, would eventually go on to become Australia's longest-serving prime minister). Here, according to Frank's son, David Menzies, is how the friendship came about:

My father Frank was in his Crown Solicitor's office in the city... Dad was a very keen amateur tenor, singing solos, and in church choirs and so forth – singing was a relaxing hobby for him. A singing friend phoned to say that he had Heddle with him in the Taxation Office. Now, on the night before, my parents had heard Heddle sing in *The Dream of Gerontius* and it was a memorable concert and Dad was overwhelmed with Heddle's superb interpretation.

So they met and immediately became friends. He and Vi came to our home on quite a number of occasions... I well remember when Heddle was leaning against the piano singing away and my mother suggested that, since it was getting late, my twin brother and I (aged 11) should go to bed. But Vi said, 'It is a night they will always remember', and so we stayed up.

And since he is still able to recall it so vividly a whole sixty-seven years later, Vi was obviously right!

Heddle and Frank had a lot more in common than singing and taxes; Frank Menzies was a veteran of the First World War, and he too had fought in Egypt and on the Western Front. Furthermore he and his wife Ruby's twin sons David and Graham, were close in age to David Nash. Soon friendship had broken out between the families. Heddle also gave Frank a number of singing lessons which, 'helped to free up' his voice and proved 'a very valuable experience for him.'

It was a friendship that would prove useful to Heddle and would continue after the Nashes eventually returned to England. A close friendship between the Nash and Menzies families continues down to the present day.

On top of tax, another problem soon reared its head: when Heddle had left England back in March he had taken with him only the repertoire designed specifically for the New Zealand tour. Once that was exhausted, he found himself unable to buy the pieces he needed, and was obliged to start borrowing new material from libraries and copying out the manuscripts by hand, an exercise that often required 'transposition to the correct key or even translation to English', for which he employed the skills of an Australian poet. The copying task was laborious, but though Heddle complained of 'tired eyes', he soon made the strange discovery that he was actually enjoying it, the skill and creative input proving both pleasing and restful. Before long he had started turning his hand-written manuscripts into little works of art, much to the joy and admiration of his accompanists who found them a delightful change from the rather scruffy pages they were accustomed to. Hand-copying manuscripts would become a favourite pursuit of Heddle's, and it seems he was already copying them as gifts. David Menzies recalls how, on a lunch visit to the Menzies, Heddle unceremoniously cleared a space on the table and started copying out some vocal music for his father. In later years, when Heddle was sufficiently impressed by any of his students, he would painstakingly copy pieces he had personally tailored to suit their particular voices, as a reward for their efforts.

But although Melbourne was showing great appreciation for Heddle's voice, actual work wasn't proving so plentiful as he had hoped. There were, of course, no permanent symphony orchestras outside Sydney and Melbourne in those days, and no permanent opera company to offer him employment. On one occasion he went all the way over to Sydney (about 500 miles) just to perform *Messiah*. The possibility of being invited back to perform in Perth he acknowledged to be out of the question: 'Sydney to Perth is 2700. That's what makes them think when they want an artist out in Western Australia, as they pay our fares and this comes expensive.' He even appears to have been obliged to return to undertake at least one singing engagement in New Zealand, where they must have been so keen to have him back, they were willing to fund his travel: 'I may have to toddle to New Zealand again this summer,' he explains, 'as there is virtually nothing doing here then, and it is not so hot just now for music. The war seems to have put paid to many musical activities here, which even in normal times are not too strong.'[29]

While Heddle was thus struggling to pick up bits and pieces of work, the rest of the Nash family were finding plenty to enjoy during their year-long sojourn. The boys were spending time on St Kilda Beach, enjoying the sun, eating fried shark and chips and becoming strong, keen swimmers. John recalled how Peter Dawson was a great friend to the family and especially 'kind to us children'. He lived at a place called Tom Ugly's Point on the shores of Sydney Harbour and took them for exciting trips along the coast in his motorboat.[30] Physically, the boys were blooming in Australia:

'[John] is taller than I am,' Heddle, the proud father reported in July 1941, 'and Australia has roughened and toughened him. He will be a six-footer for sure and is over nine stone already. David is also busy bursting his buttons and will be even bigger than John I believe. When they give me a rough house I feel like the father who said, "The only time I have ever raised my hand to my son was in self defence."'

Nevertheless, David remembers the family spending the whole time in Australia feeling homesick, constantly fretting about what might be happening in England and pining to get back.

'The radio keeps us abreast of the news,' Heddle writes, 'and it is remarkable to think that we have heard Churchill the same time as yourselves... It was good to hear that Cyril is safe. I expect Brother Allan is having a hectic ARP time just now. We don't care to think too much as it always ends in worry and I am expected to be 100% all the time, but you can understand how concerned we all are for you...'

And needless to say, Heddle was chewing himself to bits with the constant fear that, if any opportunities for tenors had arisen back home in his absence, others might be moving in to seize his crown! What's more, following the fall of Singapore, Australia itself was starting to seem not such a safe haven, its coastal fringes lying vulnerable to attack by the Japanese, a fact that had not escaped Heddle:

Anyway the whole [war] business is so absurd when you look at it from a world point of view that I feel certain it will automatically stop itself before we are much older. Everywhere, people are fighting each other. We have been lucky out here so far, but who knows?[31]

Though Melbourne audiences appear to have been continuing their love affair with him – 'Heddle Nash, who never fails to impress with his rare vocal and interpretative powers, received the reward due to a favourite in a series of appreciative recalls...' and though they were still deeming him to be 'at all times delightful', the likelihood of his taking up permanent residence had always been remote: singing engagements were never likely to have proved plentiful enough on a day-to-day basis and the tug of home appears to have been too strong.

'Life is not easy for us in my line,' Heddle reports in his letter to the Jones in July 1941, just a year after his arrival in Australia. 'I travel very little now as there are no more Broadcast Tours running since the cut of one shilling in the radio licence lost the Commission £120,000 per year... I must say we all appreciate what great possibilities were to be obtained in England. No doubt we have learnt this by leaving the place... The Aussies are tough and manners accordingly. The English kind hearts of the North I believe are only to be equalled by Aussies living in the back blocks where hospitality is a by-word. It is conspicuous by its absence in the cities...' (Heddle would only have expressed such thoughts privately, when letting his hair down in a letter home.)

It comes as little surprise that as soon as travel across the Atlantic had been declared a bit less hazardous, Heddle's face turned resolutely homeward. Towards the end of 1941, when some tickets became available on board a ship named the SS *Stratheden* sailing for Glasgow, and he got wind of it, Heddle saw an opportunity not to be missed. He was so determined to be on that ship that he turned to Frank Menzies, and with his friend's invaluable help in pulling a few strings, he managed – to his utmost joy and relief – to secure a passage for both himself and his family.

Leaving behind a memento for the Menzies of a few of his 78 rpm recordings and promising to make a point of including work by Australian composers in his concerts in Britain whenever it was appropriate (his attitude to the Australians in general did not extend to some 'very dear friends)* Heddle quit Australia. And, at a time when many musicians were only too happy to be scraping up work abroad, he set sail back home to war-torn Europe, in his own words, 'slipping in secret through the Japanese fleet'. The return journey would take them by way of the Panama Canal and into the Caribbean, where yet again they came under threat from German U-boats, especially on the prowl to pick off ships not sailing in convoy, like the *Stratheden*. Passengers were apparently deputed to keep watch, on a rota system, for periscopes. On board were some who had already suffered a hazardous time fleeing from the Japanese invasion of Singapore yet, despite all the nerve-clenching, they retained as one of their enduring memories of the voyage home on the *Stratheden* the fact that 'the famous tenor Heddle Nash' had been on board.

Fellow passengers might have been surprised to learn about some of the

---

*He kept his word, frequently featuring pieces by Horace Keats, who accompanied him on many occasions over there, as well as by the Melbourne composer Vera Buck, an especial favourite of his being *The Donkey*, set to the poem of G K Chesterton.

mischievous tricks that the tenor had been getting up to, trying to lighten the mood for his boys. On one occasion, when a Panamanian Customs launch had come alongside behaving officiously, he had seized a catapult, loaded it with a walnut off the dining table, and fired it through the open porthole at one of the uniformed inspectors' bossy backsides. Bull's eye![32]

Even more surprisingly, 'the famous tenor' had not even been able to afford the tickets. He and his family were only on board and able to return to England due to the kindness of Frank Menzies. Not only had he cut through red tape in his official capacity as Crown Solicitor, he had been generous enough, as a friend, to loan them some money!

Following their homing instincts turned out to have been the right decision, for both Heddle and his family. But on arrival they must have been harbouring a few doubts: in the early spring of 1942, Petts Wood in Kent, because of its close proximity to both London and the wartime airport at Biggin Hill, was collecting so many mistargeted bombs, it was part of the area that earned the nickname 'Hellfire Corner'!

On the music front, however, times had changed. Much to his relief, Heddle found that the importance of music as a boost to the nation's morale was now being fully recognised, and the niche that he was so well suited to fill, was ready and waiting for him. His singing was back in demand again – here, there, just about everywhere in the British Isles where he was prepared to travel.

And if there was an audience waiting to hear him sing, Heddle Nash was, as always, only too eager to hop on a train.

13

Back on the Home Front: 1942–1945

Heddle had travelled up to Glasgow from London by troop train – his usual mode of transport during the War. As usual, it had been packed out – servicemen, kit-bags, equipment – and he had been forced to stand in the corridor for most of the way, but he had been more than willing – he shouldered such discomforts as part of his War Effort.

He had been booked for two performances of *The Messiah*, with a rehearsal in the morning followed by a performance in the afternoon. The rehearsal had come and gone and all had been fine. But come the afternoon fatigue was starting to take a stealthy hold. So long as he was singing, adrenalin kicked in to keep it at bay. But after 'Comfort ye...' there comes a notoriously long wait that has been the downfall of many a bored or tired tenor. Sitting prominently exposed above the audience, on the front row of the platform, Heddle awoke to the realisation that he had just committed a cardinal sin – he had momentarily dozed off. His head was drooping forward on to his chest, he was staring down at his knees and... bloody hell! – could he have let out a snore? Acting skills clicked in. Instead of giving himself away by instinctively jerking upright, he very slowly and very thoughtfully bent forward even further, and began to re-tie his shoelace. (When he recounted this tale, it's not clear whether he was illustrating how tired he had been, or how crafty – probably a bit of both.[1])

On his return to England from the Antipodes, it seemed that war-torn Britain couldn't get enough of Heddle Nash. Bookings were pouring in at a rate that must have satisfied even him. He found himself travelling even more than before the war, the distances between venues perhaps, at first, seeming a mere cock-stride compared to the vast distances he had been covering in New Zealand and Australia. Frequently across the top of the programme would be printed the stark words AIR RAID WARNING, but neither audiences nor performers appear to have been put off, nor even keen to dive for the exit if the sirens went. Generally they opted to sit it out whilst, in the words of Jessie Wood (the wife of Sir Henry) keeping 'one ear warily conscious of the "noises off"'.[2]

From Motherwell to Accrington, Llanelly to Ilford, Belfast to Huddersfield, and a host of places in between, Heddle set about assiduously devoting himself to the task of raising the nation's morale by valiantly juggling recital, oratorio and opera. The hours when he was not actually up on the stage or platform performing got swallowed up by travel, rehearsal and organisation. Planning his complex itineraries, sourcing and booking digs or hotels, fixing up rehearsals with a pianist (Heddle could never sight-sing with ease, so this was essential), hiring props, and purchasing the necessary bits and pieces of his trade, from music scores to greasepaint-remover to sewing kits for running repairs – all those arrangements Britain's leading tenor was undertaking for himself, as can be noted from his diary of 1944. His family appear to have scarcely seen him at home, apart from occasional pit-stops, when refreshing and replenishing the contents of his suitcase and catching up on sleep obviously took top priority. A social life appears to have been non-existent, apart from the camaraderie he encountered on the road.[3]

The concerts he performed, often for charities such as the Red Cross, were largely made up of miscellaneous favourites, with numbers such as 'Road to the Isles', 'La Danza', 'The Minstrel Boy' and 'Waft her, angels' figuring frequently in his hastily jotted lists. Wartime decreed that – as in the early days – he couldn't be too fussy about the actual venues, so one night he might be performing at the Royal Albert Hall and the next some draughty school hall in the provinces.

In addition to his appearances on the concert platform and in oratorio he had managed to pick up his old links with the Carl Rosa Company and was performing for them around once a week as a guest artist. Grenville Eves recalled 'a particularly fine Faust'[4] with the soprano Joan Hammond appearing alongside Heddle, as Marguerite – 'a grand soprano from Melbourne – fine singer' was how Heddle described her. The 1944 season saw him alternating between *La Bohème*, *Rigoletto*, *Faust* and *The Barber of Seville*. When his fan Eric Rees – an enthusiastic young man in his early twenties – popped backstage at the Lyric Theatre Hammersmith to see his idol performing in the

Carl Rosa production of *The Barber of Seville*, it was a travel-weary Heddle he found slumped at his dressing table, seeking reassurance. 'Am I doing all right?' he enquired anxiously. It transpired that he had only just travelled back down to London from Newcastle by train that very afternoon and was 'still trying to remember the bloody opera!' Rees quickly reassured him that he was 'just tremendous' and adds, in brackets, 'And he was!'

Heddle had also been invited back to the Proms, and he was on the platform for the first night of Sir Henry Wood's Forty-ninth Prom season in 1943 (which would also, unfortunately, be Sir Henry's last). War had inevitably brought changes to the Proms. The traditional opening on the first Saturday after Bank Holiday had been abandoned and the concerts brought forward by a whole two months to June, to gain daylight hours and lessen the ever-present threat of aerial bombardment. The venue had changed too. Heddle found himself no longer performing at the Queen's Hall but in the now familiar setting of the Royal Albert Hall. London's favourite pre-war concert venue had fallen victim to incendiary bombs one fatal moonlit night back in May 1941, when a raid by the Luftwaffe had left in excess of three thousand Londoners killed or injured and many other public buildings damaged, including the House of Commons, Westminster Abbey, the British Museum and the Tower of London.[5]

Radio listeners tuning in to the Proms on that evening of 19 June 1943, to join the 'packed like sardines'[6] live audience, would have heard Heddle's 'elegant and stylish' rendition of 'Love in her eyes sits playing' from Handel's *Acis and Galatea*, introduced in the reasuringly familiar 'received pronunciation' of Stuart Hibberd who happened to be doing the BBC commentary that evening – and was doubtless delighted to hear his old friend not only back in action, but still in excellent voice. (Judge for yourself – excerpts from this Prom, including Heddle's solo, a solo by the pianist Moura Lympany and part of Hibberd's commentary are now available on CD.)

Heddle also took part in the 1944 Proms, but although they too opened to packed audiences, on 10 June, they would be halted by the authorities before the month was out, due to the havoc suddenly being wreaked on the capital by a vile new weapon – the V1 flying bomb, which the retreating Germans were launching from sites in the Pas de Calais and the Cherbourg Peninsula.

Up to fifteen thousand terrified Londoners a day were piling on to trains that June in an attempt to evacuate to areas out of range of the dreaded V1s, nicknamed 'Doodlebugs'. Flying in low at a speed of around 350 mph, a Doodlebug announced its presence in the sky with a noise described as 'rasping, grating' or 'droning'. If the noise suddenly cut out immediately overhead, there were just fifteen seconds to dive for shelter before it crashed out of the sky. The weapons were causing civilian death and injury, and destruction to property on a scale greater than any ever before encountered. Even more scary and demoralising, would be their successors the V2s, flying so high and so fast they were impossible to intercept. Making no noise, they came crashing down out of the sky with no warning whatsoever.

And once again it was South East London and parts of Kent that were bearing the brunt. The nickname 'Hellfire Corner' had changed to 'Doodlebug Alley'!

Although robbed of their live audiences, the 1944 Proms concerts continued over the radio, so on 23 June listeners were still able to enjoy Heddle singing Beethoven's 'Adelaïde', and on the 28th singing 'Comfort ye' and 'Every Valley' from *The Messiah*. And no one would have realised that Heddle's performance of the latter had been a serious case of mind over matter. Yet only the previous evening, at around 6.30, on one of the rare occasions when he happened to be at home and doubtless desperate for a bit of peace, Heddle himself had experienced a close shave – and his house in Town Court Crescent narrowly escaped destruction – when a Doodlebug had exploded on the recreation ground opposite with such an almighty blast it had blown his front door in! Lady Wood later recalled the incident, though she incorrectly placed it in 1941.*

On 29 August Heddle would note in his diary that his house had been damaged yet again: 'Flying Bomb cracked front ceiling badly today', he jotted phlegmatically.†

In April of 1944, Heddle had written to his fan Frank Stokes: 'I have been overworked ever since my return from New Zealand and Australia'. At the start of '44 he had flown over to Ireland for recitals with the British Music Society of Northern Ireland in Belfast and the Royal Dublin Society in

---

*'I well remember Heddle Nash coming to rehearse once looking terribly shaken – his home had been bombed overnight – but he sang in his never-to-be-forgotten style with that voice of a quality of rare beauty – although, as he has since said, "I shook and trembled for a week"!'[7]
†Like many families, the Nashes took cover under an indoor Morrison table-shelter made of quarter-inch thick steel, squashed into the back room, rather incongruously alongside the grand piano. But not many indoor shelters could have looked quite so theatrical – it had been customised with a coating of black gloss paint on the outside, to blend it in with the piano, and with typical Heddle thoroughness, been given an 'aluminium silver' treatment on the inside, to deter rust and reflect the light! (DN)

Dublin. Now he was declaring himself to be 'determined to have some time off from Duty this year, as I cannot possibly stand the strain of last year when I hardly had a day to myself'.[8]

Yet apart from Christmas Day 1944 (he was singing in Bedford on Christmas Eve and leaving Petts Wood again at 4.25 p.m. on Boxing Day evening for a Messiah in Huddersfield) Heddle appears to have had only five proper rest days off together in the whole year, which included his fiftieth birthday, taken at Colwyn Bay in August![9]

Obviously he could have cut down, but with all those bookings flowing in, and all those audiences so eager to hear him sing, in the end he chose not to. Basking in appreciation and firmly feeling that he was performing his patriotic duty, in reality there must have been no stopping him.

Another of the wartime discomforts Heddle, like other artists, had to endure, was returning to the hotel starving after an evening performance, only to encounter the bleak and daunting prospect of a CLOSED sign outside the dining room. This seems to have troubled him almost as much as the threat of bombs because he still firmly held to the belief that a singer must keep himself well nourished or his voice would suffer – 'two dinners on one plate' was what his family used to nickname him. For that reason his favourite wartime bookings had become those offering hospitality in private homes on the outer fringes of the British Isles – Ireland, Wales, Scotland, or the farming communities of the north of England, where the supply of food always seemed to be more plentiful. Not only did they feed him better, he could sometimes wangle, as part of his fee, a ham! He would bear it home triumphantly in his suitcase (along with his evening dress?) – to the delight of his family. In traditional minstrel style, Heddle literally was 'singing for his supper'![10]

Throughout the war, in addition to his live concerts, recitals and opera, Heddle was also frequently fitting in radio broadcasts such as Bandstand (relayed to the troops) and ballad programmes, occasionally partnered by such other well-loved stars as Gwen Catley and Gladys Ripley. On the whole he had to 'conform to BBC requirements as to type of programmes' and regretted that only occasionally was he able to introduce new numbers in addition to the demanded perennial favourites. In the 1944 letter to Frank Stokes, he went so far as to urge Mr Stokes – and his friends – to write in to the BBC with their requests for more variety, feeling sure that the BBC 'often listen to suggestions'.

Yet although he was regretful about not being able to extend his repertoire much over these years, Heddle knew better than most how important music becomes in people's lives at times of great stress and emotional upheaval, so he never felt himself to be 'above' performing any song that suited the powerful sentiment of the times. When the great showman Charles B Cochran[11] invited him to take part in a big charity musical extravaganza entitled *Seventy Years of Song* at the Albert Hall in support of Toc H, it was just the sort of engagement he was likely to relish.[12]

Such was the colossal theatrical clout wielded by Cochran at that time that his name alone was enough to gather together a glittering list of British stars of the day – Geraldo and his orchestra; Vera Lynn; Hutch; Ivor Novello; Stanley Holloway; Tessie O'Shea; Evelyn Laye and so forth – he even roped in the poet laureate, Robert Bridges, to recite part of Blake's *Jerusalem*!

Gathering together so many top artists on a weekday, in London, in wartime, must have seemed nigh-on impossible and Sunday performances using stage costume and dancing were strictly forbidden for some reason. Yet on the night finally selected, Wednesday 16 June 1943, all the jigsaw pieces miraculously fitted together.[13]

Heddle displayed his versatility on the night by performing in three different musical eras – first the era of 'the ballad concert' when he performed an impersonation of Sims Reeves, the greatest English tenor of Victorian times (though largely forgotten these days). He emphasised the connection between himself and Reeves by singing the ballad for which both were famous – 'Come into the Garden, Maud'. For his second appearance, in the *opéra bouffe* section, he performed an homage to Gilbert and Sullivan with 'Take A Pair Of Sparkling Eyes' – described by Cochran as a 'delicious contrast', to the preceding item – the can-can. But in the up-to-date section after the interval he found himself with a couple of very hard acts indeed to follow: the sophisticated black singer/pianist Hutch thundering out 'Begin The Beguine', and the 'Forces Sweetheart' Vera Lynn, giving her inimitable rendition of 'Yours'. How did he follow them? According to Cochran, with a 'wonderful interpretation' of 'the most popular ballad of all time' – 'I'll Walk Beside You' – backed for good measure by the two hundred voice chorus and the magnificent Albert Hall organ. The words are a bit syrupy for today's taste, but they must have jerked a few tears from an audience in wartime, especially when sung with Heddle's perfect diction and ability to sing to the heart. The great Cochran hadn't failed to appreciate the rare and irresistible audience-appeal of an operatic tenor who also knew how to interpret a ballad. (If only Heddle could have found and recorded a ballad that held the popular appeal of the First World War's 'Roses of Picardy' or 'Tipparary'.)

The honour of singing the only operatic aria of the evening fell to Eva Turner – 'One Fine Day' from *Madam Butterfly*. 'Within the scope of our programme it had to be Puccini,' Cochran memorably declared in his no-nonsense showman's fashion. 'Wagner was beyond the range of the butcher's boy, and we do not sing it in the bath.' [!]

The show won rave reviews.

As the Toc H concert illustrates, the special communication between Heddle and his audience was perhaps never stronger than during the war. And if more proof were needed of his popularity, he even had his name affectionately sent-up in the most famous radio series of the 1940s – ITMA.

Standing for 'It's That Man Again' – a phrase newspapers used about Hitler whenever he had made some new territorial gain – though why that was thought funny, or an appropriate name for a comedy series, is bewildering today – the programme certainly tapped into the nation's psyche and provided an all-important common cause for laughing and bonding in time of war. The programme was so popular it could count on a regular audience of between sixteen and twenty million. And it was jokingly said that if Hitler was having a problem deciding on a suitable time to invade the British Isles, 8.30 p.m. on a Thursday evening would be his best bet – his forces could come ashore unobserved and unopposed, because everybody in the kingdom would be indoors, listening to ITMA (including the King himself – it was reputed to be his favourite programme). There was a tale circulating at the time [14] about a man who, finding that his train was running late, was thoroughly dischuffed that he was going to miss that evening's broadcast. But he needn't have worried – it happened to be a warm summer's evening and as he walked from the station, every house had its windows open and every household was listening to ITMA: he scarcely missed a single word!

The idea of having a programme full of pomposity-puncturing puns and word-play was the brainchild of the comedian Tommy Handley, who was allowed to get away with a lighthearted jibe at the Government with his 'Ministry of Aggravation' and contributed towards the invention of a cast of rather crazy comic characters and catch phrases that everybody picked up on. There was a charlady, Mrs Mopp, who always said, 'Can I do you now, sir?' and a Colonel Chinstrap who, when offered a drink, said, 'I don't mind if I do!'

Imagine Heddle's great glee, and the immense pride and cachet for his teenage sons, when ITMA invented an opera singer, and that opera singer was dubbed – Signor Nettle Rash! It was the equivalent of being invited to guest on 'Morecambe and Wise' in the 1970s or 'The Muppet Show' in the 1980s. [15]

Yet another indication of Heddle's popular appeal during the War came when he was at last invited to appear in a movie. An intriguing prospect, even though the invite came from a British film company not of the first rank, named Butcher's Film Enterprises and there was to be no acting involved, only Heddle singing as himself in a scene set at a Promenade Concert, accompanied by the London Symphony Orchestra – something he had done often in real life. He was given a couple of songs – the romantic title song 'For You Alone', by Geehl and O'Reilly first made famous by Caruso, which was the title song of the film, and Cadman's 'At Dawning', with its refrain 'I love you', which he had first sung all those years ago as his test recording for Columbia. Described as a 'love-versus-duty romantic melodrama', the film was modelled on a Butcher's film release of 1943, entitled *I'll Walk Beside You*, with which they had enjoyed a huge success. (Heddle's invitation to appear perhaps based on his rendition of that title at the Toc H concert?) The young couple in the film were to meet and fall in love while listening to Heddle singing – not such a far-fetched idea – and the cast looked promising enough – Jimmy Hanley, Dinah Sheridan and Lesley Brook. The director was Geoffrey Household, and Butcher's Film Enterprises had had other hits with, for instance, the 'Old Mother Riley' films. *For You Alone* certainly attracted good advance reviews from the trade press. *Kinematograph Weekly* (March 1945) forecast:

> with a romantic story, a first-class cast and the inclusion of Albert Sandler and his orchestra with Helen Hill, the London Symphony Orchestra, and the famous tenor Heddle Nash, *For You Alone* will be a musical and romantic triumph.

Some of the blurbs on the flyers, however, were amazingly inventive in their desire to establish Heddle's international status and war hero credentials, going so far as to claim that he had 'topped the bill in every big city in the United States and on the Continent' and that in WWI he had commenced soldiering in his 'early teens'!...

But despite his undoubtedly proving a big and glamorous draw for the film, the enterprise was not about to set Heddle on the path to Hollywood, nor anywhere else in the film industry, for that matter. He didn't much enjoy the experience, either, though he was paid a one-off £100, which was very good for a mere two day's work by wartime standards. He is said to have found the film-making process – having been pitched straight in with no preparation – all rather hassling and vexing and rushed.[16] And although the film did strike a chord with the nation and was twice re-released, in 1948 and 1949, it never quite achieved the 'triumph' status of the trade forecasts.

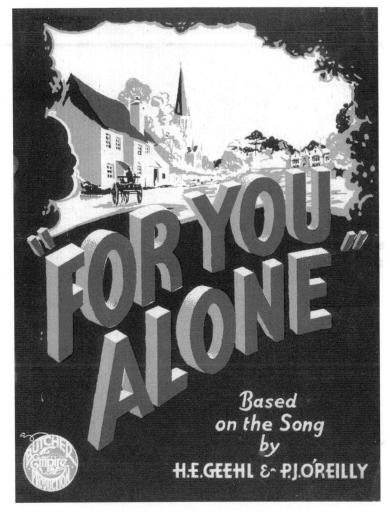

FOR YOU ALONE. A pleasing, sentimental little story about a clergyman's daughter falling in love with a naval officer and finally coming into his arms after surmounting usual obstacles.

So summarises the *Film Review* of 1945, sounding a trifle lukewarm. But it tantalisingly adds: 'With some good music.'

The film was released on 5 May 1945 but was overshadowed by powerful competition. Both *Waterloo Road* and *The Wicked Lady* from another British film studio, Gainsborough, were released in 1945, as were other classics from American studios, *I Know Where I'm Going*, *National Velvet*, *Brewster's*

Millions, The Seventh Veil, To Have And Have Not, Frenchman's Creek and – also released in that year – *Brief Encounter*. If only the characters played by Celia Johnson and Trevor Howard had enjoyed one of their illicit encounters at a Heddle Nash concert instead of in the cinema![17] The footage of Heddle singing in this film remains, unbelievably, the only known footage of him singing when still at the height of his powers.

Another of Heddle's legacies from the trenches of the First World War appears to have been flaring up during this busy period of his life and constantly threatening to strike him down. When his fan Eric Rees went back-stage to visit him after a concert up in Newcastle, Heddle was apparently complaining that he had just had 'the most terrible lumbago'. It had started between the shoulder blades and run 'all the way down my back and round the side... It was awful... I had my head stuck like this' and, according to Rees, Heddle turned his head so that his chin touched the top of his left shoulder blade (a physical impossibility, unless he'd turned into a budgerigar, but we get the picture). 'I was walking about like this for days'.

'And in that distorted position,' continued Rees, 'he went stomping and lurching around the room. It was difficult not to laugh, but I could see he was vividly reliving the agony.'[18]

But it would take more than chronic lumbago to put Heddle completely out of action.

Addressed to The Gramophone Co Ltd 19 March 1943:[19]

'HIS MASTER'S VOICE
GREATEST ARTISTS – FINEST RECORDING'
Minus the Voice of HEDDLE NASH –
Is not this statement somewhat rash?
Of all the voices rich and rare
None with his for BEAUTY can compare!
So please may this 'GREATEST ARTIST' be -
Immortalised (sic) by – HMV?

Reply from The Gramophone Co Ltd 20 March 1943 (note – by return post!)

Dear Madam,

Thank you for your letter of the 19th inst. We are wondering if you are aware of the recordings of the complete operas *Nozze di Figaro* and *Cosi dan Tutte* [*sic*] in which Mr Heddle Nash takes part. These records were made at Glyndebourne and you will find them in our catalogue under the heading of Society Records. Also, if you will refer to the catalogue of our associate, the Columbia Gramophone Company, you will see a long list of records by this celebrated artiste.

We should like to be in a position to undertake further recording with Mr Nash but we must tell you that in these days we are limited by Government order as to the number of records we can sell and, consequently, much of the repertoire we should like to record will have to wait until happier times.

May we take this opportunity of thanking you for your interest in writing.

Yours faithfully,

Heddle's recording contract had lapsed back in 1935. Nothing personal: plummeting sales figures, due to the pinchings and scrapings nationwide caused by the Depression and the emergence of radio, had put many other artists in the same position. Columbia itself had been forced to do a merger with its great rival The Gramophone Company (who owned the image and label HMV) to form Electric and Musical Industries (EMI). For Heddle and his fans this unfortunately meant that for a whole nine years – when his voice was at its finest – no recordings of it were made on to discs in a recording studio. The only recordings that exist of Heddle during that period are those made from BBC broadcasts (*Gerontius* in 1936; *Manon* in 1939 and the 1943 first night of The Proms). But despite the unhopeful-sounding response given by the Gramophone Company in the letter above, things were in fact about to change, and very soon.

In 1944 Heddle was signed up by HMV, largely at the insistence of Walter Legge (who had been so complimentary about him when writing for *The Manchester Guardian* back in 1935). Legge would eventually become the 'best-known record producer in the history of classical music' (and also marry the soprano Elisabeth Schwarzkopf). As well as running ENSA concerts throughout the UK during the war, Legge had also achieved the position of recording manager of EMI. In that capacity, he had become involved in certain negotiations with the British Council, a body that had been set up in the 1930s to combat Fascist cultural propaganda. The eventual outcome of those negotiations would be the sponsoring of a recording of *The Dream of Gerontius* by the British Council as a joint enterprise with HMV. Legge was well aware that if the project ever came off, Heddle Nash would be the likely choice for Gerontius and it is thought that he was probably making sure he signed him up in advance.

The signing was most fortuitous because it led, on 5 July 1944, to Heddle recording four of his most beautiful and successful arias with Dr Malcolm Sargent conducting the Liverpool Philharmonic Orchestra – 'Flower Song' from Bizet's *Carmen*, 'All Hail Thou Dwelling' from Gounod's *Faust*, 'Spirit so fair' from Donizetti's *La Favorite* and 'In memory I lie beneath the palms' from Bizet's *The Pearl Fishers*, the latter considered by many to be the most beautiful, atmospheric singing Heddle ever committed to disc, and described by Francis Toye, an eminent critic and biographer of the time, as the finest bel canto singing that he had ever heard from any singer of the twentieth century.

Yet the fact that Heddle's voice and interpretation were at their finest on these recordings is quite remarkable. A slight tremor should have been a distinct possibility, in view of the fact that they were cut only shortly after his first close-encounter with a Doodlebug. When he arrived at the recording studio in Liverpool, he claimed that he was still trembling from the after-shock, as described by Jessie Wood. And in the meantime it had been business as usual. Following on top of the Proms broadcast, he had popped down to perform a miscellaneous concert in Southampton and up to sing another in Rochdale and still found space to carry out repairs on his front door and fix it back on its hinges! (Apparently a local builder, inundated with work, jokingly offered to take Heddle on when he saw what a lovely job he'd done.) The day after the Liverpool recordings would see him hopping over to Cardiff to sing with the Carl Rosa in *Rigoletto* and from there he would be scooting over for concerts in Nottingham and then up to Altrincham and down to Swansea and over to Bristol...[20]

Members of Heddle's family had close brushes with two of the biggest Doodlebug tragedies of the war. On the morning of Friday 28 July 1944, son David, aged fourteen by then, was bicycling all the way home, alone, to Petts Wood from Hertfordshire, only to find that when he reached the Lewisham Clock Tower the way was barred and the air was thick with acrid smoke and particles of debris. Only a couple of hours earlier a V1 had devastated the entire market area, killing 59 people, badly injuring 300, and demolishing or damaging around a hundred commercial properties, including Marks & Spencer, Woolworth's and a Sainsbury's grocery shop. It was the worst single V1 incident in South London. Later in the year, on 28 November, Heddle's father-in-law's factory, Pearce Signs at New Cross, was involved in the worst V2 attack on Britain when one landed on the Woolworth's store at New Cross

Gate just opposite, killing 168 people and reducing it and the Co-op next door to a pile of rubble. The incident occurred around midday when Woolworth's was crowded with shoppers, many tragically queuing, it was said, in the hopes of getting one of a delivery of aluminum saucepans rumoured to have just arrived. Bodies were taken across to the Pearce Signs Factory which found itself being utilised as a temporary mortuary. (Heddle's father-in-law was immensely proud that his factory had been able to do its bit.)[21]

Heddle Nash might not have been facing death on the battlefield in this war, but he and his family certainly came in for more than their fair share of close encounters with enemy missiles.

In March of 1945, as the war drew to a close, HMV produced Heddle's beautiful recording of Richard Strauss's 'Serenade', once again accompanied by Gerald Moore at the piano, followed by a fresh and charming rendition of two delightful English songs by Jack Moeran: 'Diaphenia' and 'The Sweet of the Year' which Moeran had paid Heddle the honour of dedicating to him.

In the meantime, back at the British Council's Music Advisory Committee, while the V1s and V2s were causing mayhem, all sorts of behind-the-scenes wrangling had been dragging on. If a recording were to be produced by the Council, in conjunction with HMV, then public funds would be involved, and apparently nobody (Bliss, Boosey, Boult, Makower and later Walton, among others) could agree on which piece of music would make the best use of those funds in offering a riposte to the promotion of Beethoven, Wagner and Bruckner. It was suggested by some members of the Committee that *Gerontius* would be good propaganda in Roman Catholic countries, but its choice was by no means a forgone conclusion and things apparently got very heated indeed. So heated, in fact, that the chairman, Pamela Henn-Collins, is said to have taken off for South America, saying she wished Elgar had never composed *Gerontius*![22]

Carl Newton of the Elgar Society, in his contribution to *The Best Of Me – A Gerontius Centenary Companion*, describes the Committee's activities as 'a saga of intrigue and incompetence'; and either 'a nightmare' or 'in the nature of an Ealing comedy',[23] all depending on how you chose to look at it. But finally the Committee did resolve in favour of Elgar's *The Dream of Gerontius*. (Among the many other works considered but rejected were madrigals and lute music, Walton's *Belshazzar's Feast* and Parry's *Blest Pair of Sirens*.)

It is generally taken for granted that the artists who were invited to perform on this classic *Gerontius* recording had each been picked because, quite simply, they were the best available. Not so. Heddle himself was, in fact, the only artist who was a first choice. Even then he appears to have been ear-marked only because the BBC were keen to have him, rather than because of his considerable reputation in the part. Boult or Wood were the conductors originally mooted, with the BBC Symphony Orchestra and the Luton Choir. The now famous combination they finally signed up, Sargent, the Liverpool Philharmonic and the Huddersfield Choral Society, were not even in the running initially. Kathleen Ferrier had been first choice for the Angel, with Gladys Ripley as reserve. [24] But there's an intriguing tale of how Ferrier refused to sing the part after Walter Legge had 'taken liberties with her in a taxi'! Dennis Noble did not actually get to sign his contract to sing The Priest until just four days before they were due to record.

As for the Huddersfield Choral Society, they were in such a militant mood over so many issues (in particular the forced depletion of their ranks by weeding out the weaker singers) that Carl Newton suggests anger was as much likely to have infused their singing as the much-lauded 'community spirit'. And in all the behind-the-scenes shambles, nobody had remembered to remind Carice Elgar Blake (Elgar's daughter) that the recording was about to take place, so that when she finally arrived, she found the main hotel in Huddersfield was already crowded out by recording people, and was disgruntled about having to commute all the way from Halifax!

With all that frothing and seething going on in the background, it's interesting to see things through the eyes of a fifteen-year-old boy who happened to be loafing around the Huddersfield Town Hall while the recording itself was taking place, between 8 and 12 April.

It was David Nash's Easter holiday and he was quite used to spending his holidays whereever his father happened to be working. No one took much notice of him.

> I generally hung about and made friends with all the singers and the recording engineers, and Mrs Elgar Blake showed me how to follow a musical score. There was tension; a lot of professional and recording envy. They all seemed to me to be rather scornful of each other. The recording engineers, for instance, used to refer to Sir Malcolm Sargent as 'Goebbels'!

David took a close interest in the recording techniques:

> All the wax discs for the recording were kept in a little caravan parked just outside Huddersfield Town Hall and the wax had to be kept at a certain temperature. When you made a recording, the idea was, you made one

recording and then you played it back – which ruined it, but you could hear what came out and then you made the proper one – with fingers crossed that you were not interrupted by a low-flying plane, or a tram clanging past, or somebody getting something wrong, or coughing.

On one occasion, he recalls, a male participant had to be urgently shaken awake in case his loud post-prandial snoring ruined the recording. 'Usually it took two or three goes before everybody was satisfied.'

Heddle Nash and Gladys Ripley each received £125 for their solo contributions – not bad for five days work. Sargent got £240, Walker and Noble £30 each, the choir £300 and each orchestra member got £2/10/- (£2.50), which seems a bit mean.

But the recording was no runaway success. In the following ten years it is estimated to have sold only about 3000 copies and the British Council is said to have made a huge loss out of it – of around £2500 of public funds. Due to Legge's arrangements, HMV, on the other hand, somehow managed to end up with a £9000 profit![25] On those sales figures, it's obvious that the recording never did achieve the original aim by becoming a weapon of propaganda.

And yet, out of that highly unlikely background, with all its disparate, warring elements, there miraculously emerged a beautiful, cohesive and inspired recording – one now generally known as the Sargent/Nash recording, that has not only stood the test of time but has gone on to become a classic.

> Sargent's conducting, influenced by Elgar's, is direct, vital and urgently crafted with an inborn feeling of the work's ebb and flow and an overall picture that comprehends the piece's spiritual meaning while realising its dramatic leanness and force. Heddle Nash's Gerontius is unrivalled in its conviction and inwardness. He'd been singing the part since 1930 [sic] and by 1945 the work was in Nash's being; he sang it from memory and had mastered every facet. 'Take me away' is like a searing cry of pain from the depth of the singer's soul. Gladys Ripley is a natural and communicative Angel throughout, her flexible and appealing tone always a pleasure to hear. The Liverpool Philharmonic lives up to its reputation at the time as the country's leading orchestra (in particular the onerous string section) and the members of the Huddersfield Choral Society sing as if their lives depended on it.[26]

The extent to which Heddle was privy to all the pre-recording antics and animosities remains unknown, though obviously he can't have been totally ignorant. In the end that hardly matters though, because whatever was going on in the background, as soon as he started to sing, it would all have evaporated from his mind. Once he was singing, as critics down the years have pointed out, Heddle 'became Gerontius'.

Shortly after the Gerontius recording, Heddle, like four out of five members of the theatrical profession at some point during the war, joined ENSA (Entertainments National Service Association) and in 1945 he went to entertain troops in Belgium, France and Germany. Set up by an impresario named Basil Dean to provide entertainment for British armed forces personnel back in 1939, ENSA claimed to have been a life-line for many entertainers because it paid a good weekly wage – £10 a week for solo acts (no matter how famous) and £4 a week for members of the chorus.

Troops are said to have contemptuously nicknamed ENSA shows 'Every Night Something Awful'! The quality certainly varied and questions were asked later about whether public funds had been well spent. But sometimes audiences would be lucky enough to find themselves being entertained by top flight performers whom they might normally not have got a chance to see in civvy street. Gracie Fields, Laurence Olivier, John Gielgud, George Formby, Arthur Askey and Vera Lynn all took considerable risks by going overseas to war zones to perform. At Basil Dean's insistence, special uniforms were designed and issued for ENSA artists to wear as a precaution – there was a genuine fear that if they got captured in civilian clothes while performing in a war zone, they might be taken for spies and shot. Apparently the only artist who refused to wear the uniform was the comedian Tommy Trinder, who claimed that if he was stupid enough to get himself captured, he deserved to be shot!

Though ENSA artists had no rank, they were granted officer status, allowing them to use the mess facilities, so it turned out that Heddle had been granted an upgrade (one he was willing to accept) by the armed forces at last. And it's claimed that fellow artists who travelled with him were so delighted and impressed by the kind and diligent way he looked out for their interests and took charge of on-the-spot organisation and negotiations that they awarded him an honorary title of 'Captain'.[27]

Unfortunately the necessary course of injections and vaccinations all performers had to undergo before setting out to entertain abroad had a peculiarly adverse effect on Heddle. His vocal chords swelled up so much that by the time he arrived in Belgium he found himself 'no longer able to sing tenor – only bass'![28] But once he had recovered, he was in his element

entertaining the troops; the close contact with the audience, the informality, and the soldiers' famously thunderous appreciation being right up his street. Of course, he had performed in such circumstances before, in the First World War, when he was just a lowly private, so it comes as no surprise that he is affectionately remembered for never standing on ceremony. One time when he was inviting requests, a young soldier in the audience eagerly called out for him to sing 'that song about an elephant's ear!' He's said not even to have raised an eyebrow, but to have launched unhesitatingly into 'La donna è mobile', with its refrain 'e di pensiero'![29]

With Biddy in the garden at Petts Wood, wearing ENSA uniform 1945.

As usual, being Heddle, he soon found himself at the centre of momentous goings on. In Germany towards the end of May, he happened to be performing at Lüneburg, just after the German surrender there, when the city was suddenly abuzz with more sensational news. The notorious war criminal Heinrich Himmler, head of the dreaded Gestapo, who had sent millions to their death in concentration camps, and was billed as 'the most wanted man in the world' had been captured by the British and rumours were rife about how he had committed suicide in a house in the city, in order to avoid interrogation, by swallowing a cyanide capsule, and how his body had been hastily removed and anonymously buried by night at some lonely spot on Lüneburg Heath, to prevent the possible rise of a Himmler 'cult'.

Heddle used to claim to have met a sergeant whose thumb had been bitten by Himmler as he – the sergeant – tried to hook the suicide capsule from his mouth.[30] Recently, however, all sorts of claims have come forward – one that it wasn't Himmler himself who died, but somebody impersonating him, another that Himmler did not commit suicide at all, but was assassinated on the orders of Winston Churchill. If the latter were the case, maybe Heddle's sergeant's thumb (and he claimed he had been shown the injury) had got bitten while attempting to ram the poison down Himmler's throat?! All the new evidence and controversy arising over the last few years would doubtless have been of great interest to Heddle.

Back in England on 14 August 1945 Heddle recorded the opening recitative and aria from Handel's *Messiah*, with the Philharmonic Chamber Orchestra conducted by Maurice Miles, and that too would become one of his most sought-after, most loved and most inspiring recordings. But even then his fans were still not entirely satisfied, and one of them at least, had a bone to pick with HMV:

9th March 1946[31]

Gentlemen,

HEDDLE NASH

Though somewhat belated, I must thank you so much for the long awaited joy of your recording of The King of Tenors – HEDDLE NASH.

Might I presume upon your time by sending you just a few extracts from criticisms, then I am sure you will appreciate what a great loss to posterity it will be if our great National Asset is not immortalised for all time through your Records. It seems to us, who admire that voice so intensely, so very tragic that it is not given the publicity afforded to foreign lesser lights – not even a picture poster is displayed by your agents! Unfortunately, the majority of people need to have the good things in music pointed out to them, and I venture to think that by no other means could this object be so convincingly achieved than by a little publicity by HMV and many, many more Records by HEDDLE NASH.

Yours very gratefully,

Unfortunately the fan who sent this letter received no prompt written reply. The final paragraph has been bracketed with the words Paper restriction control. And underneath is handwritten the comment:

No action as post is not possible owing to paper restrictions.

A convenient excuse for not engaging with the fact that maybe the letter writer was making a very strong point?

14

Not so Merrie England – Reprise: 1946–1950

The war was over and Heddle had turned fifty-one, though he let it be thought that he was a couple of years or so younger – the chasm between forty-something and fifty-something being even more scary for a performer than for a normal human being. He had been working and travelling incessantly for the past three years, drawing on reserves of stamina in a way that might have drained a far younger and fitter man. Now what he was most in need of was a period of stability and recuperation. Fortunately it came – with the offer of a part in another West End operetta.

Fourteen years earlier, playing René in *The Dubarry* had given him the opportunity for financial retrenchment: now, in 1946, the part of Sir Walter Raleigh in Sir Edward German's *Merrie England* would offer a period in which he could recharge his batteries. He would be able to make the short commute from home and back each day, sleep in his own bed at night, and not have to wake up juggling scores in his head. Furthermore it would free him from the rigmarole of having to organise bookings, not to mention applying the soothing balm of having a regular pay cheque coming in. Giving eight performances a week to a West End audience is, of course, no rest cure by most singers' standards, with a matinée performance on Wednesdays and Saturdays beginning at 2.30 p.m., followed by the evening performance at 6.30 p.m., which allowed him scarcely enough time to grab a sandwich and repair his make-up before plunging back on stage. But to Heddle the sense of order and repetitiveness must have seemed just what he needed.

Merrie England had, of course, helped to get him back on his feet following the First World War, and the coincidence of undertaking the part again, after surviving a second one, can't have been lost on him.

The war had left Britain down-at-heel, drab, heavily in debt and exhausted. There was hardly anything worth buying in the shops. So what better way to spread a little cheer to an English audience, and give them a reason to part with some austerity pounds shillings and pence than with a celebration of Englishness that harked back to a more colourful, swashbuckling time when, under Good Queen Bess, England had once before 'ruled the waves' and fought off invasion? Edward German's *Merrie England* was packed with audience-appeal: rousing patriotic numbers and charming traditional folk airs, interspersed with splashes of Gilbertian/Victorian-style patter songs for a few touches of traditional humour. What's more it was a great favourite with amateur operatic societies up and down the country. And familiarity and nostalgia, at a time when people are feeling a bit punch-drunk and unsure about the way ahead, becomes very desirable.

After touring to rapturous receptions – the *Glasgow Herald* declaring it to be one of the finest operetta productions seen in Glasgow for years, and having a cast that could 'hardly be improved upon' – the show finally opened for its London run at the handsome Princes Theatre, Shaftesbury Avenue, early in 1946 (re-named the Shaftesbury Theatre in 1963). Maybe it's not by chance that the same venue, in the aftermath of the First World War in 1919, had staged a hugely successful season of Gilbert and Sullivan operas when, it was estimated, around £30,000 pounds had poured into the box office in advance bookings alone. Fingers crossed then?

The show starred Heddle Nash as bold Sir Walter Raleigh, Linda Gray (obviously not she of *Dallas* fame) as Queen Elizabeth I, Anna Jeans as Bessie Throckmorton, and Heddle's old associate Dennis Noble as the Earl of Essex.[1] The libretto had originally been written by Basil Hood, who had collaborated with Sir Arthur Sullivan on a couple of now largely-forgotten operettas, *The Emerald Isle* and *The Rose of Persia*, but for this production a new version, generally regarded as an improvement, had been devised by Edward Knoblock. Amongst all the yeomen and bowmen, the May-pole dancing and May-queenery, the show had some hauntingly memorable tunes and Heddle had arguably the best – a particularly beautiful, show-stopping song, 'The Perfect English Rose'. He sang it with such fervour, he hardly ever got away without doing an encore:

> When Mr Heddle Nash sang 'The English Rose' in the presence of good,
> bad-tempered Queen Bess, and soared at the end to an exquisite mezzo voce

As Sir Walter Raleigh, 1946.

A flat... let me say that seldom in the realm of beauty has there been such a perfect blend of music, words and voice. I doubt if there is a tenor living who could equal Heddle Nash's exquisite rendition of this loveliest of songs.[2]

(He actually did love that song himself for the pleasure it gave.[3]) But unfortunately, though Heddle recorded it in October 1945, it was never released and nobody seems to be quite certain why.

The show became such a hit that everybody who could get hold of a ticket flocked to see it. And so once again, by deciding to appear in *Merrie England*, it seems that Heddle was touching a chord with the nation.

Appearing on stage wearing a doublet and tights, as Heddle was required to do as Sir Walter Raleigh, is quite a daring venture for a man of any age, so, being slightly past his prime, he wore tights that had been discreetly padded out to enhance his legs. One evening, however, some prankster backstage thought it would be rather amusing if the padded tights 'went missing'. Heddle considered this highly unprofessional, and was definitely not amused. Knowing how much being 'in character' mattered to him, he couldn't possibly 'be' Raleigh without stalwart thighs and heroic calves. So he sat in his dressing room, folded his arms and resolutely refused to go on unless his tights were 'found'. They were, of course.[4]

Because he was singing the part of Sir Walter Raleigh (the man who first introduced tobacco to the British Isles) Heddle found he was also required to smoke a pipe on stage. Fine by him, of course; he had been a keen smoker of cigarettes, followed by a pipe, ever since World War I. Though he was becoming increasingly aware that smoking wasn't doing his throat any good – having reported in a letter from New Zealand dated 28 May 1940 'I have not smoked since reaching Wellington in the middle of April and my voice is fresher for it', and declared firmly in his diary on 13 March 1944, 'No Smoking from Today' – now he made the interesting discovery that cut-up cigars burned better than flaked tobacco in his Sir Walter Raleigh pipe. The discovery unfortunately led to him becoming a devoted cigar smoker.[5]

Heddle was no stranger to cigars, his father had smoked them. And when the family had returned to England from Australia, after William Snr's death, Heddle had found that his father had left behind a temptingly choice stock. To preserve them, they had been stored in tea leaves, so while Violet and the boys swooped eagerly on such a goodly windfall of unrationed tea, Heddle availed himself of the smokes. Heddle, it seems, had the best of the bargain – the tobacco-flavoured tea proved to be completely undrinkable, even by wartime standards.[6]

Appearing in *Merrie England* at the Princes Theatre gave Heddle the rare opportunity to take an interest in home-based matters, such as gardening. 'Digging for victory', or growing your own fruit and vegetables, had been urged on the nation to meet shortages of food imports during the war and in its aftermath, when there was still rationing and a shortage of most food-stuffs, making your garden productive remained popular. David remembers his father enthusiastically exchanging gardening tips with the neighbours, and insisting on keeping his gardening tools in tip-top condition, believing that, like woodworking tools, they should never be used by others, 'who would only ruin them'. He also thought that the exercise of digging trenches for vegetables would keep him fit. A vivid picture comes across of Heddle around that time wielding his spade furiously, attacking the Kentish soil with the utmost dedication, even to the point of exhaustion, whilst at the same time puffing away furiously on a fat cigar! Unfortunately, by the time the vegetables were ripe and ready to pick, Heddle was off on his travels again and never got the benefit of actually eating them.

As soon as he as he was old enough, David took over the care of the garden, though giving the front privet hedge a precision trim remained Heddle's self-appointed chore. Son John had definitely no inclinations towards being a man of the soil, as we learn from a dry comment of Heddle's in a letter to David: 'History was made today in Vycot garden, when John helped me to dig a trench. We forgot to photograph him on the job...'

A gala performance of *Merrie England*, in aid of the Queen Elizabeth Training College for the Disabled, in the presence of the Queen, Princess Elizabeth and Princess Margaret (Mary Pickford also in the audience) should have been the highlight of the run for him. But with typical Heddle misfortune, it was not to be. He was mortified when he was forced to retire part way through, suffering from laryngitis. And the retirement occurred before he had reached what would have been the perfect *pièce de résistance* – singing 'The Perfect English Rose' in the presence of the then immensely popular young Princess Margaret Rose. It fell to Heddle's understudy John Lewis to step in and reap what should have been 'his' moment.[7]

When the run of *Merrie England* was over, Heddle went back on the road again, frequently appearing on oratorio platforms with the greatest lyric contralto Britain has ever produced, Kathleen Ferrier, most often in *Gerontius* and *Messiah*. They would perform together until her untimely death from cancer in 1953, after a career spanning barely a dozen years. Unfortunately, only one recording was ever made of this well-loved pair performing together: Beethoven's Choral Symphony, recorded live at the Royal Albert

Hall in 1947, with the London Symphony Orchestra conducted by Bruno Walter. Heddle unfortunately left no personal reminiscences of her, but Ferrier recalled 'a riot' of a performance with Heddle in South Wales – what a pity she didn't elaborate.

They used to say that Christmas in Britain wouldn't be Christmas in these post-war years without Heddle Nash performing in the *Messiah* on the wireless or on a concert platform somewhere or other. Sir Geraint Evans recalled[9] how there would be fierce competition in Wales to obtain one of the big names for the occasion and how the name Heddle Nash was guaranteed to pack out a hall or a chapel. One Christmas, however, Violet was determined she was going to have her husband at home for a change. She was so determined that she rang Ibbs & Tillett and told them that under no circumstances whatsoever were they to take any bookings for him over the entire Christmas period, because he wouldn't be available. So Heddle found himself having to spend that particular Christmas at home with his family, trying hard to enter into the festive spirit, but according to David, looking 'noticeably dejected'.

On one occasion when he was singing in *The Messiah*, rationing restrictions and an urgent need for socks drove him to make productive use of the tenor's long wait after 'Comfort ye...' On his way to the concert venue, he had spotted a shop that was selling socks 'off ration', but he had not had time to stop. With a word to the conductor beforehand, to establish how urgent and important was his mission, Heddle discreetly exited the platform, ran to the shop, acquired his socks, slipped back on to his seat, tipped the conductor a wink to say 'mission accomplished' and carried on...[10]

His fan Eric Rees recalled hearing Heddle sing in a performance of *Gerontius* at the Albert Hall around this time and went backstage to visit him in the interval:

'As usual Heddle was wonderful,' he enthused. 'His assumption of that role was, I maintain, one of the supreme vocal achievements of the century.' But Heddle apparently commented that he wasn't finding it easy to sing that evening and Rees (vividly dredging up the conversation from his memory some fifty years later) recalls him saying,

> I've been running up and down the country for the last few weeks singing nothing but *Elijah* and *Messiah*. And that doesn't do my voice any good – they're too low for me, it pulls my voice down. I oughtn't to be singing that sort of stuff really; I ought to be singing Rossini and Donizetti, that sort of thing; that's what would suit my voice... but a man has to live, he has to support his wife and family. If you're a singer in this country, it's the

Messiahs and Elijahs that pay the bills. I'm not complaining. I do pretty well out of it; but when you come back to a thing like this you have to concentrate jolly hard to adjust and keep your voice up.

The words might not be exact, but the sentiment certainly sounds right. Rees adds that when Heddle returned to the platform he wove his usual spell as though he hadn't a care in the world. 'It was always obvious that once he started singing he became totally immersed and was oblivious to everything else.'[11]

Throughout 1946 and 1947 Heddle continued to record with HMV. He re-recorded '*Una furtiva lagrima*' from Donizetti's *L'elisir d'amore* – commenting on which, Alan Blyth, referring to the fact that he was sometimes dubbed, 'the English Tito Schipa', adds – 'here's why'. He followed that with '*L'amour, l'amour*' from Gounod's *Roméo et Juliette*, then 'How vain is man' and 'Sound the alarm' from Handel's *Judas Maccabaeus*.

On 30 January 1947 Heddle made a return to Covent Garden, after a break of more than eight long years. The Royal Opera House had finally been handed back from Mecca in October 1945 (gum free?) after long and laborious negotiations to get the enterprise up and running again.

It was not a very auspicious time to return, however, because Britain, while already struggling with shortages on all fronts, as well as bombed-out buildings and general depression, had been cruelly plunged into one of the harshest winters ever recorded. Severe frost and snow descended and held the country in an icy grip and did not let go until half way through March; the Thames froze over at Westminster Bridge; grave fuel shortages led to frequent power cuts which meant that in the rehearsal rooms and offices at Covent Garden, the lights came on for only two hours a day.

And it must have been a special challenge for Heddle, because the role he had been engaged to sing was Des Grieux in Massenet's *Manon*, one he had been performing for twenty years, and for which he had always earned such high praise, in particular for his 'youthful' and 'ardent' rendition. Opposite him, and making her Covent Garden debut in the part of Manon, was a pretty young American soprano named Virginia McWatters, who had played the part of Adèle to great acclaim in a very successful wartime Broadway version of *Die Fledermaus*, re-titled for American audiences *Rosalinda*.

According to the revered music critic Richard Capell:

Mr Nash shared the honours, with his sweet and musical singing, faultlessly phrased. 'The Dream' of the second act was a treat for the ear, and we need never ask for more of '*Fuyez douce image.*'

But Norman Lebrecht in *Covent Garden, the Untold Story*, describes McWatters as 'pretty but slight' and fifty-one year old Heddle as 'venerable' and even 'woodenly Victorian'! A bit of an exaggeration considering that Heddle was famous for having dispelled the previously 'woodenly Edwardian' image. It's possible that the author got a bit carried away in his desire to paint a vivid picture of the harsh winter and the make-do-and-mend, rag-bag image pervading the Opera House, and London in general, in January 1947. What with the icy winds and the freezing rehearsal rooms, maybe Heddle was not so much 'wooden' in the part of Des Grieux, as frozen stiff with cold?

Joking apart, the truth is probably that while Heddle was not quite so 'gallant, every inch of him' any more (by then there were a few more inches to cater for, despite rationing) and while he could no longer risk 'throwing himself on the fervours of the music' with quite such 'magnificent abandon', he still gave his best and therefore put in a sterling performance – for any opera buffs, that is, who were actually prepared to venture out into the terrible winter of the blitzed-out city, stagger through all the frost and snow, and pay good money to go to see him.

The following year, 1948, proved to be a watershed for Heddle. It started well, with a couple of good recordings for HMV – excerpts from Gounod's *Faust* and Puccini's *Tosca*, partnered by Joan Hammond, with whom he had performed very successfully during the war when they were both singing with the Carl Rosa. Then, on 7 April, at a warmer, more blossoming time of year than before, he was invited back to Covent Garden again, to reprise another of his most lauded and favourite roles, David in *Die Meistersinger*. The date happened to coincide with his silver wedding anniversary and he made the fact known to the management, who kindly honoured him with the use of the Royal Room for a celebratory party afterwards. Maybe, however, it was a mistake to highlight twenty-five years of marriage in an institution in which the word 'venerable' could trip easily off the tongue. This performance would turn out to be both a celebration and a wake, because it would prove to be his very last at Covent Garden. The institution was getting back on its feet and was starting to feel strong enough to move forward, anxious now to throw off its pre-war image, and all those who – like Heddle – had been a part of it.

Just ten days after the celebratory event at Covent Garden, Heddle – the man who 'practically lived' on trains – was wearily returning home from a routine singing engagement up north, when disaster struck. In the early hours of 17

April, he suddenly found himself a victim of one of the worst train crashes of the twentieth century.

He was heading back to London on board an express train which had started out from Glasgow at 5.40 p.m. It's not certain where he had boarded the train, but it's believed he would have been expecting to arrive eventually at Euston in the early hours of the morning, wait around for the underground, cross London to Charing Cross Station or London Bridge, then pick up a train for Petts Wood: one heck of a tiring journey, but for him, just the usual.

Picture Heddle, wrapped in a Burberry travel coat to which he had only recently treated himself, half dozing in a compartment amongst a 'fairly full load of passengers'.[12] At the ungodly hour of about ten minutes after midnight, and in a sea of blackness outside that would have registered to him as being smack in the middle of nowhere (but in fact was close to a place named Winsford, just north of Crewe in Cheshire) the train suddenly braked hard, and ground to a halt. For around seventeen minutes it sat silently idling, the passengers in the compartment doubtless glancing at their watches with pursed-up lips and buttoned-up impatience, as inexplicably held-up passengers tend to do. It would later transpire that somebody on board had pulled the communication cord 'without due cause' and the fireman and the guard, carrying lamps, had both climbed down on to the track to try to locate the coach where the action had occurred, essential for restarting the engine. But they were having difficulty. It later emerged that the culprit was a young soldier from Winsford, going home on leave for the weekend. Anxious to save himself the extra hour or two by not being carried on to Crewe, then having to make his way back to Winsford again, he had pulled the cord, and when the train stopped, had leapt off and headed for home across the fields, thinking that he had been very clever (it was a trick not unknown among servicemen in those days). The reason the rail men were having difficulty locating the coach was because the culprit had done the deed in the lavatory compartment.

There then followed a series of complications and errors – delays in putting warning detonators on the track (the guard tripped over and his lamp went out), a postal train – the 6.25 p.m. from Glasgow, happening to be running late that evening, catastrophic mistakes and mixups concerning telephone conversations and the transmission of signals, and – most tragic of all – a signalman at Winsford Station being too distracted by heating his supper to be really certain about whether the passenger train had actually passed by or not.

The outcome of it all was that the postal train, estimated to have been travelling at around sixty miles per hour, received none of the warnings it should have received, and had no chance to brake to less than forty-five to fifty miles per hour before ploughing straight into the back of the stationary passenger train.

At around twenty-seven minutes past midnight, Heddle, bored and weary, but fortunately travelling, as was his custom, in one of the centre coaches, suddenly and without warning, experienced the tremendous force and noise of the collision. The centre coaches, which didn't have their brakes on, were propelled some seventy-five yards up the track. He found himself being flung forward against the compartment's pull-down wooden table, the impact of its corner coming into sharp contact with his abdomen. Yet he was lucky. The rear coach and half of the coach ahead of it were demolished and the first four vans of the postal train were severely telescoped. In all twenty-four passengers were to lose their lives. Fourteen more severely injured passengers would be detained in hospital.

The first doctor didn't arrive on the scene until just in excess of three quarters of an hour later (some delay being caused by the fact that when the

The scene of the Winsford train crash at dawn.

guard from the passenger train ran to the signal box at Winsford Junction to report the accident, the signal man there, unaware that anything was at all untoward, could not understand his 'confused account in Scottish dialect'!) In the meantime Heddle joined other passengers in clambering down on to the tracks and stumbling back down the line, in all the dangerous confusion of thick darkness, towards the mangled metal heap of wrecked coaches, to try to help the injured. A year or two later he intriguingly made a note referring to having been 'nearly killed twice in twenty minutes'[13] – whether that refers to some danger he encountered on his mercy mission in the precarious and nightmare conditions of the wrecked carriages remains unknown, but looking at the chilling daylight photos of the crash, and realising what he and the other helpers must have been up against, it seems like a strong possibility.

When a shattered Heddle finally made it home to Petts Wood the following day, his new light-coloured travel coat was a write-off – heavily stained with blood from the casualties.[14] Yet interestingly, he had managed to keep his presence on the train a secret from the press. In David Nash's opinion, his father would have felt that his involvement in the tragedy would have been 'bad for business' in those days, so he remained anonymous. Heddle must have quietly made certain that he was with the uninjured and walking wounded who were eventually carried on to Crewe an hour or two later, and from there he proceeded home with as little fuss, and as fast, as possible.

The young soldier who had pulled the communication cord, in remorse, 'played the man',[15] three days later, giving himself in to the police on his return to Newcastle. But his only punishment was eventually to be fined £5 for pulling it 'without reasonable cause', and being ordered to pay £6.5s costs, because it was decided that though 'to some extent' his irresponsible act was 'a primary contribution to the unfortunate sequence of events which followed',[16] it had not been the direct cause of the disaster. Responsibility for that was found to lie with the signalman at Winsford Station, busy heating his supper, who gave 'Train out of Section' to Winsford Junction for the passenger train, and accepted the postal train, although the passenger train had not actually passed his box. It has been rather sensationally claimed that the twenty-four people who died in this crash did so as the result of 'the activation of a safety device', but that was clearly not entirely the case.

As for Heddle, when he later went for a check-up with his GP, he was not only warned that delayed shock might set in, but made the alarming discovery that he had not escaped injury himself. In his own personal collision with the pull-down refreshments table, he had sustained an injury to his pancreas. Shortly afterwards, he discovered he was being plagued by great thirst, and was sent to nearby Farnborough Hospital for a diagnosis. There it was found that as a result of the injury his diabetes had become severe. So just at a time of life when he especially needed to be able to draw on his fullest resources health-wise, Heddle learned that he would have to start injecting himself with insulin on a daily basis. And he would have to continue doing so for the rest of his life.

'Sometimes,' he told his son, when at a low ebb, 'it seems as though the gods just don't want me to sing.'[17]

Stuff and nonsense! Within days he was back on his feet, back on trains and back at work. 21 April found him up in Glasgow with the Carl Rosa, performing the role of Alfred to Ruth Packer's Violetta in La Traviata and earning praise for his 'easy stage presence', and his 'dramatic and clear singing' with 'every word distinct'![18]

In November and December of that year, again with Gerald Moore at the piano, Heddle went on to record some of his loveliest and most popular songs: first, Handel's 'Silent Worship' and then 'Linden Lea', a Dorsetshire poem by William Barnes, set to music by Ralph Vaughan Williams. They were two of his own favourites, and he often performed them in public. For many, they are simply the most exquisite versions of these delightful songs ever recorded. His love for 'Linden Lea' especially would be shared in the 1950s and 1960s by thousands of school children who learned to sing it on the BBC radio schools programme 'Singing Together', introduced by William Appleby. In the same recording session Heddle, who was always keen to promote Liszt's songs, also put to disc Liszt's *Liebestraum* and '*O quand je dors*'. His voice might be thought to have lost a little of its bloom by this stage in his career, but, as Alan Blyth points out, 'we are consoled by the maturity of his art and skill'.[19]

It was following a performance of *Gerontius* later that year in Nottingham that Heddle, having just put on a mesmerising performance, was approached by a member of the audience. 'My friend and I were both taken by his father,' he recalled '...we were both bowled over by the experience and were walking on air. We went out past the artistes' dressing rooms and there was Heddle Nash, leaning against the door jamb. My friend's father said, "A marvellous performance, Mr Nash. Thank you very much indeed". "Thank you. All in a night's work, you know," was the reply. I can't remember the effect on us at the time but I have never forgotten the great man's words or his performance.'[20]

Thankfully, the gods had still not succeeded in putting a stop to Heddle's singing, yet.

15

The Vinyl Years

As Heddle fought hard to conceal his health problems, the feeling began to take hold in certain quarters that his voice was past its prime. True, it had lost some of its bloom, but it was still, one might argue, the most delightful tenor voice in the country and his desire to connect with an audience remained unabated. But the year was 1950 and Britain was standing on the threshold of a new era. The mood among the movers and shakers was for change: it was high time, they felt, that the nation put war and austerity behind her and turned her battered and impoverished face towards the shiny new future that they sincerely hoped awaited in the second half of the twentieth century. So although it was only six years since Heddle had recorded such delights as 'In memory I lie beneath the palms' and five years since his definitive recording of *The Dream of Gerontius*, he was to learn that he now carried about him too strong an association with World Wars and Depression for his image to be one that suited the mood of the moment. Yet again, after all his valiant efforts, Heddle Nash was about to fall victim to the times in which he lived.

A Festival of Britain was mooted, with a nod to the Great Exhibition a century earlier, but designed to be more of 'a people's exhibition', one which would give the nation 'a tonic'. Its aim was to celebrate British achievement in history, industry, science and the arts and the plan was for it to take place in the cheery summer months of May to September 1951, on the South Bank alongside the River Thames. A blitzed and derelict area of land was designated for transformation into a 'dream of the future' with exciting, though temporary examples of architecture, realised in such iconic structures as The

Dome of Discovery and the Skylon. All the musical items for the Festival were to be staged in a newly built-for-the occasion Royal Festival Hall, which was to be the only permanent piece of architecture on the site and built at the huge cost (for the time) of one million pounds.

One of the items chosen to be performed at the Festival Hall as part of this celebration of Britishness was *The Dream of Gerontius*. This should have been a fine moment for Heddle, a reward for his stalwart patriotism. But somewhere along the line, the organisers took the controversial decision not to offer the part of Gerontius to Heddle Nash. Instead they offered it to Webster Booth – a fine enough singer, but not one who had been chosen by Elgar, or one who had made the part so thoroughly his own in the way that Heddle had. At that time he was perhaps best known for broadcasting as half of a husband-and-wife singing team of Anne Ziegler and Webster Booth (Britain's answer to Hollywood's Jeanette Macdonald and Nelson Eddy). Heddle instead received an invitation to sing the less prestigious Elgar piece, *The Kingdom*. It hurt.[1]

Meanwhile, behind the scenes at HMV the support of even his former champion Walter Legge appears to have been on the slide. Heddle's contract at HMV was renewable on a yearly basis and there seems to have been some question hanging over whether it should be renewed for the year 1949–50. Maybe Heddle picked up on HMV's less than enthusiastic mood because he did not jump to sign that year; in fact he delayed for several months. His belated decision to sign prompted an internal memo to Mr Albu, Artists Dept. dated 20 September 1950, which it is fortunate that Heddle never saw because here is an example of hard-nosed business in action: After ruthlessly commenting that he believed Heddle to be 'past the stage' at which they could 'afford to use an orchestra', Legge goes on the suggest that Heddle might record 'The Faery Song' from *The Immortal Hour*, the attraction of that particular item being that it would involve no more expense than the hire of a harpist![2]

For some unknown reason, Heddle never actually recorded 'The Faery Song' anyway. More's the pity, because that hauntingly beautiful song, with music by Rutland Boughton and words by Fiona Macleod * is said to have have suited his voice beautifully – and it would have sounded especially well with the delicate backing of a harp! But he was struck down by the tenor's plague – a heavy cold.[3] In fact he made no further recordings until March and April of 1952, after his contract had been renewed again for a final year. He was then

***

*'How beautiful they are, the lordly ones...' One pictures a fey Scots lady penning the words, but Fiona Macleod was in fact the nom de plume of a man named William Sharp.

accompanied in a series of English songs, not by a harp, but by Gerald Moore on the piano in inestimable form. The recordings included exquisite renditions of songs by Vaughan Williams, German, Elgar, Quilter, MV White, Cadman and Balfe, whilst 'The Road to the Isles', arranged by Kennedy-Fraser, was sung by Heddle with a Scottish accent, fading away into the distance, an effect he always achieved in his live performances by slowly wandering off stage and singing increasingly pianissimo over his shoulder. He then wound up the session with Cadman's 'At Dawning', which proved to be not only the song he had sung on his test recording for Columbia back in 1926, and in the film of 1945, but also the very last he would ever record, because this turned out to be his final session in the studio. Sadly so, for all these recordings show a maturity of interpretation that puts them among the finest he ever made.

Further evidence that Heddle's voice and stamina were both still holding up, despite the diabetes, the weaknesses left by the First World War, and the general wear and tear of a hectic life, is the fact that he continued to sing arduous programmes at Celebrity Concerts. Sir Geraint Evans gives a lively insight into what Heddle's busy professional life would have been like in the early 1950s, describing how he would often take the 'Messiah Special', as the Paddington to Fishguard train became known 'usually on Thursday mornings, because "Celebrity Concerts" and oratorio tended to be held on nights when towns had their early closing day.'[4]

Sir Geraint explains how many of the leading singers would meet up on the platform, including Joan Cross, Isobel Baillie, Elsie Suddaby, Mary Jarred, Heddle Nash, Norman Walker and various others. The train would stop at Newport, then Cardiff, Bridgend, Swansea and so on along the line, and every time it stopped one or two of the singers would get off to travel on to different parts of the valleys, or to towns in west Wales, to keep their engagements:

> I thought it an honour to be part of such a distinguished company. Some had years of experience for their fifteen-guinea fee, out of which they paid their own expenses... More importantly, they knew how to behave as professional artists, and I gained a great deal of experience from working with them.
>
> At Celebrity Concerts we really had to give our all, to sing our guts out in operatic ballads and every sort of song, but as long as there were some good high notes everybody was delighted, not least in Wales.

A concert at which Heddle would have been 'singing his guts out', in this case for Whitehaven and District Music and Arts Association (in association with the Arts Council of Great Britain) in February 1950, reveals a programme which would tax any tenor. Yet he probably performed it for around the fee cited above, £15/15s/od:

Programme

I

Ombra mai fu (Xerxes)	
Recit.: O loss of sight } Air: Total eclipse } (Samson)	
Recit.: My arms } Air: Sound an alarm } (Judas Maccabeus)	*Handel*
Un aura amorosa (Cosi fan Tutte)	
Ah! lo veggio (Cosi fan Tutte)	*Mozart*

II

Adelaide	*Beethoven*
Rosebud in the Heather	
Whither	*Schubert*
Atlas	
Oh, quand je dors	*Liszt*

III

Indian Love Song	
Love's Philosophy	*Delius*
To the Queen of my Heart	
In the Dawn	*Elgar*

IV

Go, lovely Rose	
Wild Cherry	*Quilter*
Love's Secret	
The Wind	*Bantock*
So Sweet is shee	*arr. Dolmetsch*
Pretty Phyllis	*arr. Owen Mase*
Why so pale and wan, fond lover ?	
Love is a Bable	*Parry*

Although his family were aware of the shadows hanging over Heddle's health in the early 1950s, and the despondency he felt at times, overall he retained his zest for singing and for life in general. It had become a matter of great pleasure to him that both his sons were doing him proud in their adult life, and were now paying him the biggest compliment of all – receiving tuition from him in the hopes of following in his footsteps by pursuing a singing career.

John had first opted for his great childhood love of aircraft by becoming an apprentice with Handley-Page and qualified as an aeronautical engineer, ending up on the design team. 'He has no time for singing at all,' Heddle reported back in 1944 when John had first become an apprentice. 'His one love is aeroplanes!'[5] But eventually the 'Heddle' music in John's blood proved too strong and he won a scholarship to the Guildhall School of Music, where he studied with Heddle's old friend and colleague Norman Walker, while simultaneously having lessons from his father. To Heddle's great delight John eventually won the prestigious 'Queen's Prize', which set him on the road to a very successful career as a leading baritone, singing with the Carl Rosa, Sadler's Wells and the ENCO. David went up to Cambridge and also for a time studied singing with his father, appearing with him at Sadler's Wells before joining the cosmetics firm Elizabeth Arden.

But for a time, as John once explained: 'Music at my father's house in Petts Wood sometimes got complicated. The singing went on for a large portion of the day. Father's dog would howl! It got taken for many a walk in the woods.' On one occasion when David was playing and singing with great gusto, a chunk of the ceiling fell down – probably latent bomb damage – one hopes. Pieces of plaster were discovered still lodged inside the grand piano when it was restored a number of years later. Unsurprisingly, it was often Heddle himself who undertook the dog-walking, a chance to enjoy some peace and solitude, down in the woods at the end of the road. Alternatively he would retire to the garden shed where he took solace in a silent smoke, or shaping a piece of wood.[6]

It was during the long vacation, the summer before graduation, when David was on a scheme which took him away for a summer stay at Heidelberg University, that his father wrote him a couple of cheerful letters in which the voice of the warm family man comes across. The opening sentence will sound familiar to many dads communicating with a twenty-two year old son spending time abroad:

Friday August 15th 1952

...I note your money has arrived so there is no need to worry Petts Wood Bank about it. The Albert Hall Proms went off well on August 6th and reception was fine. John is on his way home today from St Ives where he sang two performances of *Tom Jones*. I have just been rung up to be told by a contralto that he has thrilled everybody.

Our show of *Merrie England* is slowly creeping forward & by next Tuesday we should have more definite news of contracts. [It didn't actually come off in the end.] They have lost Linda Grey, however, to another show.

David Nash.

Sorry to hear about the rations. However, do not stint yourself on food. Those are orders... By the way David, your letters have been commented upon as being very interesting by all who have read them. If you have time – a short resume of your adventures and exploits at Heidelberg would be amusing to keep by you. Who knows? You may become an author – on the side.

It's nice to know you have friends from Caius with you & so not entirely on your own... and we are glad you like walking. It is one of the best hobbies you could have.

He hands over to Violet who reports that Dad (Heddle) is very well and 'saucy' and digging his way to health.

Monday August 25th 1952

.... Come home when you think fit. If you want another day – take it. All well here. We are just scooting off to the Carlton Cinema in Orpington to see the Marx Bros in a film & have a laugh at their 'tommy rot'. Weather quite hot and oppressive with thunder clouds. We went to Seaford on Saturday for the day & will do it again when you come home. They have built up the Promenade to hold back the sea & instituted chalets at 5/- per day where you can cook for yourselves on a Primus.

Should like to be with you for a stroll round Heidelberg. No more news. All well here.

Love from Dad (In Haste)

Another telling letter written by Heddle in 1952 managed to survive for many years in a biscuit tin in the recipient's garden shed in Larne, County Antrim, Northern Ireland. An overcrowded memory and untypical lapse in organisation must have prompted the following, dated 22 January 1952:

Dear Miss Crossey-O'Boyle,

Re. Larne Choral Society. February 7th, 1952

Messrs Ibbs & Tillett have given me your address. Miss Cheselden says she sent me a programme to fill in. This I may have done in the rush of correspondence but I have no record of it in my diary. If you have the programme, will you please let me know what is put down? Otherwise I am afraid I must ask you to let me know your wishes as to numbers of appearances and type of songs required.

I propose catching the 7.55 pm train from Euston on February 6th arriving Larne 9.15 am on February 7th. As I have no accommodation booked for that night, will you please arrange that for me? I should also like to know the name of the Concert Hall and time of rehearsal and performance.

Am looking forward to being in Northern Ireland again after a very long period.

Yours sincerely

On the reverse of the letter, in a different handwriting someone has written:

Varied Programme
– Take a pair of sparkling eyes

– Faery Song
– Serenade F. M. of P
– Oh maiden my maiden

It's interesting to note how, at the age of fifty-seven, and in poor health, Heddle was arranging to undertake such an overnight journey in the bleak month of February, including crossing the Irish Sea, followed immediately on arrival by rehearsals and an arduous evening's recital, all at an unknown venue and trusting in his hosts to have arranged him a bed for the night!

Disappointingly, although his photo appeared on the programme, he never actually made it to this particular venue after all, his place being taken at the last minute by Trefor Jones. It's for sure Heddle would have got there if he could, and it seems likely that he was struck down by one of his heavy colds. After wondering what Heddle's fee might have been at that time, Mr Wilson Logan, who kindly supplied the letter, points out: 'the travel arrangements are interesting, the overnight train from Euston to Stranraer, and then the ferry, arriving in Larne the next morning. I wonder what a tenor of the quality of Heddle Nash (if there is one?) would cost today?' Hopefully more than the equivalent of £15/15/- forked out by the Welsh Valleys!

The year 1954 found Heddle attached to the English Opera Group, whom he found very much to his liking – 'a very nice and gentlemanly lot'. He was performing the role of Hawthorn in the opera *Love in a Village* by Arthur

Oldham who was a former private pupil of Benjamin Britten. When it was first staged by the English Opera Group, *Love in a Village* had been dismissed (according to Oldham's obituary notice in *The Guardian*) by one London newspaper as 'once Britten, twice shy'. Also according to *The Guardian*: 'It took time, plus a nervous breakdown and a period working as a messenger in the BBC's newsroom to recover from such slights.' Oldham, however, had finished with opera for good and went on to make his name as a choirmaster in Edinburgh and Paris.

As for Heddle, even a performance as Hawthorn at the Barnstaple Devon Festival on 1 August 1954 was not to be without its dramas. The week before he had been staying at the seaside bungalow of friends at Ogmore-by-Sea, near Bridgend in South Wales and had slipped on wet grass, fallen, and hurt his shoulder. In pain, he had presented himself at the local hospital where they had X-rayed the shoulder, diagnosed 'arthritis' and advised him to go away and keep exercising it. The pain, however, just got worse. In agony now, Heddle returned to the hospital where this time the diagnosis was very different – a cracked collar bone. He was put in plaster with his right arm fixed 'bent and horizontal'. Yet he still went off to Devon, somehow managed to get into his costume, and went on stage to perform.[7]

Shortly afterwards Heddle had a concert engagement up in Buxton, Derbyshire, and off he went again and fulfilled that contract too, standing on the platform with his arm still in the bent and horizontal position. His son David recalls having to accompany his father up there as 'baggage handler and minder'!

That same year, 1954, though still delighting audiences and apparently having lost none of his zest for performing, Heddle finally followed the route that so many singers have taken in their later years to augment their income: he accepted a teaching appointment at the Northern School of Music in Manchester. The teaching was to be on a daily basis, which meant he would have to travel all the way up from Kent, teach his pupils and then travel back again – a long and hectic working day for anybody, but especially so for a sick man now sixty years old. And around the teaching, he would still be travelling to perform complex concert programmes. What was driving him to keep going, instead of sinking into a dignified and well-earned retirement? Not entirely the desire to communicate: despite that glorious voice, although he 'did pretty well', he had never been in a position to put much into savings, so money as well as vocation would have remained a strong motive. Not that he short-changed his audiences in any way – they still felt they had been privileged to share a magical experience.

In addition to teaching pupils at the Northern School of Music, the most noteworthy of whom was the tenor John Mitchinson, Heddle picked up a few private pupils in Manchester, including the comedian Ken Dodd. Anybody not a fan of Ken Dodd's singing voice might be wise to look away now...

In Stephen Griffin's biography[8] Ken Dodd acknowledges a debt to Heddle: 'I'm very proud that I had six singing lessons from Heddle Nash; he told me I was a tenor, I'd always thought I was a baritone.' So it seems Heddle actually played a part in producing such hits as 'Happiness', 'Tears' and 'Love Is Like a Violin'. He had died before his former pupil's rendition of 'Tears' lodged itself in the charts for six months in 1965 and achieved sales figures of around two million. Heddle would have given his eye teeth for a hit that size! Nevertheless, ever generous to his fellow artists, he would no doubt have been genuinely 'tickled pink' on Ken Dodd's behalf.

Proof that Heddle was still in excellent voice comes in a lovely description from Charles Corp,[9] who heard him singing at, of all places, the Church of St Mary, Shipley, Sussex, in 1956. United with the Burrell family in grief, Heddle had never lost touch with them following the death of Anny Ahlers over twenty years earlier, and this is thought to have been the third concert he had given there. A week before the concert he went down to rehearse with the Reverend Cecil Cochrane, the Director of Music at Christ's Hospital, who was to accompany him, and Charles was fortunate enough to be present at the rehearsal:

> The rehearsal took place in the Singing Room at Christ's Hospital. It had excellent acoustics, resonant, but not too much so. HN's voice sounded quite wonderful in there. The voice did not seem to be connected to the singer at all. It was just running around the room like a ball of silver. The man standing there singing did not seem to be making any particular effort, the sound was just 'there.'

But Charles was amazed to learn afterwards that Heddle apparently could not sight-sing music:

> I heard that Cecil Cochrane handed HN a book that had the words of the Hymn but the tune was not the usual, familiar one. Cecil Cochrane played the familiar tune and HN sang away quite happily. When they had finished, Cecil Cochrane pointed out to HN the fact that he was not playing the tune that was in front of him. HN told him that he learnt everything by 'ear'.

Heddle could never sight-sing with ease, and preferred to rehearse a piece over and over until he had it firmly in his memory.

In 1957 Heddle took up a second teaching post, as Professor of Singing at the Royal College of Music in London. By all accounts he thoroughly enjoyed teaching his students and encouraging them, sometimes even welcoming them into his own home. 'Never let go of your music!' was a practical piece of advice he always gave; leave it lying around, he warned, and somebody would be sure to nick it.* 'Use your toes to beat time – no one will notice – and count like fury!' was another. And he advised them to learn as many scores as they could in advance, because later on, if they became successful, they wouldn't have the time. By learning in advance they would ensure that they would always be ready, if called upon at short notice. Being prepared had certainly paid off well for Heddle (he had personally acquired a mind-boggling reper-toire of twenty-four operas,[10] not to mention numerous oratorios and songs). To encourage students who were doing particularly well, he would produce one of his painstakingly handwritten scores as a reward. And on one occasion, when a highly promising but impoverished student was offered work but had no evening dress to perform in, Heddle kindly lent his own – gratefully received, even though it was a little too short in the arms and legs.[11]

It was while Heddle was teaching at Manchester, in 1954, that the young David Menzies arrived from Australia to do postgraduate work in Dentistry and stayed with the Nashes for a while. He remembers walking over to Petts Wood Station with David to meet Heddle off the train, and noticing how he had still retained a slight Cockney accent. That evening, they all sat cosily together listening to the radio premiere from Manchester of Sir John Barbi-rolli conducting Vaughan Williams' 8th Symphony. The scene sounds very 'post-war England', but the truth is that in the outside world big changes were already afoot and Heddle must have been acutely aware of them.

The previous year Elvis Presley had already cut his first disc and that very year of 1954, Bill Haley recorded 'Rock Around the Clock' – the new era of Rock 'n' Roll and youth culture was on its way. Back in 1950 the record company RCA had introduced the first vinyl 12" LP, and followed that with the 7" single in 1951. That would be the beginning of the end for those heavy 78 rpm and 80 rpm shellac discs on to which Heddle had recorded all his

---

*Sir Geraint Evans was also the recipient of Heddle's advice, and made a point of abiding by it: 'I liked to have a score by me in a performance, remembering Heddle Nash's advice: "You never know when you might want it. Even if you only sit on it."' *A Knight at the Opera*

music for Columbia and HMV. By the end of the 1950s, stereo vinyl would have established itself as the dominant medium for recorded music. Potentially that would leave Heddle's beautiful recordings as dead as dodos, the discs themselves likely soon to run the risk of being heat-moulded into fashionable plant-pot holders or fruit bowls, or later have their centres cut out and turned into trendy coasters!

Throughout the 1950s Heddle had been taking pride and pleasure in making appearances with his son John. They had sung twice together in *The Barber of Seville* on television and performed in concerts. 'Singing duets is always a joy,' John once pointed out.[12] 'Since each duet has potentially twice the impact of a solo, if only the singers will work together. With father this was hardly a problem, and we included many opera duets in the concerts.' (*La Bohème*, *The Pearl Fishers* and the sparkling 'Supper Duet' from *Die Fledermaus*.) A few times they even performed together back at the Pier Pavilion in Llandudno. (Coincidentally John claimed to be on stage performing there the very night Heddle died.) 'When I gave up engineering and took up singing,' John said, 'I met almost universal friendship from musicians of his generation – and still meet it. I cannot think of a greater tribute to him. He was universally loved in the profession.'

Back in 1951 Heddle had sung the role of Dr Manette in a radio broadcast on the BBC Third Programme of an opera by Arthur Benjamin, libretto by Cedric Cliffe, named *A Tale of Two Cities* and based on Charles Dickens' book of the same name. The opera had won a prize at the Festival of Britain, but although critics such as Eric Blom in *The Observer* were hoping that a stage production would soon follow, that did not occur. It wasn't until 1957 that it was finally staged by the New Opera Company, at Sadler's Wells. Arthur Benjamin was not only particularly keen that Heddle should repeat the part of Dr Manette in the stage version, but that all three singing members of the Nash family should take part. He hoped that John would sing the part of Sydney Carton and Heddle too would have dearly loved it, but unfortunately, due to John's contractual difficulties, John Cameron eventually undertook Carton and was to prove a big success in the production, along with Ruth Packer, who sang the role of Mme Defarge. David Nash, however, did take part, much to his father's pride. The opera as a whole was received enthusiastically, attracting no less than seven curtain calls at its premiere. Heddle had just turned sixty-three that summer and to be involved in such a success at that point in his life must have been a tremendous boost.

A Tale of Two Cities was, not surprisingly, to be Heddle's final opera, but needless to say, he would not be bowing out on a whimper:

Heddle as Dr Manette in A Tale of Two Cities.

Heddle Nash's experienced artistry made a living figure of Dr Manette.[13]

Powerful exchanges – Madame Defarge and Dr Manette in the tribunal scene are tremendous.[14]

Heddle Nash a superbly convincing Dr Manette – uncomfortably so in the terrifying moment when his newly-restored reason begins to crumble under the venomous gaze of Mme Defarge.[15]

The opera was televised the following year, in 1958, starring John Cameron, Heather Harper and Heddle Nash.

Yet 1958 was to be a bitter-sweet year for Heddle. Just after Easter of that year, the sixty-four-year old, still best-loved 'king of English tenors', who was thoroughly enjoying his pupils and endeavouring to continue earning a living by delighting his audiences, received a letter from a very high-up person at the Northern School of Music in Manchester, the contents of which must have made his stomach contract.[16] It still makes painful reading.

The letter regretted to inform him that among candidates for the following year there were none who were either 'uncommitted to other teachers' or who would 'do him credit'. And as the majority of his present students would be leaving at the end of the coming term, they could not continue the existing arrangement concerning travel and subsistence. Heddle is reminded that he is 'in the nature of a luxury' and that, 'where there are budgets to balance', they are 'not justified in having such a luxury' unless they can make the fullest use of it.

After *A Tale of Two Cities* Heddle continued to fit in the odd recital, or a *Messiah*, but increasingly from 1958 onwards he found he was being obliged to spend more and more time at home. Sometimes he would go on long walks around the Kentish countryside in an attempt to hang on to some degree of fitness, and he began to look forward to Saturday afternoons when his favourite programme was on TV. Ever a man of surprises, just like his father before him, this remarkably kind and gentle man turned out to be a huge fan of – wrestling! Even more surprisingly, so was the local vicar, and furthermore, the vicar and the lyric tenor would occasionally find huge enjoyment in going off together to live wrestling bouts, cheering on the 'goodies' and vociferously booing the 'baddies'. Heddle's taste in reading ran in a similar 'goodies' and 'baddies' vein: he was particularly partial to the thrilling adventure stories of John Buchan, Jack London and G H Henty where, unlike in real life, the goodies always managed to come out on top.[17]

In 1961, though approaching the age of sixty-seven and knowing that he was seriously ill, Heddle ordered himself a couple of new suits, plus – still optimistic of fulfilling more engagements – a whole new set of evening clothes.[18] In March of that year he travelled all the way up to Yorkshire to sing in a performance of – what else? – *The Messiah*. We have no report of how well he performed, but his loyal fans, who looked upon him as an old friend, were probably as delighted as always by his superb diction and the unmistakable quality of his voice. After Yorkshire he ventured even further afield, up to County Durham to act as a judge at the Darlington Music Festival.

Those two appearances proved to be Heddle's last.

On 13 August, only four months after singing his last *Messiah*, the 'best Messiah in the business' died, a victim of lung cancer.[19]

For many of his fans, the last sighting and the enduring memory of Heddle would have been similar to that so touchingly described by Eric Rees:

The last time I saw him was at Enfield, with the Enfield String Orchestra, in 1956 or 1957. At the close of the concert Heddle treated us to several delicious encores; last of all came Kenneth MacLeod's famous 'Road to the Isles'. At the beginning of the final refrain he began to walk slowly off the stage, finishing by singing the last line pianissimo over his shoulder as he disappeared into the wings. That was my very last sight of him. God bless him. He was a great artist and a lovely man.[20]

Heddle was laid to rest in the impersonal and sprawling cemetery at Chislehurst in Kent, under a headstone carved from York stone, in the simple shape of a soldier's cross. At the base of the cross were carved the words: 'I fell asleep, and now I am refreshed', taken, appropriately, from *The Dream of Gerontius*.[21] A memorial service, held at St Sepulchre's Church at Holborn Viaduct[22] included Ralph Vaughan Williams' *Serenade to Music*. Some of the students taking part were ones who had been studying with him at the Royal College of Music, others represented the profession. The Lesson was read by another well-loved BBC announcer friend, Frank Phillips, and the Appreciation was delivered by his old singing colleague Roy Henderson.

Sixty-seven is not the most appropriate age for a celebrity to die, at least so far as the length of obituaries is concerned. It is better by far, as measured

in column inches, to die young and be remembered at the height of one's powers, like Heddle's former supremely gifted partners Kathleen Ferrier, or Anny Ahlers, or else to live to a venerable old age and be remembered with nostalgic affection, and perhaps even be the recipient of some sort of honour for staunch patriotism and dedication to improving the standards of British singing, by a grateful nation. 'Sir Heddle Nash' – how dashing that sounds, and how sad that he was never the recipient of such an appropriate accolade – or indeed, of any official accolade at all.

But maybe it was fitting that Heddle, destined, in the words of Bruno Walter, to be born in the wrong place at the wrong time, should also die at the wrong time too, at the start of the Swinging Sixties, when all emphasis was on the Rock 'n' Roll beat of the 'here and now' and before his career had had a chance to be seen in retrospect in all its glory.

Yet a voice as special as Heddle Nash's was never destined to be easily forgotten. In the minds of all lovers and enthusiasts of great singing, his memory was bound to simmer on. And over at EMI the death of this aristocrat among singers, who was hailed as the 'Voice of Mozart', whose voice was 'unsurpassed in elegance and charm' and whose 'early records are still regarded as the finest Mozart singing by a tenor on disc'[23] did not go unnoticed. Although they had paid him no royalties at all for over two years, and would eventually calculate for his executors that the outstanding sum they owed to his widow was a paltry £21:17s:9d,[24] within two weeks of his death an internal memorandum was circulating to the effect that since his death had created a fresh surge of interest, perhaps they should try to organise an EP record of the tenor arias from *The Dream of Gerontius*, providing they had the necessary metal parts to do a good job.

Gradually, over the years, most of the recordings Heddle committed to those old shellac discs were to become digitally re-mastered and eventually available on CD. Forgotten old broadcasts would also be dug out, refurbished and put on to CD. His distinctive voice has survived. For anyone who cares to sample what 'Britain's best and most-loved tenor' of the pre-war years once sounded like, it lives on, as spine-tinglingly bright and fresh and full of the minstrel-like appeal as in his heyday; though of course, in the words of a fan fortunate enough to have attended a number of his live performances, 'that is no substitute for the living presence of a great artist.'[25]

As for Heddle himself, for whom 'singing was his life', he would be downright thrilled to know that fifty years after his death, his voice is still giving pleasure. And he would probably give a wry shrug at the news that, what's more, his silver voice is still managing to rake in a bob or two!

Notes

ABBREVIATIONS: HN *Heddle Nash*; DN *David Nash*; JHN *John Heddle Nash*; VN *Violet Nash*; MN *Mary Nash*; JN *Joan Nash*; IB *Isobel Baillie*

Introduction

1 Gerald Moore's autobiography *Am I Too Loud?*
2 DN
3 *Birmingham Post* 11 Apr. 1928
4 *Manchester Guardian* 29 Nov. 1928
5 HN letter to Frederick Gaisburg 10 Dec. 1935 (supplied by DN)

Chapter One

1 The *Daily Mirror : To-day's Gossip* Nov. 1933
2 Cockney accent anecdote DN
3 Joseph Nash's dates, background, early movements and change of name traced from *Census Records of England and Wales*
4 Maria Heddle's Orphir background, move to Edinburgh and marriage to Joseph Nash traced from *Scotland's People*
5 Jessie McKenzie also traced to Edinburgh through *Scotland's People.*
6 Jessie singing anecdote DN

7 Eric Rees unpublished fragment written for *The Record Collector* 1996 (supplied by DN)

8 Joseph and Maria in Deptford: *Census Records of England and Wales*

9 *Stamford Library maps of London and its Suburbs*

10 Census Records of England and Wales

11 *Charles Booth's survey into life and labour in London 1886–1903 (Alexandra Street and Vansittart Street refs. Notebook B368 P.55)*

12 Joseph's death by drowning discovered from his death certificate.

13 Report on inquest in *Kentish Mercury* Jul. 1887 (Lewisham Local History Archives)

14 Information on receiving-houses on Grand Surrey Canal from *Dickens's Dictionary of London* 1879

15 Occupations and whereabouts of Maria, Amy and William following death of Joseph *Census Records of England and Wales*

Chapter Two

1 Harriette Carr's background, early married life of William Nash and birth of children *Census Records of England and Wales*. Additional material DN

2 From a fragment jotted down by one of Heddle's fans, Frank Stokes

3 HN's boyhood pranks from jottings of JHN in preparation for his show *Best Messiah in the Business* (supplied by JN)

4 The accompanist and répétiteur Mary Nash, daughter of Frank, who also inherited the Heddle music gene and for whom Heddle was 'the perfect uncle'

5 Maria reverting to 'Naish' and death at Congresbury from *Parish Records* online

6 Amy's whereabouts: *Census Records of England and Wales*

7 Notes supplied by VN for lecture on HN by Grenville Eves March 1972, under the chairmanship of Sir Keith Falkner (supplied by DN)

8 Blackheath Road School from photographs of exterior and a woodwork lesson in progress 1906 (London Metropolitan Archives)

9 HN's scholarship certificate (supplied by DN)

10 Westminster School anecdote: DN

11 Mercers' School from DN and *Mercers' School History* (*Old Mercers' Club* – on-line)

12 DN

13 Bungled attempt to win scholarship to Royal College of Music DN

14 Until 1904 known as Goldsmiths' Technical and Recreative Institute, founded in 1891 when it was dedicated to 'the promotion of technical skill, knowledge, health and general well-being among men and women of the industrial, working and artisan classes'

15 Certificate from Goldsmith's College (supplied by DN)

16 Description of 65 Wickham Road from the Nash family photo album and DN

17 HN, from jottings in preparation for Lecture Recitals entitled *Trials & Triumphs of a Singing Career* at Cheadle Green Institute (Hallé Club) Oct. 1956 and *Trials and Experiences of an Operatic Career* at Walker Art Gallery (Liverpool Opera Circle) Oct. 1957 (supplied by JN)

18 DN

19 DN and article by WS Meadmore *Gramophone* Apr. 1937

20 From jottings of HN in preparation for recitals (as above)

Chapter Three

1 DN

2 Estimate of HN's height by DN and MN was c 5'10", but off-stage people seem to have found him a little shorter than expected. Photographic evidence suggests perhaps closer to 5'9".

3 HN's notes for the recitals in Cheadle and Liverpool, 1956, 1957

4 Signaller WWI – Worcestershire Regiment website

5 DN

6 A S Benbow 9th Company Imperial Camel Corps Brigade, Imperial War Museum Dept. of Documents

7 Capt WR Elliot *The Second Twentieth*

8 Ferruccio Bonavia *The Listener* Apr. 1943

9 Elgar drew not only from his imagination and Cardinal Newman's poem, but from his own early brushes with tragedy, which included the early deaths of two of his brothers.

10 Sinking of the *Ivernia: Daily Mirror* 5 Jan. 1917 and 27 Jan. 1917

11 DN

12 Ferruccio Bonavia *The Listener* April 1943

13 Gerard J De Groot *The First World War*

14 DN

15 Capt WR Elliot *The Second Twentieth*

16 According to claims made later, the unfortunate offender might find that he had been 'accidentally' placed within range of enemy fire.

17 DN

18 Capt WR Elliot *The Second Twentieth*

19 DN

20 Gerard J De Groot *The First World War*

21 DN

Chapter Four

1 DN, MN

2 Details about William Nash Snr DN

3 Ashok Kumar *Snooker and Billiards Dph Sports Series,* Discovery Publishing House

4 DN

5 Background to Violet and the Pearce family DN

6 Singing said to have cured his stutter: jottings of JHN for show *Best Messiah in the Business*

7 Marie Brema anecdote retold by Susan Rutherford in *The Prima Donna and Opera*

8 Regrets about not having full musical course: jottings of HN for recital at Manchester

9 Visits to Covent Garden VN, rcounted to Grenville Eves for 1972 lecture

10 John McCormack, Gracie Fields, George Formby...

11 Shanklin Isle of Wight booking and Gaieties Around England: HN jottings for recital

Chapter Five

1 Story of Scala Theatre from *London Theatres and Music Halls 1850–1950* Diana Howard, and *The Theatres of London,* Mander and Mitcherson

2 Believed to be César Cui's *Puss in Boots*, Rossini's *L'occasione fa il ladro* and *La gazza ladra,* and Respighi's *La bella dormente nel bosco*

3 Teatro dei Piccoli: *The Puccini Problem: Opera, Nationalism and Modernity (Cambridge Studies in Opera)* Alexandra Wilson. *Old Show in Manhattan* Apr. 1941 at *Time.com.*

4 *Popular Science Monthly* Jun. 1933

5 *Old Show in Manhattan* Apr. 1941 at *Time.com*

6 According to the *New York Times*, attended by a highly distinguished audience of statesmen, actors, painters, foreign ministers and important foreign residents.

7 *Popular Science Monthly* Jun. 1933

8 From jottings of HN for Manchester recital

9 Maria Signorelli states in her essay *A History of the Little Theatre* that the show ran for two months, but in *Stage Musical Chronology: The 1920s* compiled by John Kenrick the actual number of performances is listed as 16, which bears out *HN*'s note that 'the show ran for a short time only'

10 *Popular Science Monthly* Jun. 1933

11 Information about gift from William Snr DN, MN
The Podrecca Puppets now form part of the collection of the famous puppeteer Maria Signorelli.

Chapter Six

1 HN's lodgings in Milan: DN and a note in family photo album

2 HN's jottings for Cheadle and Liverpool recitals, 1956, 1957

3 HN jottings as above

4 As above

5 Early repertoire: Larry Lustig article for *The Record Collector* Mar. 1996 and HN's notes as above

6 IB autobiography *Never Sing Louder Than Lovely*

7 IB *Never Sing Louder Than Lovely*

8 Edele Nascio: G B Shaw's article in *Everybody's* entitled 'We sing better than our grandparents' 1950

9 'I'll show these foreigners I can sing as well as they can': VN for Grenville Eves lecture March 1972

10 DN

11 Christopher Fifield *Ibbs & Tillett: The Rise and Fall of a Musical Empire*

12 Christopher Fifield *Ibbs & Tillett: The Rise and Fall of a Musical Empire*

13 HN jottings for Cheadle and Liverpool recitals 1956, 1957

14 Audition at Old Vic: DN and VN, as recounted to Grenville Eves for lecture (above) 1972, though it is likely that he only stepped into the part of the Duke at a slightly later stage

15 Performance as Duke of Mantua: HN notes for recital in Manchester

16 HN's relish in word-play DN

17 IB *Never Sing Louder Than Lovely*

18 The conductor Charles Corri

19 DN

20 DN

21 DN

22 Esmond Knight *Seeking The Bubble*

23 Alan Blyth *The Recorded Legacy*

24 Letter from Columbia Records 8 Jan. 1926 (supplied by DN)

Chapter Seven

1 John Lucas *Thomas Beecham: An Obsession With Music*

2 *Romeo and Juliet* anecdote from Alan Blyth's notes for HMV Records

3 DN

4 BNCO broadcast of Jules Massenet's *Manon: Manchester Guardian*

5 Atmosphere at Queen's Hall: Robert Elkin *Queen's Hall 1893–1941*

6 HN letter from Italy to brother and sister-in-law Bob and Gladys Jones 22 May 1928 (supplied by DN)

7 Maggie Teyte *Star On The Door*

8 DN

9 Elizabeth Schafer *Lilian Baylis: A Biography*

10 VN, for Eves lecture 1972

11 HN jottings for Cheadle and Liverpool recitals 1956, 57

12 DN

13 Information on London Delius Festival: John Lucas *Thomas Beecham: An Obsession With Music*

14 John Lucas *Thomas Beecham: An Obsession With Music*

15 The Astoria is now the Carling Academy. Information taken from its website

Chapter Eight

1 DN

2 *The Daily Mirror* Sat. edition Feb. 1929

3 Grenville Eves lecture 1972

4 IB *Never Sing Louder Than Lovely*

5 Maggie Teyte *Star On the Door*

6 Correspondence between the Secretary and Treasurer and Mayor Sept 1935 – 'we should make a small profit but it will not be anything very much' (Worcester Local History Archive)

7 DN

8 In the magazine *Everybody's* 1950

9 *The Manchester Guardian*

10 Conversation retold by Anthony Boden *The Three Choirs: A History Of The Festival*

11 DN

12 Robert Elkin *Queen's Hall 1893–1941*

13 In a performance at the Royal Festival Hall in April 1952, for example, with the Goldsmiths' Choral Union, a member of the audience noted how he took a wrong turn at the end of the *Sanctus fortis* section (Charles Corp)

14 Sir Joseph Henry Wood *My Life of Music*

15 *The Times*

16 *The Daily Telegraph*

17 Neville Cardus *The Delights of Music – a Critic's Choice*

18 IB *Never Sing Louder Than Lovely*

19 Frances Donaldson *Royal Opera House, Covent Garden: In the Twentieth Century*

20 Maggie Teyte *Star on the Door*

Chapter Nine

1 Highly regarded English composer/conductor now largely remembered for his involvement in film work – including *Whisky Galore* and *Kind Hearts and Coronets*

2 VN for Grenville Eves lecture 1972

3 *The Manchester Guardian*

4 *Theatre World* Nov. 1932

5 DN

6 *The Daily Mirror*

7 DN

8 James Agate *Immmoment Toys*

9 *Daily Mirror: To-day's Gossip* 16 Apr. 1932

10 *Daily Express* 25 Jun. 1932

11 *Daily Express* 22 Sep. 1932

12 *Die Verliebte Firma (The Firm in Love)* 1932. The second film to be directed by Max Ophuls

13 *The Manchester Guardian*

14 DN

15 In those days attempted suicide was a criminal offence

16 *The Daily Express: Dubarry's Last Curtain* 21 Mar. 1933

17 *The Guardian* 19 Mar. 1933

18 Dec. 1938 the tragedy was being revisited by Sharpe of the Flying Squad in *The Star*

19 *Daily Express* 24 Apr. 1935

20 *Daily Express* 9 Jan. 1935 when he is quoted as saying that the receiving order came as an 'absolute surprise'. But Scott would have found his money affairs reduced to small-fry compared with those of bankrupt King Zog of Albania, fighting to save his tottering throne, and awarded considerably more column inches, on the same page

21 Divorce petition 1935 *National Archives*

22 *The Daily Express* 19 Oct. 1935

23 Stuart Hibberd's oration at HN's funeral

Chapter Ten

1 Stella Gibbons *Cold Comfort Farm*

2 Spike Hughes *Glyndebourne*

3 DN

4 DN

5 First Night Programme 1934: 'now the acoustics have been corrected (at a cost of a few pounds), so that, at last, they are marvellously good... the result of the application of Science, of elementary Physics, and chiefly of commonsense'

6 Spike Hughes *Glyndebourne*

7 John Julius Norwich *Fifty Years of Glyndebourne*

8 HN notes for recital 'Tonsils out in 1934. A month later Glyndebourne singing all day'. Additional information DN

9 Spike Hughes *Glyndebourne*

10 *The Manchester Guardian*

11 *The Manchester Guardian*

12 Spike Hughes *Glyndebourne*

13 Letter to HN Glyndebourne

14 DN

15 Mitchell and Reed *Letters from a Life*, Vol.I

16 Recounted by Sir Geraint Evans *A Knight at the Opera*

17 DN

18 Bruce Norman *Here's Looking at You*

19 Fischer's account: *Library and Archives Canada*
20 *Television* Aug. 1934

Chapter Eleven

1 *The Manchester Guardian*
2 *The Daily Mirror* 22 May 1935 'If Covent Garden does not applaud Lily Pons, the world's smallest prima donna, she threatens to applaud herself...'
3 *The Daily Mirror* 24 May 1935 'Pocket Prima Donna's Triumph'
4 According to John Lucas in *Thomas Beecham: An Obsession With Music*, Beecham was commonly rumoured to have added a rude word after 'Shut up you –' which the press felt was too indelicate to print.
5 HN letter to Frederick Gaisburg (supplied by DN)
6 There are many accounts of this hoax
7 John Lucas in *Thomas Beecham: An Obsession with Music* states that Harold Holt, business manager of the LSO was involved with Beecham in cooking up the scheme
8 Leech Collection (1935–1955) at the British Library's National Sound Archive
9 HN had performed with Dua in *La Bohème* at the Royal Opera House the previous year. Dua performed the parts of Benoit and Alcindoro. *Royal Opera House Programme* 5 Oct. 1935
10 DN
11 DN
12 DN
13 Alan Blyth *The Recorded Legacy*
14 Letter 22 Oct. 1938 (supplied by DN)
15 IB *Never Sing Louder Than Lovely*
16 VN for Eves lecture 1972
17 DN
18 Stuart Hibberd *This is London*

Chapter Twelve

1 Three Choirs Festival 1939 *DN*. Friends of Worcester Cathedral Concert from programme (Elgar Birthplace Museum Archives)
2 Eric Rees was a friend of Megan Thomas as well as fan of HN. Quotation taken from Rees letter to Alan Blyth 28 May 2007

3 Violet letter from NZ to her sister Gladys Jones and brother-in-law Bob in Petts Wood 28 May 1940

4 IB *Never Sing Louder Than Lovely*

5 Sinking of *Lancastria Daily Mirror* 30 Jul. 1940

6 Impromptu Menuhin concert from DN

7 From biographical notes Souvenir Programme, Wellington Town Hall 27 Apr. 1940 (supplied by Charles Corp)

8 IB *Never Sing Louder Than Lovely*

9 New Zealand itinerary from collection of IB (supplied by Charles Corp)

10 IB *Never Sing Louder Than Lovely*

11 *NZ Evening Post* 25 Jun. 1940

12 Walter Nash anecdote DN

13 Letter from William Nash Snr written from a nursing home in Falmouth, Cornwall 23 May 1940. He died two days later on 25 May at Falmouth (supplied by DN)

14 MN

15 HN letter to brother and sister-in-law Bob and Gladys Jones in Petts Wood 28 May 1940

16 *The Age* 15 May 1940

17 The Australian-born bass-baritone, remembered these days especially for his gutsy rendition of songs such as 'The Road To Mandalay' and 'The Floral Dance'.

18 *The Age* 15 May 1940

19 Broadcasting tour itinerary from HN letter to Bob and Gladys Jones, written from *Hotel Esplanade* Perth 13 Sep. 1940

20 DN

21 HN letter to Bob and Gladys Jones 13 Sep. 1940

22 HN letter to Bob and Gladys Jones 13 Sep. 1940

23 DN

24 *The Age* 11 Oct. 1940

25 DN

26 *The Sun* 13 Oct. 1940

27 *The Herald* 11 Nov. 1940

28 *The Sun News-Pictorial* 27 Oct. 1941

29 Letter to Bob and Gladys Jones 25 Jul. 1941

30 Jottings of JHN for show *Best Messiah in the Business*

31 Letter to Bob and Gladys Jones 25 Jul. 1941

32 DN

35 DN

Chapter Thirteen

1 *Messiah* anecdote *DN*
2 Jessie Wood *The Last Years of Henry J Wood*
3 Details about bookings from 1944 pocket diary of HN (only diary known to be still in existence. Supplied by DN). Also taken from HN letter to Frank Stokes 5 Apr. 1944
4 Grenville Eves, notes for lecture on HN 1972
5 Yet even with the Fire Service at full stretch, the Queen's Hall might have been saved, but for a tragic shortage of water, due to damaged mains. By dawn all that remained of London's favourite concert hall was the outer walls, giving it the appearance of a Roman arena. Many of the valuable musical instruments, left there overnight by members of the Philarmonic Orchestra had been incinerated (Robert Elkin *Queen's Hall 1893–1941*)
6 BBC CD of 1943 Prom concert
7 Doodlebug encounter from HN 1944 diary, Jessie Wood *The Last Years of Henry J Wood* and DN
8 HN letter to Frank Stokes 5 Apr. 1944
9 HN diary 1944
10 DN
11 Cochran's stagings included the famous *Cochran Reviews* and the musicals *Bitter Sweet, Evergreen* and *Anything Goes!*
12 TOC H stood for Talbot House, the first such venue established in Belgium in the First World War. The organization aimed to provide home comforts for the troops on a rank-free basis. 'Toc' was the signaller's version of the letter T.
13 Details about *Seventy Years of Song* from Charles B Cochran *Showman Looks On*
14 Anecdotes about ITMA from Tom Hickman *What Did You Do In The War, Auntie? The BBC At War*
15 DN
16 DN
17 Unfortunately, the only copy of *For You Alone* that has been traced is in Los Angeles, the UCLA Archives, part of the Mel Tormé donation. (Mel Tormé was a huge film buff.) At the time of writing it can only be viewed by appointment. However the BFI have now placed the film on

their Most Wanted list, so hopefully another copy might be discovered in the near future and, at long last, it might become possible to see Heddle performing at the height of his fame.

18 Extract from an account written for *The Record Collector* Mar. 1996
19 Letters supplied by David Nash
20 HN's diary 1944
21 DN and Pearce encounters with Doodlebugs DN and further information from the many reports of the incidents on-line
22 Carl Newton *The Best Of Me – A Grontius Centenary Companion* ed. Geoffrey Hodgkins
23 Carl Newton's full and excellent account can be found in *The Best of Me* Part V (*The Nightmare of Gerontius: The Story Behind A Famous Recording*)
24 Heddle is always quoted as having unhesitatingly chosen Gladys Ripley as his favourite Angel – she had lived a very full life and 'knew what it was all about'.
25 Carl Newton *The Best of Me* Part V as above
26 *Gramophone* Classical CD Guide
27 JN
28 HN's Jottings for Cheadle and Liverpool recitals 1956, 57
29 MN
30 DN
31 Letter supplied by DN

Chapter Fourteen

1 The many tales about what great rivals Nash and Noble were seem to have been largely exaggerated, although both occasionally took delight in stirring up the myth. The truth of the matter seems to be that although they were never bosom pals, they really did enjoy singing together
2 Beverley Baxter
3 DN
4 MN
5 DN
6 DN
7 *Daily Mirror* 29 Mar. 1946
9 Sir Geraint Evans *A Knight at the Opera*
10 DN

11 Eric Rees article for *The Record Collector* Mar. 1996
12 *The Ministry of Transport Railway Accidents Report On The Collision at Winsford* His Majesty's Stationery Office 13 Jul. 1948
13 HN's notes for Cheadle and Liverpool recitals, 1956, 1957
14 DN
15 *The Manchester Guardian*
16 *The Manchester Guardian*
17 DN
18 *Glasgow Herald* 22 Apr. 1948
19 Alan Blyth *The Recorded Legacy*
20 Ted Clark in a letter written to Alan Blyth. Accounts of Heddle making a similar response come from other parts of the country, including Stroud, so perhaps HN made something of a habit of it?

Chapter Fifteen

1 DN
2 Memo supplied by DN
3 Memo supplied by DN
4 Sir Geraint Evans *A Knight at the Opera*
5 HN letter to Frank Stokes 5 Apr. 1944
6 DN
7 DN
8 Stephen Griffin *Ken Dodd: The Biography*
9 Tenor, singing teacher, friend and archivist of Isobel Baillie
10 VN
11 DN
12 JHN notes for show *Best Bloody Messiah in the Country*
13 Evan Senior
14 *The Times*
15 Frank Granville Barker on a repeat performance the following year with Amy Shuard as Mme Defarge
16 Unsigned letter Royal College of Music Archive (admin correspondence of Cox and Miss Redhead 1956/7)
17 DN
18 DN
19 Like Richard Tauber before him, in 1948
20 Eric Rees article for *The Record Collector* 1996

21 Violet would not join him there for a further thirty-two years. She died aged 93 in 1993

22 St Sepulchre at Holborn Viaduct is known as the National Musicians' Church. It is where the young Sir Henry Wood learnt to play the organ and contains his ashes. There is a Musicians' Book of Remembrance.

23 Obituary in *The Daily Express* 15 Aug. 1961

24 Correspondence between Executors and The Electric & Musical Industries Ltd. 1961–62 (supplied by DN)

25 Rev Richard Blakeway-Phillips letter to Alan Blyth 4 May 2006

Acknowledgements

I owe a huge debt of thanks to David and Liz Nash for their patience, encouragement, enthusiasm and sheer dogged determination to help me to root out the facts – sometimes with surprising results! They shared my excitement over discoveries and added the elements of friendship and fun.

I am also grateful to Joan Nash (widow of HN's eldest son, the baritone John Heddle Nash, for supplying John's angle and so kindly allowing me to use some of the jottings he made about his father), and Heddle's niece Mary Nash, for giving me her reminisences of 'the perfect uncle', as well as other interesting family snippets.

Paul Campion, who assisted Alan Blyth with *Heddle Nash: The Recorded Legacy*, I thank for starting the ball rolling by very kindly putting me in touch with David Nash.

David Menzies and Charles Corp both provided me not only with vivid anecdotes but also with enthusiastic encouragement and some excellent photographs. Sue Hamilton Blyth generously gave me permission to quote from the late Alan Blyth's writings on Heddle. To Bryan Crimp I am exceedingly grateful for permission to quote from the autobiography of Isobel Baillie and to Nöel Goodwin for permission to quote from the autobiography of Sir Geraint Evans. Carl Newton, Anthony Boden and Mr H Wilson Logan kindly allowed me to make use of their material, while Larry Lustig, editor of *The Record Collector* and Nash afficionado, gave me permission to quote from an article written for that magazine by the late Eric Rees. The Reverend Richard Blakeway-Phillips and Ted Clark both provided lively memories. Paul White I thank for being a good friend, as well as for meticulously picking over the manuscript. Barbara Cleverly encouraged me with her enthusiastic support. The Allen family I thank for being understanding when I constantly slipped back into the twentieth century to be with another man. Lastly my thanks go to Robert Pritchard at Jubilee House Press for championing the book and enabling me to 'publish against the tide', and to Bree Wright for all her hard work.

Quotations from Gerard J De Groot *The First World War* are reproduced with the kind permission of Palgrave Macmillian, those from Christopher Fifield *Ibbs & Tillett: The Rise and Fall of a Musical Empire* have the permission of Ashgate Publishing Group, while permission to use the material on the soprano Sarah Fischer came from the Library and Archives of Canada.

I should also like to thank all who gave me assistance at the following institutions: the London Metropolitan Archives, the British Library Newspaper Archives, Colindale, the Elgar Birthplace Trust Archives, Broadheath (Sue Fairchild), the Royal College of Music Archives (Helen Hopper), Lewisham Local History Library, Worcester Local History Library, the National Archives, Kew, the BBC Written Archives Centre, Caversham (Jeff Walden), the National Portrait Gallery, London (Bernard Horrocks) and the Glyndebourne Archives (Julia Aries).

A special acknowledgement goes to my late mother, for introducing me to Nash at a very early age.

Picture Sources

Bibliography

Agate, James, *Immoment Toys: A Survey of Light Entertainment on the London Stage 1920–1943* Jonathan Cape 1945

Baillie, Isobel, *Never Sing Louder Than Lovely* Hutchinson 1982

Blyth, Alan, *Song on Record: Vol I Lieder* Cambridge University Press 2006

Boden, Anthony, *A History of the Three Choirs Festival* Sutton Publishing 1992

Brown, George Mackay, *Winter Tales* John Murray Publishers Ltd 1995

Cardus, Neville, *The Delights of Music* Gollancz 1996

Cochran, Charles B, *Showman Looks On* Dent 1945

Donaldson, Frances, *The Royal Opera House in the Twentieth Century* Weidenfeld and Nicolson 1988

Elkin, Robert, *Queen's Hall 1893–1941* Rider & Co. 1944

Elliot, Capt. WR, *The Second Twentieth* Facsimile of the original published jointly by The Naval & Military Press Ltd and The Imperial War Museum.

Evans, Sir Geraint & Goodwin, Noel, *A Knight at the Opera* Michael Joseph 1984

Fifield, Christopher, *Ibbs & Tillett: The Rise and Fall of a Musical Empire* Ashgate Publishing Ltd 2005

De Groot, Gerard J *The First World War* Palgrave Macmillian 2001

Franklin, David, *Basso Cantate* Duckworth 1969

Gibbons, Stella, *Cold Comfort Farm* Penguin 1998 (first pub. 1932)

Griffin, Stephen, *Ken Dodd: The Biography* Michael O'Mara 2007

Hibberd, Stuart, *"This Is London..."* Macdonald And Evans 1950

Hickman, Tom, *What Did You Do In The War, Auntie?: BBC at War, 1939–45* BBC Books 1995

Hodgkin, Geoffrey, *The Best of Me: A Centenary Companion* Elgar Editions 1999 and Lewis Freeman

Hughes, John Graven, *The Greasepaint War : Show Business 1939–45* New English Library 1976

Hughes, Spike, *Glyndebourne* David & Charles 1981

Knight, Esmond, *Seeking The Bubble* Hutchinson 1943

Kynaston, David, *Austerity Britain 1945–51* Bloomsury Publishing PLC 2007

Lebrecht, Norman, *Covent Garden: The Untold Story* Simon & Schuster Ltd. 2000

Legge, Walter, *Words & Music* Routledge 1998

Lucas, John, *Thomas Beecham: An Obsession With Music* The Boydell Press 2008

Mitchell and Reed, *Letters From A Life Vol I: 1923–39: Selected Letters and Diaries of Benjamin Britten* Faber and Faber 1991

Moore, Gerald, *Am I Too Loud?* Penguin Books Ltd. 1974

Neill, Dibble, Trowell, *Oh My Horses!: Elgar, the Music of England and the Great War* Elgar Editions 2001

Norman, Bruce, *Here's Looking At You: Story of British Television, 1908–39* BBC Books 1984

Norwich, John Julius, *Fifty Years of Glyndebourne* Jonathan Cape Ltd 1985

Rutherford, Susan, *The Prima Donnas and Opera 1815–1930* Cambridge Studies in Opera 2006

Schafer, Elizabeth, *Lilian Baylis: A Biography* University of Hertford Press 2007

Teyte, Maggie, *Star On The Door* Putnam 1958

Wilkinson, Roni, *Pals on the Somme 1916* Pen and Sword 2006

Wood, Sir Henry *My Life Of Music* Gollancz 1938

Wood, Jessie, *The Last Years of Henry J. Wood* Victor Gollancz Ltd 1954

Alan Blyth's *Heddle Nash :The Recorded Legacy* gives a comprehensive account of all HN's recordings, complete with a disc of his own favourite Nash recordings and many delightful comments, made in his inimitable style. (pub. by Alan Blyth 2007)

Index

Midgely, Walter 2
Mildmay, Audrey *see* Christie, Audrey
Moeran, E J 26, 31, 116, 203
Moore, Gerald 2, 92, 115–16, 203, 221,
 225
Mullings, Frank 89, 91

N

Nash, Allan (brother) 18, 49, 187
Nash, Amelia (great-aunt) 7–8, 9, 12
Nash, Amy (aunt) 13, 15, 21
Nash, David Leonard Heddle (son) 25,
 50, 78, 103, 105, 120, 140, 143, 160,
 162, 171, 178, 180–3, 184, 185, 187,
 202, 204–5, 214, 215, 221, 228–9,
 232, 235
Nash, Douglas (brother) 18, 21, 49
Nash, Frank (brother) 18, 49
Nash, Harriette (mother) 17, 19, 20, 21,
 49–50, 178
Nash, John Dennis (son) 25, 85, 123,
 158, 171, 178, 180–3, 187, 214, 227–8,
 235
Nash, John Heddle *see* Nash, John
 Dennis
Nash, Joseph (grandfather) 7–11,
 13–14, 16, 19, 21, 50, 51
Nash, Leonard (brother) 18, 27, 30, 33,
 35, 39–40, 42, 48, 49
Nash, Maria (grandmother) 7, 8–11,
 13–15, 20–1
Nash, Mary (niece) 20
Nash, Violet (wife) 22, 53–4, 57, 64–5,
 67, 71, 73, 75, 77, 82, 96, 103–5,
 120, 129, 158, 160, 171, 178–82, 213,
 215, 229
Nash, Walter 177
Nash, William (father) 13–16, 17–18,
 20–2, 23, 24, 25, 27–8, 50–1, 53, 67,
 178, 213
Nash, Winifred *see* Vernon, Winifred
Natzke, Oscar 174, 179–80
Negri, Pola 101
Newton, Carl 203, 204

Noble, Dennis 89, 91, 162, 204, 205, 211
Norman, Bruce 150
Novello, Ivor 32, 101, 196

O

Oldham, Arthur 232
Oldham, Derek 101
Olivier, Laurence 81, 206
operas, operettas and oratorios:
 A Tale of Two Cities 235–7
 Acis and Galatea 193
 Alexander's Feast 94
 Carmen 147–50, 202
 Cavalleria rusticana 91
 Così fan tutte 4, 139–40, 144, 154,
  162
 Der Rosenkavalier 136–7, 154, 159
 Die Entführung aus dem Serail
  144, 166
 Die Fledermaus 42, 115, 118, 136,
  162, 216, 235
 Die Meistersinger 3, 106–7, 111, 126,
  159–60, 163, 180, 217
 Die Zauberflöte 79, 82, 144
 Don Giovanni 95, 111, 145
 Don Pasquale 176
 Elijah 107, 154, 174, 215
 Faust 79, 84, 93, 163, 174–6, 192,
  202, 217
 Frederica 118
 Gianni Schicchi 115
 Il barbiere di Siviglia 70, 115,
  144–6, 152–4, 159
 Jeptha 28, 176
 Judas Maccabaeus 176, 216
 King Olaf 174
 L'elisir d'amore 70, 84, 216
 La bella dormente nel bosco 63
 La belle Hélène 134
 La Bohème 4, 70, 81, 93, 97, 111,
  114, 118, 155–6, 158, 159, 192, 235
 La Cenerentola 154
 La danza 115
 La Favorite 202